THE 10 COMMANDMENTS OF MONEY

LIZ WESTON is the number-one most-read personal finance columnist on the Internet, according to Nielsen Net Ratings. She writes twice weekly for *MSN Money,* and authors the "My Two Cents" column for *AARP the Magazine* and "Money Talk," a weekly column that is syndicated in newspapers nationwide. She lives in Studio City, California.

Praise for *The 10 Commandments of Money*

"A wonderful basic personal finance book [with] enough counterintuitive ideas to keep even people who know a bit about personal finance reading further."   —*The New York Times*

"*The 10 Commandments of Money* is simply jam-packed with information, Web sites, names, do's and don'ts. . . . All in all, this book is a fact-filled, commonsense approach to dealing with the everyday money issues we all need to address."   —*New York Journal of Books*

"You want Liz Weston on your money management team."
                                                      —*USA Today*

"*The 10 Commandments of Money* is . . . a perfect read as a personal finance primer. Weston's solid and occasionally humorous writing shines through as always, and it is her strength writing about these topics that takes this book from being yet another personal finance book to being an enjoyable read that I would recommend."   —TheSimpleDollar.com

"In *The 10 Commandments of Money,* Weston lays out nuanced new rules for financial life based on her own observations of the real world and real consumers. Where other authors get it wrong, Weston gets it right. She digs into the data like nobody else. . . . *The 10 Commandments of Money* is like your Boy Scout guide to being prepared."
                                        —Elisabeth Leamy, *ABC News*

"This book is money manna from heaven, and Liz Weston is the financial sage of our times. She's revised the tired truths about finances and offers up smart, timely advice on paying off debt, investing for retirement, setting up a real-world budget for years to come, and more. I'd follow her anywhere!" —Beth Kobliner, author of *Get a Financial Life*

"Financial columnist Weston provides a workable happy medium between fear and fecklessness . . . A godsend for the financially befuddled, bewildered, or just plain anxious." —*Publishers Weekly*

"Amid all the clutter of personal finance books, twenty-four-hour financial reality shows, and hucksters screaming stock tips, *The 10 Commandments of Money* really stands out. It's a great education in real-world personal finance, yet easy to read for the non-expert. It's a guidebook to improving your financial health without simplistic solutions or one-size-fits all formulae. It tells us what we need to learn from the Great Recession and market meltdown without preaching or proselytizing. It's a big dose of financial/investment/life wisdom in a little book."
—Bob Veres, editor and publisher of *Inside Information* and columnist for *Financial Planning*

THE 10 COMMANDMENTS OF MONEY

Survive and Thrive in the New Economy

LIZ WESTON

A PLUME BOOK

PLUME
Published by the Penguin Group
Penguin Group (USA) Inc., 375 Hudson Street, New York, New York 10014, U.S.A. •
Penguin Group (Canada), 90 Eglinton Avenue East, Suite 700, Toronto, Ontario, Canada
M4P 2Y3 (a division of Pearson Penguin Canada Inc.) • Penguin Books Ltd., 80 Strand,
London WC2R 0RL, England • Penguin Ireland, 25 St. Stephen's Green, Dublin 2,
Ireland (a division of Penguin Books Ltd.) • Penguin Group (Australia), 250 Camberwell
Road, Camberwell, Victoria 3124, Australia (a division of Pearson Australia Group Pty.
Ltd.) • Penguin Books India Pvt. Ltd., 11 Community Centre, Panchsheel Park, New
Delhi – 110 017, India • Penguin Group (NZ), 67 Apollo Drive, Rosedale, Auckland
0632, New Zealand (a division of Pearson New Zealand Ltd.) • Penguin Books (South
Africa) (Pty.) Ltd., 24 Sturdee Avenue, Rosebank, Johannesburg 2196, South Africa

Penguin Books Ltd., Registered Offices: 80 Strand, London WC2R 0RL, England

Published by Plume, a member of Penguin Group (USA) Inc. Previously published in a
Hudson Street Press edition.

First Plume Printing, January 2011
1   3   5   7   9   10   8   6   4   2

FIGURE CREDITS: Page 17 and page 18, copyright © 2009, Pew Research Center. "Luxury
or Necessity? The Public Makes a U-Turn": http://pewsocialtrends.org/pubs/733/
luxury-necessity-recession-era-reevaluations.

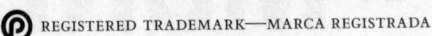 REGISTERED TRADEMARK—MARCA REGISTRADA

The Library of Congress has catalogued the Hudson Street Press edition as follows:

Weston, Liz Pulliam.
The 10 commandments of money : survive and thrive in the new economy /
Liz Weston.
p. cm.
Includes bibliographical references and index.
ISBN 978-1-59463-074-3 (h.c.)
ISBN 978-0-452-29762-3 (pbk.)
1. Finance, Personal. I. Title. II. Title: Ten commandments of money.
HG179.W4752 2011
332.024—dc22   2010037171

Printed in the United States of America
Original hardcover design by Catherine Leonardo

To Will, as always

ACKNOWLEDGMENTS

Too often author acknowledgments are like those overlong acceptance speeches at the Academy Awards: you want someone to start up the orchestra to drown them out.

So I'll keep this short.

I need, want and desire to thank *MSN Money* for its generosity in allowing me to excerpt my columns for this book.

Working with my editor, Meghan Stevenson, and her boss, Caroline Sutton, was an unexpected delight. Although I wasn't responsible, I applaud Meghan for transforming her wine budget into a 401(k) contribution.

This is the part where I start to gush about my agent, Stephen Hanselman, of Level5Media. Tim Ferris is right: Stephen is the best agent in the world—period. I count among my luckiest days the day that we met. (And publicist Stephen Crane, thank you for arranging the introduction.)

And now to burble on about my family: my ever-present, ever-loving, ever-supportive husband and our darling daughter, who waited with varying degrees of patience for Mommy to finish the Darn Book so she could get her first dog.

Finally, Ralph Waldo Emerson said that our growth is seen in the successive choirs of our friends. If that's the case, I must be seventeen feet tall, because my chorale consists of amazing women who freely offered love, encouragement and forgiveness when I dropped out of sight for months to write this book. Marla, Barb, Kelly, Melissa, Bambi, Morgan, Aldina, Kathy: thank you.

CONTENTS

INTRODUCTION

The financial crash and subsequent recession exploded many people's ideas of how money was supposed to work. Assumptions—about risks and rewards, markets and returns—lay in ashes. People saw the value of their biggest assets, their homes and their retirement portfolios, plummet faster and farther than they'd ever thought possible.

Even the safest-seeming investments, including savings accounts and money market funds, suddenly didn't feel so secure as banks failed and financial firms "broke the buck," letting money funds lose principal. With the speed of a catastrophic wildfire, the financial crisis whipped through the economy and around the world, plunging economies from prosperity to despair seemingly overnight.

The worst financial meltdown since the Great Depression left many people reeling, frightened for the future and despairing that they would ever meet their goals. The terror wasn't limited to the little guys. Many of the pundits and personalities who had been cheerleading the bubble years gave in to panic as well. Instead of offering wisdom, they preached hysteria. Some predicted utter ruin while others abruptly changed their strategies and advice, insisting that what used to work no longer would.

In a way, they were right. The money rules that emerged during the stock and real estate bubbles were ill conceived, dangerous and unsustainable. Particularly scary was the notion that risk no longer mattered or could be eliminated—that real estate always rose in price and so did stocks, if you held them long enough.

Other ideas took hold that were equally wrong and scary: that credit card debt was somehow "normal," that traditional mortgages no longer made sense, that borrowing a fortune for education was "good" debt. But many of the solutions prescribed at the height of the crisis—such as shunning stocks entirely, making big plays in gold, ignoring credit card debt to pile up big cash reserves—were equally misguided.

These notions grew up in part because of our great and long-standing ignorance about money, a financial illiteracy that makes us vulnerable to the illegal cons of scam artists as well as the legal ones perpetrated by Wall Street, lenders and corporations.

What's needed now is some sanity rooted in personal responsibility. There are new rules of money that will help you avoid making critical mistakes, survive the bad times and thrive in the good ones. There are easy lessons you can learn now about how money works and how the economy really functions that will help you make smarter choices for years to come no matter what life throws your way. Most of all, there are important truths you can absorb about how much power you have to control your own destiny—truths that can help you separate the helpful from the hysterical and move forward with confidence.

These aren't necessarily the money rules your parents learned, or their parents. The realities of finance have changed too much for old-school strategies to have much relevance.

Let's take just one example. For previous generations, "living within your means" was a fairly simple formula. You put aside 10 percent or so of your income for a rainy day and lived on the rest.

Consumer credit wasn't widely available. The closest most people got was an account at their local grocer that they could pay off once a month or a layaway plan at their favorite department store. If you did get a loan, for a car or a home, the lender was pretty conservative about how much you could borrow.

All that has changed.

Instead of just saving for a rainy day, people now have to save enough to cover most of the costs of their retirement—a period that can last decades, instead of just a few years. Traditional pensions are disappearing, and even employer help in the form of company matches in 401(k) plans has disappeared at some firms.

Then there's saving for college. Instead of a luxury for the elite, a college education is now a necessity for most. Although college can be a tool for economic advancement, these days it's also required if you don't want to slip down the financial ladder. Because of changing job markets and employer requirements, the son or daughter of a union worker who had only a high school diploma must now have a two-year degree, and more likely a four-year degree, simply to match the parent's earning power and benefits. But the costs of college have exploded, far outpacing inflation and the ability of many families to pay. Medical and housing costs have soared as well, taking much bigger chunks of workers' paychecks than in the past.

At the same time these changes were occurring, the availability of consumer credit was soaring. Between 1990 and 2007, credit card debt rose fivefold as card issuers competed aggressively to sign up new customers and extend more and more credit to the ones they had. Lenders' standards got looser and looser. The idea that a lender wouldn't let you take on a loan you couldn't afford became a joke. With sophisticated analytics, credit scoring formulas and a whole market system designed to whisk risk away from lenders and onto investors, what the borrower could afford became an afterthought, and then lenders didn't think about it at all.

All this credit papered over the crisis many American families experienced: their incomes stagnated while their costs rose. Median household income peaked in 1999, according to the U.S. Census Bureau, and a decade later inflation-adjusted incomes still hadn't bounced back. For many families, borrowing became the way to stay afloat and maintain the lifestyle they thought they'd already achieved.

Credit got tougher to get as lenders pulled back from their Great Recession losses. But it is still possible to get a far bigger mortgage or auto loan than you can comfortably afford. It's still possible to get in over your head with credit card debt. Meanwhile, lenders have come up with new ways to snare people with short-term borrowing—payday loans, payday "advances" and "bounce" protection—that can quickly upend a budget with triple-digit interest rates.

So, millions of people are struggling with finances that simply don't work. They cut out the lattes and the dinners out, if they were ever indulging in those, and they still barely skate from paycheck to paycheck. Even if they're doing better and setting a little money aside, they're plagued by the worry that they're not saving enough, not doing enough to make sure they won't end their days in deprivation and want.

Equally altered are the rules by which corporations function. Behavior that previous generations would have condemned as scandalous, predatory or even illegal is now considered the corporate norm. That means that we, as consumers and investors, have to be vigilant as never before if we want to keep the money we worked so hard to earn. Personal financial literacy—educating ourselves on the realities of the new world we live in and implementing the financial strategies that will work in it—will allow us to prosper no matter what.

In this book, I'll guide you through the ten most important things you need to know to make your money work. These ten commandments of money are principles distilled from more than fifteen years of writing about money and helping literally millions of people get their finances on track, first as a newspaper columnist for the *Los Angeles Times* and eventually as the most-read personal finance columnist on the Internet. (I'm a twice-weekly columnist for MSN Money, where portions of the following chapters first appeared.) I'm also a graduate of the Certified Financial Planner training program, and that education was invaluable, but my advice is guided just as much by interactions with readers and their real-world problems.

Because of all that experience, I believe these ten principles will help you create the life you want. But this isn't Mount Sinai, and I sure as heck am not Moses. And I need to warn you that you should be wary of what I call the Money Fundamentalists.

In a world where money has become so complex and confusing, many people long for simple answers. "Just tell me what to do!" is a familiar chorus in the personal finance realm. And there are people who are happy to tell you *exactly* what to do—even if they don't know you or your financial situation. These people spout advice that appears to leave no room for doubt: "All debt is bad!" "Invest in real estate!" "Put all your money in gold!"

Some of these advice givers genuinely believe they've found the one key to a successful financial life. Others are just salesmen, trying to grab attention in a crowded market so they can sell their version of snake oil. Few of those spouting simplistic solutions have anything resembling a comprehensive financial planning background.

If they had, they would know that money, like life, isn't painted in black and white strokes. There's lots of nuance and gray. A piece of advice that works great with one person might be a disaster, or completely unnecessary, for another. For example, some people simply can't handle credit cards. No matter what they do, they wind up maxing out their plastic if they have access to credit. The best solution for them is to close their accounts and live a cash-only lifestyle.

Other people, though, develop the discipline to use credit responsibly and pay their balances in full every month. Telling these folks they have to cut up their credit cards is kind of like banning drinking because a few people become alcoholics (and we know how well the little experiment of Prohibition fared). Simple answers may be comforting, but they're usually no match for the complex situations we have now.

In any case, I hope as you read this book that you'll find my suggestions, guidelines and advice to be helpful. But despite my phrasing this advice as commandments, you shouldn't take what I or any other financial pundit has to say as gospel. Do your research, investigate your options, reflect on your own situation and use your common sense. Employ what works for you—or, as recovering alcoholics would say, "Take what you like and leave the rest."

THE 10 COMMANDMENTS OF MONEY

Create a Budget
That Works in the Real World

THE OLD-SCHOOL RULES:
Live within your means.

THE BUBBLE ECONOMY RULES:
Live to the max, with easy low payments.

THE NEW RULES:
Use the 50/30/20 budget to know what
you can really afford and what you can't.

The first step in creating a financial plan that works is to create a budget that works. But as the financial world has gotten more complex, so, too, has the budgeting process, and many people wind up flailing. People's situations vary so widely that there's no cut-and-dried answer to "How much should I be spending on X?"

THE TRADITIONAL ADVICE GOES SOMETHING LIKE THIS:

- Gather up your pay stubs and bill statements from the last few months.
- Carry a notebook and pencil for a few weeks so you can write down every expenditure that's not captured in your bill statements.
- Combine your notebook entries with your bills to see where your money is going.

- Don't forget to budget savings for retirement, college savings, emergency funds, your next car purchase, your next vacation . . .
- Slice and dice and tweak until you have a budget that matches your income—at least until the next expense comes along that you forgot to account for and that blows your whole plan out of whack.

This track, trim and retrench method actually can work if you're persistent about it and if your basic expenses are reasonable relative to your income.

If your overhead is too high, though, the hours you spend crafting and trying to follow a budget are going to be a huge waste of time. Now, frankly, there is so much more to keep track of than there used to be that formulating this kind of budget can also make you a little crazy. You simply won't have the ability to simultaneously

- cover your current bills,
- pay off your past (your debt),
- save for the future (retirement, college, emergencies) and
- enjoy your life today.

One or more of those four categories will wind up getting sacrificed, no matter how good your intentions or how much time you spend fiddling with a spreadsheet.

On the other hand, I can't tell you exactly how much you should spend in any given category. A twenty-something with no debt might be able to afford a much bigger rent payment, relative to her income, than a family juggling car payments, student loans and child care. A homeowner in the Northeast will almost certainly spend more on utilities than his counterpart in California. People covered by traditional pensions can get away with saving less of their incomes for retirement than those who have a 401(k) with no match, or no workplace plan at all.

There is, however, a budget system that can work on just about any income and in virtually every situation. It will give you the flexibility you need to help you live your life while building financial security and minimizing the chances a setback will send you over the edge.

It was created by Harvard bankruptcy professor Elizabeth Warren, who based it on her years of studying families on the brink. The budget is simple, if not easy. It's the 50/30/20 budget. Here's how it works:

You start with your after-tax income. That's your gross pay minus any wage-based taxes, such as withheld income tax, Social Security and Medicare taxes and disability taxes. If your employer deducts other expenses from your paycheck, such as 401(k) contributions, health insurance premiums and union dues, add those back into your net pay to get your after-tax income.

INSIDER TERMS

401(k): A workplace retirement plan that allows employees to contribute pretax money to various investment options. The money grows, tax deferred, until it's withdrawn. Many 401(k) plans—and their cousins in the not-for-profit world, 403(b)s—offer a company match, where the employer also contributes money to the worker's account. Theoretically, a 401(k) can provide more money in retirement than a traditional pension plan, but many people mess up by starting too late, saving too little, cashing in their plans when they change jobs and taking either too much or too little risk with their investments. We'll discuss 401(k)s more in the chapter on retirement.

You aim to limit your "must-have" expenses to 50 percent of that after-tax figure. "Must-haves" include all the basic expenditures you really need to make each month: outlays for housing, utilities, transportation, food, insurance, child care, child support, tuition and minimum loan payments. Not sure if an expenditure is a must-have? Here's the key: If you can delay a purchase for a few months without serious consequences, it's not a must-have. If you're contractually obligated to pay something (a credit card minimum, child support or a cell phone bill), then it *is* a must-have, at least for now. I'll go into this in further detail later in the chapter, but here is how I would break down the basic must-haves:

Expense	Consequence of not paying
Rent or mortgage	Eviction or foreclosure process begins
Utilities	No water, heat, electricity
Car payment; transportation costs	Car is repossessed; you cannot to get to work

Expense	Consequence of not paying
Child care	You cannot leave home to get to work
Child support	Child's welfare is threatened; possible legal action
Tuition	Education at risk
Food	Hunger; medical problems
Minimum loan payments	Credit score damage; possible legal action
Insurance premiums	Loss of insurance, which can lead to debt or bankruptcy in the event of illness or accident

Your "wants" can consume 30 percent of your after-tax pay. Vacations, gifts, entertainment, clothes, eating out and other expenses are all "wants." Some bills you pay might overlap the two categories. For example, basic phone service is a must-have. But features such as call waiting or unlimited long distance are wants. Internet access and pay television are two other expenditures that can feel like must-haves but usually are wants, unless you're on some kind of long-term contract. Remember, if you can put off the expenses without major fallout, or you can find a substitute, it's a want rather than a must-have. You may really love your broadband connection, for example, but if you had to live without it you could still access your e-mail at the local library or coffee shop. You may find your smartphone to be an incredibly useful and handy device (I sure do), but that doesn't make it a must-have unless you're on a contract. If you're paying month to month with no contract, it's a want.

Savings and debt repayment make up the final 20 percent of your budget. To achieve financial independence and minimize the chances of disaster, you need to get rid of consumer debt, save for retirement and build your emergency fund. Any loan payments you make above the minimum belong in this category, as do contributions to your retirement and emergency funds.

On my Web site, AskLizWeston.com, you'll find a link to a calculator that can help you create your 50/30/20 budget. But here are some theoretical examples to give you an idea how this might work.

Jamal is fresh out of college with an after-tax income of $3,000 a month. He has a minimum student loan payment of $200, his employer-subsidized health insurance costs him $75, his bus pass to work costs him $100 and groceries set him back $225. So far, his must-have expenses add up to $600 a month, so he should spend no more than $900 a month on rent and utilities if he wants his must-haves to equal no more than 50 percent of his after-tax income.

Under the 50/30/20 plan, he'd have $900 a month to spend on eating out, clothes, vacations and other wants. The remaining $600 should be earmarked for retirement savings and debt payoff. Since Jamal has no other debt and his student loan rates are low, the entire $600 can be devoted to savings.

Maxwell and Minnie are in a whole different boat. They bring home a lot more—their combined after-tax income is $8,000 a month—but they have more bills, including a mortgage ($2,400, including taxes and insurance), credit card bills ($150 minimum payment) and a car loan ($400), as well as more insurance needs (life and disability coverage that costs $300 a month, as well as health insurance that costs about the same). They spend another $450 on basic groceries and utilities (lights, water, gas, sewer), bringing their must-haves to the 50 percent mark of $4,000. They spend $2,400 on their wants—everything from their cable TV subscription to holiday presents—and the remaining $1,600 is split between retirement savings and extra payments against the credit card debt.

Now let's change the scenario a bit. Let's say Max and Min didn't know about the 50/30/20 plan. They just signed a $450-a-month lease on a new car and bought smartphones that lock them into a two-year contract at $150 a month, bringing their must-haves to about 58 percent of their income.

There isn't much wiggle room in their other must-have expenses. They may be able to bring down their food and utility expenses a bit, but not enough to compensate for the $600 in additional costs to which they've committed themselves.

On the car lease, they're pretty much stuck. It's tough to get out of one of those without a serious black mark on your credit. Max and Min could back out of the cell phone deal and pay the early termination fees, which as of this writing range from $150 to $350 per phone. When money is really tight, that can be the best of bad options, since returning to basic phone service or a prepaid plan can save you enough to offset the fee within a few months. But Max and Min might decide the phone service is something they want to keep.

So the way to compensate would be to either make more money—Max and Min would need to bring in an additional $1,200 a month to get their must-haves in line—or trim the "wants" category to compensate. In time, Max and Min could restore more balance to their budget as their incomes rise and as they pay off their credit cards and car loan. If they resist the urge to add more financial commitments, they eventually could get their must-haves below 50 percent.

Mia's situation is more critical. She's a single mother with two young children and a pile of debt: credit cards, medical bills, student loans, a car loan. She bought her house during the boom years and was approved for a mortgage that eats up more than 50 percent of her $4,500 after-tax income. Child care costs her $1,000 a month and her minimum loan payments are another $200. These must-have expenses alone total more than 75 percent of her after-tax pay. Add in groceries, utilities, health insurance, auto insurance and gas to get to work, and she has virtually nothing left over. Is it any wonder her credit card debt is growing and she has nothing saved?

There are no easy fixes for Mia's situation. She can't eat out less than she already does, which is never, and niceties like cable television, a broadband Internet connection, new clothes and vacations were cut long ago. She may be able to trim child care costs by finding a cheaper provider, but that wouldn't help her enough to solve her budget problem.

What's really dragging her down is the house and her debt. She simply can't afford her home. If she could get approved for a mortgage modification that reduces her payment to 31 percent—the percentage used in federal modification programs to determine affordability—she might be able to struggle through until her income rises a bit and her kids are in school, reducing child care costs. If not, letting go of the house is probably the most sensible option. She also needs to talk to a bankruptcy attorney about her debt. While her student loans likely couldn't be wiped out and she'll need to keep her car loan so she can get to work, a bankruptcy filing could eliminate her credit card debt and medical debt, giving her enough breathing room to pay her other bills.

There are plenty of situations where it's tough to keep the must-haves under the 50 percent mark, such as when you're unemployed. Or you may decide to make certain trade-offs to preserve an expense that's important to you. For example, you might opt to stretch for a few years to pay for quality child care when your children are little, knowing the costs will drop when they reach school age.

But to make your budget work, you'll need to cut back on the *wants* to compensate, and spend less on vacations, clothes, toys and entertainment. Cutting back on the savings and debt repayment category isn't advisable, unless you've already paid off all your toxic (credit card) debt, have a fat emergency fund and have been saving prodigiously for retirement.

On a practical level, most people won't be able to go on for years without a nice vacation or new clothes. The occasional modest splurge is not what is going to ruin your budget. The underlying consistency will carry you through. But even if you do decide to push the 50 percent mark, you probably don't want your must-haves to go much above 60 percent or so. And even then, beware of accepting a situation where your must-haves remain above 50 percent of your after-tax income for more than a few years. It's tough to achieve long-term financial stability if your money isn't balanced. So although you may want a nicer house, a sweeter ride or a private school education for your kids, the wiser course in the long run would be to choose options that you can comfortably afford—within the 50 percent limit.

A WORD ABOUT CHARITABLE GIVING

MOST OF US FEEL it's important to give back. Some of us feel so strongly about charitable giving that it's a "must-have" part of our budgets. If your giving is unbalancing your budget or causing you to sink into debt, however, you need to rethink that approach. You may be able to volunteer your time and skills instead of giving money, for example, until you're on sounder financial footing. If your contributions are part of a commitment you've made to your religious organization, such as a tithe, talking with your religious leader can help you craft a plan that keeps your commitment at the center of your life while still making progress on your finances.

Corralling must-have expenses is essential to making your budget really work. But many people find the prospect daunting because their must-haves are eating the lion's share of their income.

They didn't think about the dangers of too much overhead when they decided where to live, what car to buy or how many kids to have.

They locked themselves into certain expenses and now they're drowning in bills.

Here's a typical scenario. Jules and Julia meet and marry. Their parents tell them it's okay to stretch to buy their first home, so they wind up with a mortgage that eats up half their take-home pay.

Then Jules's car dies, and they go out to buy a replacement. New cars are expensive, though, and the additional payment really puts a strain on their finances.

Then Julia gets pregnant. Now, in addition to a monster mortgage and a big car payment, they have to figure out how to pay for the hospital bills, Julia's maternity leave and ongoing child care.

No wonder there's no money left to save for retirement, contribute to the baby's college fund or pay off the credit card debt they racked up furnishing the house and paying for repairs before Jules's car finally bit the dust.

In families like these, must-have expenses might eat up 75 percent, 80 percent or even more of after-tax income.

The usual advice—to stop buying lattes, eat more meals at home and trim the cable bill—just won't cut it. Their budget *can't* work because their overhead gobbles up too much of their income.

If that describes your situation, and you can't boost your income enough to bring the must-haves to the 50 percent mark, the only real solution is to make some big and probably unwelcome changes in your lifestyle. You may have to move, get a roommate or a tenant, give up a car, change your child care arrangements. The only way for you to get ahead, in other words, may be to take a big step back.

By the way, I'm deliberately not including an exhaustive list of ways you can "trim your spending now!" I've discovered such lists seem to trigger real resistance in many people. They start thinking, "I can't do that. . . . I certainly won't do *that*. . . . Is she out of her *mind*?"

This is the "Yeah, but" syndrome, as in "Yeah, but that won't work in my case," and once it starts it's hard for you to absorb any other pertinent information.

In any case, it's not up to me to tell you how to live your life or spend your money. It's up to you to do some soul-searching—and research (I've provided some resources later in the chapter to help you get started)—and then make some decisions about your spending, even if it means accepting some pretty big changes in your life.

I suspect that the reason no one wants to hear this type of advice is because most people feel that they're already living below the lifestyle that they deserve. Here I am, telling them they have to cut back from that.

If it's so hard to keep to the 50 percent limit, why do it? Several good reasons:

- **It gives you flexibility.** Your income could drop by half and you'd still be able to pay your essential bills. When your must-haves eat up more of your income, you have less ability to cope with setbacks such as layoffs, reduced work hours or unexpected expenses.
- **It helps you know what you can and can't afford.** If you're considering adding a loan payment or other contractual obligation to your overhead, you simply check to see if it would push you over the 50 percent mark. If not, you can consider adding the payment; if so, you don't.
- **It gives you balance.** Limiting your overhead allows you to have money for the pleasures in life, such as dinners out and vacations, without stress. It also allows you to get out of debt and save for your future.

Alan wrote to me about the trade-offs his family had opted to make. He and his wife owned a home in Southern California, near all his relatives. But when his wife got pregnant, they decided they really wanted her to stay home with the baby—and that they couldn't swing that with the high cost of Southern California living.

"We ultimately decided in mid-2006 to relocate to Spokane, WA, where we purchased a home for cash, paid off vehicle loans and credit card balances, and had a tidy fund left over," Alan wrote. "We have remained free of consumer debt since, but the huge benefit is that now our very existence is much more flexible in terms of minimum income required."

Even losing his job for a few months didn't turn into a crisis, since they had manageable living expenses plus emergency savings. But Alan acknowledges there are other costs.

"This has truly been a life-changing decision for the better, but . . . we are now 1,000 miles from the nearest relative, and returning to California if we wanted to probably is not feasible for a long, long time."

I've heard from many others who have struggled to hold on to unaffordable homes, resisting the idea that they might have to give up and sell or let the house be taken in foreclosure. Once they let go, though, they often discover the disruption in their life is more than offset by the sense of relief and calm they get from having a budget that's finally under control.

One woman who worried about how a move would affect her kids discovered that the change wasn't easy, but had its unexpected upside. "They're happier because I'm happier," is what she finally concluded.

THE MATH IS THE MATH

OCCASIONALLY, I'll hear from someone living in a high-cost city such as New York or Los Angeles who is convinced that the math should be changed for residents of those areas. Don't I know how much a decent apartment costs? they'll demand. The 50/30/20 plan might work for people in the Midwest, they sniff, but not in the Big City.

I do understand that it's more common for people to spend more on the basics, particularly housing, in high-cost areas. I'm a long-time resident of Los Angeles, where a recent study found that half of local residents spend 40 percent or more of their income on housing costs.

But the high cost of living here doesn't change the math. If you spend more than 50 percent of your after-tax pay on must-haves, you have to cut back in other areas if you want your budget to balance. If you want a truly balanced *life*, though, the smart approach is to cut your must-haves instead.

And you're not required to spend 40 percent or 50 percent of your income on rent, no matter where you live now. You could find a cheaper place, get a roommate or (gasp) move to another neighborhood or even another city. In short, you have choices. Failing to exercise them won't change the math, but it will affect your odds of financial success.

HOW TO BUDGET IF YOUR INCOME ISN'T REGULAR

Most budgeting advice is based on the idea that you have a steady, predictable income. But that's not the case for a huge chunk of U.S.

workers. About a quarter of us are self-employed. Many more have variable hours and thus variable incomes. A growing number work project to project, with paychecks that are steady only as long as the gig lasts.

My husband and I have dealt with all these situations. I left the *Los Angeles Times* in 2002 to start my own company. Before he became a college professor, my husband was a successful freelance illustrator and then worked in animation, where frantic bursts of activity and fat paychecks would be followed by weeks or months of unemployment. We both well know the uncertainty of the variable-income life, the pain of having clients who pay late or not at all and the extra burdens of paying for your own benefits.

The best way I've found to budget with a variable income is to start with the past. Look back over two or three years' worth of tax returns and ascertain the after-tax average of what you made over that period (find the "total income" listed on your federal income tax return and from that subtract your "total tax," then subtract the "total tax" from any state and local returns you filed for the same years). If it was $30,000 one year, $60,000 the next and $45,000 the next, for example, your average was $3,750 a month ($135,000 divided by 36 months).

Another method is to base your budget on the lowest amount of income you reasonably expect to make in the coming year. This is usually the more conservative approach and a good one to use if you're just starting out as a freelancer or if you suspect trouble is ahead—if your billings are down, for example, or your industry is shrinking.

In the months when your income exceeds your budget, it's essential to squirrel away much of that extra money to use in the lean months. What you don't want to do is ramp up your overhead costs unless you have good reason to believe the good times will last. You also need to save sufficiently to cover your taxes and make the dreaded "quarterly

INSIDER TERMS

Estimated tax payments: Payments you may be required to make every three months to the IRS if your tax withholding on your income is insufficient. Estimated tax payments are typically required of people who are self-employed, who have sideline businesses and who otherwise have a substantial amount of income not subject to withholding, such those with investment income.

estimated payments"—tax deposits that are typically required four times a year. Worker bees usually have most if not all of their income taxes withheld by their employers, but the self-employed need to estimate and pay these taxes as they go along. Failing to make your quarterly estimated tax payments can result in a huge tax bill, plus penalties, come April 15.

This is one of the many reasons you really need to hire a tax pro if you're self-employed—not just to help you with those pesky estimated tax filings, but to be a trusted year-round resource. A good CPA or enrolled agent can help you decide on the best structure for your business (sole proprietorship? S corporation? C corporation? limited liability company?), take full advantage of the tax breaks business ownership offers and get you set up with the right retirement plan. Get referrals from business-owning friends, from your local CPA society and from the National Association of Enrolled Agents (www.naea.org). It does costs money, but it is worth it.

INSIDER TERMS

Enrolled agent: Tax preparers who are qualified to represent you in dealings with the IRS. Many enrolled agents are former IRS employees and they typically charge less for their services than CPAs (certified public accountants), making them a more affordable option for many freelancers and small business owners.

WRESTLING YOUR BUDGET INTO SHAPE

If you're looking for ideas on how to trim expenses, you're in luck: there is a wealth of free and low-cost resources brimming with tips, tricks and suggestions.

You can start with two books that are probably in your local library: Amy Dacyczyn's *The Complete Tightwad Gazette* and Mary Hunt's *Debt-Proof Living*. You'll probably find other books worth checking out in the same section, but these two women are the queens of stretching a buck. Dacyczyn retired from advice giving way back in 1996, but her approach and most of her suggestions are still relevant. Hunt runs a Web site at www.debtproofliving.com that's well worth checking out.

SPEAKING OF ONLINE RESOURCES, SOME OF MY FAVORITE BUDGET-TRIMMING IDEA SITES INCLUDE:

Bargaineering (www.bargaineering.com). Jim Wang's blog offers plenty of good personal-finance content along with reviews of banks, credit card offers, books and products.

The Centsible Life (www.thecentsiblelife.com). Written by a stay-at-home mother of four young kids, this site is packed with ideas about cutting costs as well as musings about raising children.

Consumerism Commentary (www.consumerismcommentary.com). Track blogger Flexo's net worth as he and partner Smithee write about saving money on everything from banking to travel.

The Dollar Stretcher (www.stretcher.com). If this site has had a major redesign since its launch in 1996, I missed it. But you don't need fancy graphics when you have a huge library of articles and tips about saving money. Even black-belt frugality experts will find new information here.

Get Rich Slowly (www.getrichslowly.org). Blogger J. D. Roth dug his way out of debt and tells you how you can, too. An active community of readers provides additional insights and commentary.

The Simple Dollar (www.thesimpledollar.com). Like Roth, Trent Hamm has experienced and conquered debt. He grew up in poverty and understands how early deprivation can lead to later disasters with money.

Smart Spending (articles.moneycentral.msn.com/SmartSpending). MSN Money's "Smart Spending" blog remains one of my favorite places to check for savings tips, commentaries on frugality and a roundup of good deals around the Web.

Wise Bread (www.wisebread.com). A variety of voices enliven a site devoted to helping you "live large on a small budget." In addition to personal finance and frugal living, Wise Bread provides commentary on careers and "life hacks."

If you're looking specifically for tips on trimming food costs, you'll find a treasure trove of wonderful sites. Among them: CouponMom.com (www.couponmom.com), Hot Coupon World (www.hotcouponworld.com), Mommysavers (www.mommysavers.com) and Be Cents Able (becentsable.blogspot.com).

These sites link to other relevant sites and blogs that you can explore. I'm constantly stumbling across new voices and ideas; every time I think all the money-saving tips have been explored, someone comes up with a new one.

All this information can be overwhelming, of course, and figuring out what will work for you and what won't can be a trial-and-error process. It can help to brainstorm with a trusted, thrifty friend or to join a community of like-minded people who can support and guide you. Many of the sites listed here have groups of dedicated readers who share ideas in forums and through comments. My advice: keep an open mind and be willing to consider the options presented. A solution that may first strike you as extreme or unworkable may be exactly what's needed to kick your budget into shape.

And if you want to see what's possible when people are committed to financial freedom, check out the voluntary simplicity movement. These folks are committed to cutting their expenses to the bone so they can save enough to say good-bye to full-time work decades before most of the rest of us will be ready to retire. Many have already achieved that dream and spend some of their free hours helping others to achieve the same goal.

INSIDER TERMS

Voluntary simplicity: A lifestyle choice to reduce consumption, often dramatically, in order to live more simply for spiritual, health, environmental and/or economic reasons. Many proponents of voluntary simplicity question the materialism of modern life, which they say leads to overspending, overwork (as people have to work harder to pay their debts), more stress, strained relationships and damage to the environment as resources are used to create unnecessary material goods that often wind up in landfills.

TWO SITES TO EXPLORE INCLUDE:

Financial Integrity (www.financialintegrity.org). This is the site run by the New Road Map Foundation and Vicki Robin, a coauthor of the seminal voluntary simplicity guidebook *Your Money or Your Life*.

The Simple Living Network (www.simpleliving.net). Followers of voluntary simplicity will find just about everything they need here, including articles, discussion forums and links to a range of like-minded sites.

People in the voluntary simplicity movement use a variety of approaches to saving money, which often include ditching unnecessary expenses (pay TV, expensive cell plans), shopping at thrift stores and yard sales, growing some of their own food and getting creative about managing housing costs. I know people who have:

- Lived in boats, RVs and campers
- Moved in with their parents or their adult kids
- Shared a house with another family or group of adults
- Managed apartment complexes or campgrounds in exchange for free or discounted rent
- Served as caretakers for ranches or vacation homes
- Opted for homes that were far less than what they could afford

Take Janine and Brad Bolon. In their thirties, they decided to shoot for financial independence—while living in Southern California and raising four kids. Brad's colleagues bought homes in gated communities, but the Bolons opted for a 1,500-square-foot town house in a less-affluent area of Woodland Hills. Janine shopped at thrift stores, carefully managed their food budget and kept utility costs low by using air-conditioning on only the hottest days of the year. She also homeschooled the kids, which she says helped save money by reducing outside pressures for them to keep up with the latest clothing styles and toy trends.

They lived on less than a third of Brad's $110,000 income and put the rest into savings. After eight years, they had enough to pull the plug. They sold their home, paid cash for a house in Utah and launched a new life untethered to the usual nine-to-five.

Their savings would allow them to quit working for pay entirely, the Bolons say, but now they work by choice in their own businesses, which allow them to set their own hours and still spend plenty of time with their family.

Voluntary simplicity clearly isn't for everyone. Most of us will choose a lifestyle with more comforts, even though it means working longer. But knowing what's possible can help you challenge some of your beliefs about what's really a must-have in your life and what's not.

WANTS VS. NEEDS

"I need a new car." "We need a bigger house." "Baby needs shoes."

We use the word "need" a lot when what we're really talking about is a "want." The issue is more than just semantics, since the words we use can have a powerful effect on the options we choose.

Take the idea that you "need" a new car. The reality is that no one needs a new car; brand-new vehicles are actually a luxury. In some areas with poor public transportation, you can argue that you need a car, but no one needs a new one; there are plenty of used models available, ranging from real clunkers to almost-new lease returns. By telling yourself you need a new vehicle, you're cutting yourself off from the many more affordable options you could have considered.

Our true needs are relatively few and include shelter, food, clothing, transportation and companionship. But shelter can range from a cardboard box under a bridge to a palace. Food can be soup from a local homeless shelter or a dinner at Per Se. Clothing can be hand-me-downs or designer. Transportation ranges from your feet to a private jet. Whatever we choose above the minimum for survival is a want.

And our wants are endless. Once one is satisfied, we'll focus on another, or on an upgrade to the first. You've heard people say of others, "They're never satisfied." Well, none of us is. Any periods of satisfaction are short-lived, and then we move on to the next desire. Understanding that is the key to mastery over our budgets and our money.

Because we can't have it all, we have to decide which desires are most important to fulfill. We have to sift through our ever-changing, ever-renewing wishes to determine which are fleeting and not worth indulging and which are truly close to our hearts. If you love to travel, for example, you may decide it's worth giving up other wants so you have the money for plane fares and hotel rooms. If family life is close to your heart, you may forgo fancy vacations or a nicer house so you can have more kids or spend more time at home. Fortunately, when we're careful and conscious about money, our choices get clearer and the decisions get easier to make.

Interestingly, you could see this happening on a broad scale during the recession that began in December 2007. The Pew Research Center for years has been tracking what household conveniences and services people consider necessities and which are considered luxuries. Between 1996 and 2006, the proportion of people who considered such items as clothes dryers, air-conditioning and microwaves to be necessities climbed sharply.

But once the recession hit, people obviously changed their minds about what's truly a luxury. Check it out:

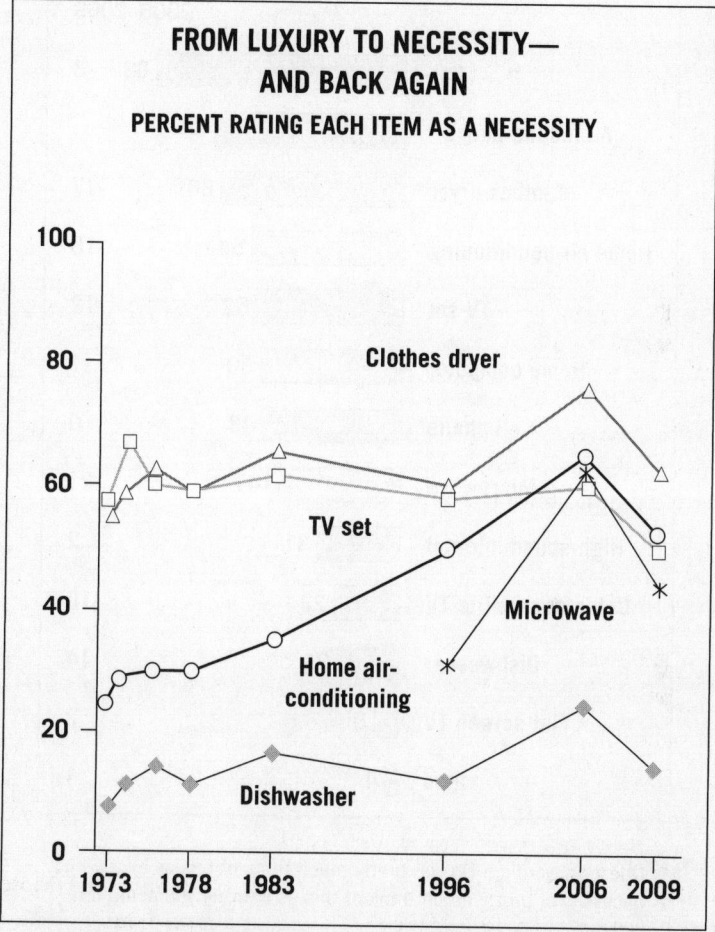

**FROM LUXURY TO NECESSITY—
AND BACK AGAIN**

PERCENT RATING EACH ITEM AS A NECESSITY

Source: 1973 to 1983 surveys by Roper; 1996 survey by *Washington Post*/Kaiser/Harvard; 2006 and 2009 surveys by Pew Research Center.

Question wording: Do you pretty much think of this as a necessity or pretty much think of this as a luxury you could do without?

For the first time, substantial majorities no longer considered microwave ovens, televisions or air-conditioning to be can't-live-without items. The percentage who cited clothes dryers and dishwashers as necessities dropped sharply as well.

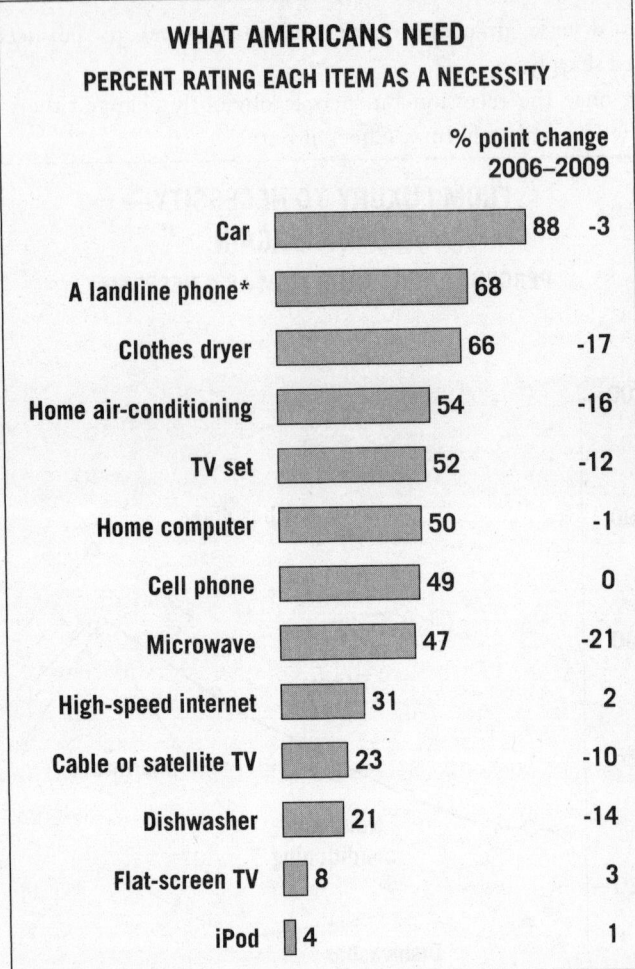

WHAT AMERICANS NEED

PERCENT RATING EACH ITEM AS A NECESSITY

% point change
2006–2009

Item	Percent	% point change 2006–2009
Car	88	-3
A landline phone*	68	
Clothes dryer	66	-17
Home air-conditioning	54	-16
TV set	52	-12
Home computer	50	-1
Cell phone	49	0
Microwave	47	-21
High-speed internet	31	2
Cable or satellite TV	23	-10
Dishwasher	21	-14
Flat-screen TV	8	3
iPod	4	1

*Landline phone question was asked only in 2009.
Question wording: Do you pretty much think of this as a
necessity or pretty much think of this as a luxury you could do
without?

Now, none of the items on the Pew survey is truly a necessity in any objective sense. Our ancestors certainly got along without cars, phones and televisions. Even today, billions will live their whole lives without these luxuries.

But the dramatic change in Americans' attitudes about these items underscores how changed circumstances can alter the way we view our expenditures and possessions. And that little bit of insight can make a huge difference in how we choose to spend our money in the future.

MAKING BUDGETING EASIER

While computers and Internet access aren't necessities, they certainly make managing a budget a lot easier.

One of the best tools for managing your money is Quicken personal finance software ($60 to $100, depending on the version). This program helps you create your budget as well as retirement, college savings and debt payoff plans. It will retrieve all your financial transactions from checking, savings, credit and investing accounts and help you categorize them so you can see exactly where your money is going. Its cash flow feature can show you upcoming expenses so that you're never caught short.

As wonderful and full-featured as this program is, it's not for everybody. Its many features may be overkill for some users and there is a bit of a learning curve in getting the program set up and running.

Fortunately, there are plenty of other options. Sites like Mint.com (a service from Quicken) and moneyStrands offer transaction-tracking and budgeting features for free. These sites gather and categorize your transactions automatically so you can see at a glance where you stand.

It's pretty easy to set up an account, although you need to be comfortable with the idea that your financial information will "live" on their secure sites, rather than being downloaded only into your home computer. I am, since I realize my home computer is likely more vulnerable to a hacker than an encrypted financial site, but you'll want to familiar yourself with any site's privacy and security policies before you entrust it with your online IDs and passwords.

If you're not ready for automation, you can still use your computer to help you. PearBudget (at www.pearbudget.com) and Microsoft, among others, offer downloadable budget templates that allow you to enter your transactions yourself. I'll warn you, this is a lot of work, and only the most detail-oriented will keep up the effort required. For the rest of us, automation is the way to go—and transaction tracking is just the start.

PUT EVERYTHING ON AUTOMATIC

The fewer decisions you have to make, the better.

If you have to decide every paycheck whether or not to save, you're likely to find "better" things to do with that money. If you have to remember to pay twelve or fifteen separate bills every month, sooner or later you're going to forget one—risking late fees, penalty interest rates and even damage to your credit scores.

INSIDER TERMS

Credit scores: These are three-digit numbers lenders use to help gauge your creditworthiness. Credit scores are calculated using the information in your credit reports on file with the three major credit bureaus. The leading credit scoring formula is called the FICO, although there are more than one hundred different credit-scoring formulas in use. FICO scores range from 300 to 850, with higher scores indicating a lower risk of default.

That's why it makes a lot more sense to put most of your saving and spending decisions on automatic.

To do that successfully, though, you have to set up a system you can trust. Here's how to do that.

Set up true overdraft protection. People who resist automation usually tell me they need to "control" when bills get paid. What they usually mean is that they're not sure they'll have enough cash in their account to pay the bill when it's due, which is a legitimate concern—but one that's easily rectified with a good transaction-tracking system and true overdraft protection.

Overdraft protection links your checking account to a savings account, credit card or line of credit. If a transaction exceeds your checking account balance, money to cover it is transferred from the linked account. You pay an annual fee for the service, typically $10 to $50, plus any interest charges incurred if the linked account is a credit card or credit line. With credit cards, you may also pay a "cash advance fee" of 3 to 5 percent, which is why linking to a savings account or line of credit is usually a better option.

Unfortunately, in recent years many banks replaced true overdraft protection with "bounce protection" or "courtesy overdraft," both of which work quite differently. Instead of taking the money from one of your own accounts, the bank "lends" you the amount of the over-limit transaction and slaps you with a $35 fee. A single lapse could lead to multiple fees, making this system far more profitable for the banks. Many banks also manipulate how they process your checks, ATM withdrawals and debit card purchases to boost fees: they reorder transactions to process the biggest transactions first, to drain your account and increase the odds that subsequent transactions would bounce, thus incurring more fees.

The Federal Reserve has since told banks that they can no longer sign people up automatically for bounce protection and that customers must "opt in" to the service. (Banks can still process your daily transactions any way they like, however.) Unfortunately, too many people still don't realize that there is a better alternative and choose bounce protection over true overdraft protection. If you're not sure what you have, call your bank; if your checking account isn't linked to a savings account, credit line or credit card, ask for that service. If your bank doesn't offer it, look for a new bank—this protection is that important to your financial life.

Keep some padding in your checking account. To reduce the chances you'll ever need to tap your overdraft protection, always keep a cushion of cash there that you don't spend. If your bills are relatively modest or you're just starting out, $100 may be enough. If big transactions regularly whip in and out of your account, though, $500 or $1,000 is preferable.

Enable alerts. Most banks allow you to set up e-mail or text alerts so you're notified when your account falls below any minimum you set. If you keep some cash in a linked savings account, you can quickly transfer money to cover any impending shortfalls. (Many banks allow you to make transfers from your cell phone, either via text or through a smartphone app.)

Set up automatic payments and transfers. Start by "paying yourself first." If you're contributing to a retirement plan such as an IRA, set up a transfer so that money is whisked into the appropriate account shortly after each payday. If you're beefing up an emergency fund, set up another transfer for that purpose.

Then tackle your bills. If a bill payment is exactly the same dollar amount each month (such as with most mortgages, auto loans and student loans), you can use your bank's online bill payment system to set up a recurring payment. If the amount varies, you can arrange with the biller to have the total taken directly from your checking account or charged to a credit card—but only use a card if you'll pay it off in full. You don't want to pay finance charges to cover regular bills.

To pay the credit cards themselves, consider having at least the minimum payment deducted automatically from your checking account each month. You can always make a second payment later to pay off or pay down the balance.

Or you can simply have the whole balance deducted from your checking account. After using automatic payments and the minimum payment option for years, I've now switched all our credit cards to the "pay balance in full" automatic option. Our statements give me plenty of notice about when our payments are due and how much they will be; I simply add an upcoming transaction to our transaction-tracking system and make sure there will be enough money in the account to cover it.

You definitely want to limit what companies are authorized to scoop money out of your account, however. Some billers—gyms and phone companies among them—are notorious for continuing to reach into your account after you've asked them to stop. And retailers don't have the best reputation for safeguarding your important financial information. Some of the biggest database breaches in recent years have occurred among retailers or the companies used to process their payments.

Financial services companies, including banks, brokerages and credit card companies, in general do a better job of complying with laws governing electronic transactions and of safeguarding data. They're not perfect, heaven knows, but they've certainly got a better track record than retailers. If I don't trust a biller, I have the bill charged to one of our credit cards, and I pay that off every month. (A bonus is that all those bills charged to our cards help us generate more rewards points for travel and other goodies.)

Regularly check in with your transaction-tracking system. Once you've got your system set up, it takes just a few seconds to sign in and see where you stand. Many of us make this part of our daily routine, but even weekly check-in should be enough to avoid major problems.

Consider the two-checking-account system. If you have trouble figuring out how much you need to leave in your account for bills and how much is available for other spending, you can eliminate much of the guesswork by using two checking accounts.

You can have your paycheck deposited into one account that's primarily for paying regular bills, then arrange for an automatic transfer so that your weekly spending money is routed to a second checking account.

Or you can turn it around so that enough money to pay bills is carved out of your primary checking account each paycheck, leaving whatever's left as "play" or spending money.

There are some drawbacks to the two-account approach. It may take a few months to determine the right amount to transfer each payday, particularly if you have a lot of variable bills (or you forget about a big nonmonthly bill, like an annual insurance premium). You also need to keep track of two account balances, instead of one.

But you can tell much more easily how much cash you have available for spending on groceries, gas, clothes, entertainment and other "non-bill" expenses.

If your bank won't give you a second checking account for free, consider using the no-minimum, no-fee online payment accounts offered by Internet banks including ING Direct, EmigrantDirect, HSBC Direct and FNBO.

WHY YOU SHOULD CONSIDER AN ONLINE BANK

VIRTUALLY ALL BANKS THESE DAYS have online access, but true online banks are a different animal—and their proliferation has been a huge boon for consumers.

Online-only banks don't have to pay for real estate and a big fleet of tellers, so they can keep costs low. There are typically no minimum balances required for opening and maintaining an account, and you don't have to worry about account or maintenance fees. Online banks make it easy to transfer money, so you can easily move cash around as you need it. And your deposits are covered by FDIC insurance, just like at other banks.

Opening a savings account at an online bank typically takes about five minutes. You link it to your checking account at a brick-and-mortar bank, transfer your initial deposit and are good to go. Many online banks also offer checking accounts with free online bill pay and ATM fee reimbursement.

Obviously, you have to be comfortable handling your banking transactions online. If you need a lot of handholding or face time with a teller, you may still want to do most of your banking with a brick-and-mortar bank, but you could still use an online bank for your savings.

WHY YOU NEED SAVINGS "BUCKETS"

In another recent Pew Research Center poll, one-third of respondents reported an unexpected expense in the previous year that seriously set them back financially. Of those who reported such surprise bills, the big expenses cited most often were:

- Medical (34 percent)
- Cars (24 percent)
- Housing (20 percent)

Here's the thing, though: Medical bills, car expenses and home costs aren't really unexpected—at least they shouldn't be. If you have a body, a car or a home, sooner or later it's going to cost you.

Predicting exactly how much you'll have to pay can, of course, be tricky. And forcing yourself to sock that much away can be even trickier. But you can reduce the odds of a budget-busting expense with smart planning—and fortunately, online banking technology can make this much, much easier.

Here's how: treat your big unexpected bills like the ones that come every month.

Start by opening a savings account at an online bank. Like at traditional banks, your deposits are covered by the Federal Deposit Insurance Corporation (FDIC), but unlike at traditional banks, you're typically not charged account fees (such as a monthly fee if you don't maintain a minimum balance). Most allow free transfers between your online account and your brick-and-mortar checking account.

Once you have an account set up, you can easily open additional accounts (often called subaccounts or targeted accounts) for different goals and purposes. Any bill that you receive less than monthly, for instance, is a good candidate for its own subaccount. That might include insurance premiums, property tax payments, estimated tax payments and vehicle registration. You may want to set up accounts for major upcoming expenses: vacations, holidays, a home down payment, as well as those inevitable car, home and medical bills.

Fund these accounts by figuring out how much you'll need annually, then dividing it by the number of paychecks you get. (More on that in a minute.) Set up an automatic transfer to sweep money from your checking account into the appropriate savings subaccount. For example, let's say you spend $800 on a typical Christmas, including presents, entertaining and decorations. If you get paid every other week, with 26 pay periods a year, you could set up an automatic transfer of $31 after every pay period to be deposited in your holiday subaccount. That is, of course, if you start with your first paycheck in January and your goal is in late December. If you get a later start, you'll have to divide the sum you need by the number of paychecks remaining until your goal.

Before I switched to the bucket system, I had all the savings for insurance, taxes, repairs and emergencies funneled into one account, which made it hard to figure out if we really had enough saved to cover expected contingencies. When I started separating our savings into subaccounts, I discovered we didn't have quite enough to cover our upcoming life insurance premiums plus our property taxes without dipping into the repair or emergency funds. Instead, I calculated the shortfall and how much time we had left to save for them, then boosted the amounts that were being transferred into our insurance and property tax accounts. Once those bills were paid, I adjusted the transfers back down to the amounts that would cover the bills the next time they came due.

Another good reason for separate buckets or subaccounts: many of us have a squishy idea of what constitutes an emergency. It's too easy to raid the one big pot and then discover you don't have enough cash to cover the big bills when they arrive. When you have separate buckets, it's easier to keep a strict hands-off policy on those emergency funds so they're only used when they're needed—such as when you've lost your job.

Separate accounts also give us that instant gratification so important for staying motivated to save, according to financial planner Robert Pagliarini. Setting up these smaller pots and making regular deposits give us tangible proof that we're making progress toward our goals.

"When you rip open your account statements or view them online, you'll know that every dollar in each account is earmarked," Pagliarini says. "You'll know exactly how much you've saved and how much more you need to save."

It should be pretty easy to determine how much to save for those not-monthly-but-still-regular bills, like taxes and insurance. But how about the three expenses I mentioned earlier—car costs, home costs and medical bills? Here's how to estimate:

Car costs. If your car is five years old or less, check out Edmunds

.com's "True Cost to Own" feature, which tracks how much recent models are likely to set you back in maintenance, repairs and other costs.

A new Honda Civic, on average, is estimated to cost a Los Angeles resident $3,499 in maintenance and $773 in repairs over the next five years. Combine those costs and you should be setting aside $854 a year, or about $71 a month, into a separate account earmarked for auto costs. With a five-year-old model, the average costs go up to $4,944 for maintenance and $2,581 for repairs over five years. That means you should be setting aside about $125 a month. If it sounds like more than you'll need, well, then, you'll have a down payment for a newer car that much sooner.

What if your car is older? Collect your maintenance and repair receipts from recent years, figure out a yearly average and then inflate that by at least 10 percent. You also can ask a trusted mechanic what repairs are likely to be in your future, and add those costs as well. You can have this conversation the next time you bring the car in for a repair or ask for a checkup, something that will typically cost you $75 to $150. Consider it an investment in your car's future.

Home costs. Saving for home maintenance and repairs requires a slightly different technique.

Homeowners quickly learn that big expenses come with the territory. A new roof or furnace, for example, can set you back thousands of dollars. But you typically won't face such big bills every year. So the trick is to start saving early so that you have a stash ready for such costs. Many homeowners got out of this habit because they could tap home equity or use low-rate credit cards. But with lenders clamping down in both areas, savings is once again the best way to go.

How much to set aside? Financial planner and author Eric Tyson recommends a simple guideline: set aside 1 percent of your home's purchase price each year to pay for inevitable repair and maintenance costs. If you paid $250,000 for your home, you should be saving $2,500 a year, or about $208 a month. You won't use up that money each year, Tyson says, but eventually you're certain to face an expense that uses up every dime you've accumulated.

What if you're a renter? You may not have to pay for a new furnace, but you'd still be smart to set aside some money for moving expenses and a deposit on your next place. That way you're prepared if the landlord jacks up the rent, converts it to condos, loses the place to foreclosure or turns the apartment next door into a crack den.

Medical bills. How much you should set aside depends on the details of your insurance, such as:

- Your deductible (if any)
- Your out-of-pocket maximum (if any)
- Your co-payments

You can find out these details by reviewing your policy (your insurer may have the details online) or talking to your company's human resources department. Chances are good these details will change every year, so stay up-to-date.

Some policies require you to pay the first $1,000 or more of your medical bills out of your own pocket before coverage kicks in, but then everything after that is paid for, or your co-pays are capped at a certain dollar amount. You'd be smart to try to save at least the full amount of your deductible, if possible, and, ideally, your total out-of-pocket maximum. Other policies require you to pay only a portion of each bill—say, 20 percent or 30 percent—but may not have any cap on how much you'd have to shell out in a year. Your exposure to big bills in that case could be catastrophically high. Even if you don't have an out-of-pocket maximum, you should try to save enough to cover what you spent last year on co-payments, plus a few hundred dollars more, to cover your most likely expenses. (And if you have a choice, you might consider switching to a less risky policy.)

Check your vision and dental coverage as well. Chances are, it's pretty limited. The yearly benefit on a dental policy, for example, is often just $1,000 to $1,500, which could be exhausted in one complicated procedure. Unfortunately, the older you get, the more likely those procedures become, so you'll want to save some extra for those.

If your employer offers a flexible spending account (FSA) for medical expenses, you should definitely take advantage of that to put aside pre-tax money using a deduction from each paycheck. But contribute only what you're likely to spend that year, since flexible account savings that aren't spent are lost forever. Knowing what you spent last year can give you a guideline for how much to contribute this year. Add in any treatments you know lie ahead, like braces for your kids or crowns for your own teeth. You also should know that the rules regarding FSAs have changed; as of January 1, 2011, you can no longer spend the money on over-the-counter medicines, and starting in 2013 the amount you can contribute will be capped at $2,500.

Another option is a health savings account (HSA). If you're self-employed or your company offers HSA-compatible policies, you could combine a high-deductible policy with one of these special tax-advantaged savings accounts. The good news is that any money you don't spend can be saved for a future year. For more details, talk to your tax pro and check out the Treasury Department's page of information on HSAs at www.ustreas.gov/offices/public-affairs/hsa/.

INSIDER TERMS

Health savings account (HSA): A tax-advantaged savings account, available to people enrolled in a high-deductible health insurance plan, that allows tax-deductible contributions for paying medical expenses. If unused, the money can be rolled over from year to year. Only certain insurance plans are eligible and the amount of each year's contributions is limited by law.

Otherwise, additional cash for medical bills should be funneled into your medical savings subaccount.

All this assumes you have health insurance. If you don't, predicting your expenses with any degree of accuracy will be tough. You can use the past few years' health care spending as a guide, but understand that one accident or illness could trigger catastrophically high expenses. If that happens, you may wind up in bankruptcy court. Medical debt contributes to two-thirds of consumer bankruptcies, according to research by Harvard's Elizabeth Warren.

Given what I've told you about the 50/30/20 budget, you may be wondering whether these transfers for repairs and medical bills are considered must-have expenses, wants or savings.

In our family, I count them among our must-have expenses, since they're required to properly maintain ourselves and our property.

Saving for future expenses acknowledges the reality that we can't always predict what our lives will cost. But we're always better off having extra savings to meet our needs than scrambling at the last minute to come up with the cash. Many people forgot that lesson during the boom years when credit could be counted on to fill the gap, but we've since been reminded how important it is to have that cushion.

ACTION STEPS

We've covered a lot of ground in this chapter. Here's a reminder of what you need to do now:

- Aim for a spending plan where your "must-have" expenses don't exceed 50 percent of your after-tax income, wants are corralled to 30 percent and you're saving or repaying debt with the remaining 20 percent.
- Use the Web to find a wealth of money-saving tips.
- Track your spending using Quicken, an online tracker like Mint.com or Yodlee or other budgeting software.
- Set up true overdraft protection and reject expensive "bounce protection" or "courtesy overdraft."
- Set up savings "buckets," preferably at an online bank, for each of your goals and irregular expenses, including car, home and medical costs.
- Automate bills and savings transfers.

2ND COMMANDMENT

Create a Survival Plan with Cash and Credit

THE OLD-SCHOOL RULES:
Save for a rainy day.

THE BUBBLE ECONOMY RULES:
Who needs savings? Leverage to the max!

THE NEW RULES:
Build both your cash savings and your access to credit
for maximum financial flexibility in emergencies.

I've lived through a few earthquakes, including the devastating 1994 Northridge temblor in California, and I can tell you: you're never really ready.

You might have your emergency supplies laid in and your evacuation route planned out, but when a really big earthquake hits, you can't quite prepare for the absolutely primal fear that washes over your body. It's when the shaking stops and you can take action that the value of advanced preparations becomes obvious. While others are freaking out, you calmly take action—tending to loved ones, securing your property, breaking out the supplies to cope with the loss of services you've until now depended on. You are prepared.

The financial crisis that erupted in 2008 exposed how very many people were unprepared for an economic earthquake. But some people endured better than others. Even as home values plummeted, credit tightened and unemployment soared, they had what it takes to endure and in some cases even profit from the fallout.

Those resources extend far beyond the much-touted emergency fund. Although a big pile of cash can help, it's not essential and it's certainly not enough. What counts is your overall financial flexibility—the resources you can command to help withstand a crisis, even one that's unexpectedly severe or long lasting.

Of course, you may not feel in control right now. You may think it's difficult or impossible to cope, given your income and circumstances. But I'm going to disabuse you of that myth and show you exactly how to do it, starting right now.

CASH IS NOT ALL YOU NEED

Emergency funds got a lot of attention after the financial crisis really hit. Financial writers noted how our personal savings rate suddenly soared from nearly zero to over 4 percent, and then kept climbing. Some pundits decided the usual advice to have three to six months' expenses saved wasn't enough—now you needed eight months, nine months, a year's worth of cash on hand. If ever a piece of advice was designed to depress and discourage the typical American family, that was it.

INSIDER TERMS

Personal savings rate: The percentage of after-tax income that households save. While similar to the national savings rate—a measure of what households save, as a percentage of the value of all goods and services produced in a year—the personal savings rate does not include most retirement savings and is thus considered a better measure of how much Americans are putting aside for emergencies.

THE MAJORITY OF U.S. HOUSEHOLDS DON'T
EVEN COME CLOSE TO HAVING "ENOUGH"
SAVINGS ON HAND:

- Forty-three percent of households have less than $1,000 in liquid savings, according to SMR Research, a market research company.
- Twenty-eight percent live literally paycheck to paycheck, an ACNielsen poll found, with no savings whatsoever.
- Just three in ten households have a cash hoard that would

> tide them over for a minimum of three months, according
> to Ohio University researchers.

That's terrible, right? And a great excuse for financial experts to lecture people that they're not doing enough.

Sometimes, though, I wonder whom these experts think they're talking to—maybe investment bankers who get fat bonuses or lottery winners. It would be nice if some of those experts would consider the financial realities of the typical household before they rush to condemn those who don't have a huge cash stash. The reason more people don't have three months or more saved up is because it's hard—really hard—for most households to accumulate that much money.

Let's say you spend about $40,000 a year. By getting strict about your budget and trimming your expenses, you reduce your costs 10 percent to $36,000 a year, or $3,000 a month. If you put every penny of the $4,000 you trimmed into savings, it would take you more than *two years* to save three months' worth of expenses, or $9,000. And that's if you don't have any financial setbacks in the meantime that would force you to tap those funds.

Furthermore, many people who are realizing their need for an emergency fund are also dealing with other important financial issues. They may have credit card debt or not be saving enough for retirement. Carving cash out of their budget for emergency savings will and should take a backseat to those important priorities. For these families, saving for emergencies has an unacceptably high opportunity cost.

"Opportunity cost" is a term in economics that means what you give up in order to get something else. If you make saving for emergencies your top priority over debt payoff or retirement savings, the opportunity cost you could pay might be enormous. It makes no financial sense, for example, to have money sitting in a savings account earning a puny interest rate while you have credit card debt accumulating at double-digit rates. Paying down your credit cards lowers your interest costs and typically frees up space on your credit lines that you could use again in an emergency.

EMERGENCY SAVINGS VS. CREDIT CARD DEBT: THE CLEAR WINNER

One of the more absurd pieces of advice floating around during the recession was that people should stop paying down their credit card debts in order to build up their emergency funds to cover eight or nine months' worth of expenses.

Now, if you're in imminent danger of losing your job, conserving cash makes sense. But for most people, the opportunity cost of taking such advice is pretty horrifying. Let's use the example of the family that's trimmed its spending by $4,000 a year. Building up a nine-month reserve would take this family nearly seven years (81 months). If they were simultaneously carrying $20,000 in credit card debt at 18 percent interest, building that emergency fund would cost them more than $16,000 in finance charges.

If they instead applied their newfound savings to their credit card debt, they could be debt free in two and a half years (30 months) and pay less than $5,000 in interest. Then they could start applying the money they had been paying to the credit cards toward their savings.

Assuming they had been paying $833 a month to the cards (an initial minimum payment of $500, plus $333 from the spending they trimmed), they could have a nine-month reserve saved up in just 32 additional months. In other words, they would be debt free *and* have a fat emergency fund in *less time* (62 months) than if they had focused solely on building up their savings (81 months).

Another common, and unfortunate, bit of bad advice is that folks should put their retirement savings on hold while they save for emergencies. But such a shortsighted approach can quite literally cost you a small fortune.

Let's assume you're single, you're making $50,000 and your company would match 50 percent of your 401(k) contributions up to 6 percent of your salary (the most common match). By not contributing 10 percent of your salary, you're forever giving up $1,500 in free money (the match) plus paying an unnecessary $1,250 in extra income taxes each year (assuming you're in the 25 percent federal bracket).

The biggest cost, though, is the future tax-deferred earnings you've forgone. Each year you don't contribute, you're costing yourself $65,000 in future retirement money (assuming your contributions, plus the match, grow at an 8 percent annual rate for thirty years). Once they're gone, you can't get back those opportunities to receive a match or to set your money growing as early as possible.

That doesn't mean emergency savings shouldn't be one of your priorities. But while you're building your fund, and even afterward, you'll want to have access to credit. Those who hate debt in any form may recoil from this advice, but the truth is that credit can be an incredibly helpful tool. Like any tool, it can be misused. But properly deployed, it can be a lifesaver.

High-end financial planners know this. That's why they often have their affluent clients set up a home equity line of credit (HELOC) to be left open and unused in case of emergency. Job searches tend to take longer when you make six figures or more. Planners know that if their clients lose their jobs, they could be out of work for many months before an equivalent position comes along. Having access to a HELOC allows these clients a lifeline to tap if their emergency savings fall short.

INSIDER TERMS

Home equity line of credit (HELOC): A revolving account that functions much like a credit card, allowing borrowers to repeatedly draw down and pay off a variable-rate loan. Because they are secured by the equity in a home, HELOCs are mortgages that typically qualify for tax deductions on the interest paid on the first $100,000 borrowed.

HELOCs typically cost nothing to set up, and most have relatively low annual fees ($50 to $100 is typical). The interest rate is low, and you don't have to pay any principal during the first ten years or so you have the line. So if your interest rate is 7 percent, you can take about $70 of every $1,000 you borrow and use it to make your payments until the crunch passes.

You do, of course, have to have enough equity in your home to convince a lender to approve your application—or to prevent an existing lender from closing, freezing or reducing the limit on your account. The amount of equity required increased substantially after the financial crisis arrived. Before the crunch, lenders would allow you to borrow 100 percent or more of your home's value. These days, 80 percent loan-to-value is the limit for most, although some lenders won't allow you to tap more than 60 to 65 percent of your home's value in areas hard hit by foreclosures. ("Loan-to-value" means your limit on the credit line plus the balance of your mortgage.)

It's also essential that you not use your HELOC for other, nonemergency spending if its purpose is to supplement your cash savings. Any dollar you borrow prematurely is a dollar you won't have access to when you need it.

If a HELOC isn't an option, credit cards can provide a lifeline. Credit cards typically come with higher interest rates, but their minimum payments are fairly low, usually 2 to 4 percent of the balance monthly. And credit cards have a feature that home equity lines lack: if you wind up filing for bankruptcy, balances on unsecured debts like credit cards may be erased, while secured debts like mortgages and HELOCs can't be discharged.

INSIDER TERMS

Secured vs. unsecured debts: Secured debts are linked to an asset that the borrower pledges as collateral for the loan. If the borrower fails to pay, the lender can take the asset as full or partial payment of the remaining balance. Mortgages and vehicle loans are examples of secured debts. Unsecured debts are not linked to any asset. Credit cards, medical bills and personal loans are examples of unsecured debt.

Clearly, you don't want to use your cards if you know you won't be able to pay your debt. But once again, they can keep you from going under when things go wrong and you're not adequately prepared.

The "cash plus credit" approach acknowledges that life can surprise us. Even someone who thought he was adequately prepared, with six or nine or twelve months' worth of savings, can find a job search lasting longer than he expected. Or multiple crises can hit at once. After Hurricane Katrina, for example, many people found themselves both homeless and jobless because the disaster destroyed businesses as well as neighborhoods. Even absent a natural disaster, life can throw you curves, such as a disabling accident or illness that makes it hard to work, cutting into your income while increasing your medical bills. Appropriate insurance can help, of course, and we'll talk about that in an upcoming chapter. But it's foolish to believe you can plan for every contingency, which is why I recommend you shoot for a generous amount of financial flexibility in your life, such as cash plus credit equal to twelve months' worth of must-have living expenses.

I think you'll find the more cash you have on hand, the better you'll sleep at night. A preliminary goal, once your retirement savings and debt payoff plans are on track, might be to accumulate emergency savings equal to three months' worth of must-have expenses, and you'll probably want to grow your stash from there. But your access to credit can be a useful proxy for a fully funded emergency account while you're building your savings.

You'll want to be extremely judicious about how you use your credit. In a crisis, you'll need to cut your expenses to the bone before you do anything else. If you're living on the 50/30/20 budget, you can and should cut back to must-haves only, suspending extra debt payments and any "want" purchases until your situation improves. You don't want to drain away your precious equity, pile up massive credit card debt or wind up filing for bankruptcy simply because you refused to adjust your lifestyle.

You also need to realize that this advice isn't for everybody. If you're a chronic overspender who can't be trusted with credit, you're better off going the all-cash route. All the lines of credit in the world won't help you if you've maxed them out before the crisis comes.

But most people should at least think about the alternatives to tide them over as they're building their traditional emergency funds. Let's

OTHER RESOURCES THAT ENHANCE YOUR FINANCIAL FLEXIBILITY

ANY OF THE FOLLOWING can dramatically reduce your economic vulnerability, allowing you to raise money in a hurry:

- Family or friends willing to lend or give you money
- Objects or collections you can easily sell (good jewelry, furs, firearms, vehicles) either to a dealer or through resources such as Craigslist and eBay
- Cash-value life insurance policies that you can borrow against or cash in
- Nonretirement investments you can borrow against or cash in
- In-demand skills that would allow you to get a second job
- A work-at-home partner who could get a paying job
- A side business that can generate more income

Some of these resources are hard to quantify, and I wouldn't deduct any of them from the twelve-month financial flexibility fund. But it's good to know what alternatives you have if the you-know-what really hits the fan. If you have plenty of these options, you may feel more comfortable with a smaller cash fund. If you have few, you may want to accelerate your savings plan.

hope you never need them, but if you do, you may be very happy you have them.

HOW TO SAFELY BUILD YOUR ACCESS TO CREDIT

Just when many people needed to tap their credit thanks to rising unemployment, lenders began taking that credit away. They shut down, froze or lowered limits on millions of credit cards and home equity lines of credit. Some lenders began "chasing down the balance" on customers they considered risky. Every time those customers paid off a chunk of their debt, the lenders would lower their credit limit by an equivalent amount.

This practice hurt customers in two ways. First, the customer lost access to credit that could have been useful in an emergency. Second, lowering credit limits made the customers look perpetually maxed out, which was typically bad for their credit scores. And good credit scores are the key to building your access to credit and leveling the playing field with lenders.

At the same time some people were losing their credit lines and having their accounts closed, others were still being offered low-rate credit card and balance transfer offers because of their excellent credit scores. If their issuers did try to raise their rates or lower their limits, these prime-credit candidates could often get the moves rescinded simply by threatening to move their business elsewhere.

People with good credit also enjoyed some of the lowest mortgage rates on record, even as those with poorer credit found themselves cut off from home loans. Many lenders lifted the score needed to get the best rate from 720 to 740, while Fannie Mae, the giant mortgage-buying agency, lifted its minimum score requirement from 580 to 620.

GOOD CREDIT HELPS IN OTHER WAYS. AFTER ALL, CREDIT INFORMATION IS USED BY:

- Insurance companies to evaluate applicants and set premiums
- Cell phone carriers to decide whether to sign you up for service
- Utilities to determine whether to charge you a deposit, and how much
- Landlords to decide who gets apartments
- Employers concerned about higher risk of theft from those with troubled finances

Clearly, cultivating good credit scores is an essential twenty-first-century skill. The good news is that it's possible to boost your numbers if you have a handle on your finances and you know how credit scores work.

After all, the median credit score is 711 on the 300 to 850 FICO scale, which is the score used by most lenders. That means half the adult U.S. population has a higher score and half has a lower score. Thirty-seven percent have scores over 750, and 18 percent have scores above 800, according to Fair Isaac, the company that created FICO scoring.

To boost your scores, you need to keep in mind that:

You can't raise your scores if your finances are still in free fall. If you're unable to pay your bills, you certainly can't fix your credit. Real credit score repair will have to wait until your financial crisis has been solved and you have enough money to cover your expenses, plus some extra to begin paying down your debts.

You can't raise your scores if you don't use credit. Credit scores try to predict how well you're likely to use credit in the future by how well you've used it in the past. So while living a cash-only lifestyle may do wonders for your wallet, it won't help your scores. Without continuing use of some type of credit, eventually your credit reports won't even generate credit scores.

You don't have to pay credit card interest to achieve great scores. "Using credit" is not the same as "carrying a balance on your credit cards." Carrying a balance is expensive, bad for your finances and usually unnecessary. Many of us who have achieved 800-plus scores pay off our balances religiously, and we know you can build and keep great credit scores without ever paying a dime of credit card interest.

You can't expect overnight results. You're likely to see improvement in your scores within thirty days if you pay down significant chunks of your credit card debt. But otherwise, credit repair takes time, and how much time depends on the many details of your credit reports. If you have serious black marks, such as bankruptcies or foreclosures, you can see significant improvement in your scores as time passes but you may have to wait until those negatives drop off your credit reports before you can join the 700-Plus Club.

Now that you understand the basics, you can use the following techniques to get your scores over 740.

Patrol your credit reports. Your credit scores are based entirely on the information in your credit reports on file at the big three credit bureaus: Equifax, Experian and TransUnion. Serious errors in those reports can depress your scores.

INSIDER TERMS

Credit bureaus: Privately run companies that collect credit and other information about individuals. This information is sold to authorized users for a fee and used in a variety of contexts, from making credit card offers to background checks for employment decisions. The three major credit bureaus are competitors and don't collect or report information the same way, so your credit reports at each of the three are likely to be somewhat different.

You can get your reports once a year for free from AnnualCredit Report.com; you can buy subsequent copies directly from the bureaus or from MyFICO.com. Dispute any serious errors, such as:

- Accounts that aren't yours
- Reports of late payments when you paid on time
- Bankruptcies older than ten years or accounts that were wiped out in bankruptcy but are listed as still due
- Other negative information that's older than seven years (the seven-year clock typically starts 180 days after the account first went delinquent)

Get a major credit card, or two, or three. Retail cards and gas cards can help you build your credit history initially, but to get your scores into 700-plus territory you'll want at least one (and probably two or three) major cards: Visa, MasterCard, Discover or American Express. If you can't qualify for a regular credit card, consider a secured version, for which you make a deposit with an issuing bank. You can find offers at CardRatings.com, CreditCards.com, LowCards.com, CardHub.com and IndexCreditCards.com, among other sites. Just make sure the card reports to all three bureaus, and try to get a card that converts to a regu-

---

INSIDER TERMS

Secured credit card: These cards are secured by a deposit you make at the issuing bank. Your credit limit is typically equal to the deposit you make. The best secured cards report to all three credit bureaus, don't charge up-front fees and have annual fees under $100.

---

lar credit card after twelve to eighteen months of on-time payments. If you have only one or two major credit cards, consider adding another. The initial application may temporarily ding your scores 5 points or less but the added credit line should improve your scores, and your financial flexibility, over time.

Get an installment loan. The FICO formula likes to see both revolving accounts (credit cards) and installment accounts (mortgages, auto loans, student loans, personal loans) on your credit reports. If you don't have any installment loans showing up on your reports, consider applying for a small personal loan and paying that back over time. If your credit scores aren't good enough to get an unsecured personal loan, talk to your local credit union about a secured version. Often called a share-secured loan, this type of borrowing is backed by money you place in a credit union savings account or certificate of deposit. The interest rate you pay is typically a few percentage points above the rate you earn on your money. These loans may be easier to get than bank loans, since credit unions are often willing to look at more than just your credit scores, according to Susan Tiffany, the director of consumer publications for the Credit Union National Association. Credit unions "don't treat credit scores as the only source of information about you," Tiffany says. "They're looking for ways to say yes. Are you responsible with your checking account? Are you demonstrating that you're trying to be a regular saver? Those behaviors can help."

INSIDER TERMS

Installment loans: Installment loans allow you to borrow a set amount of money and pay it back over time with a set number of scheduled payments. The interest rate and amount of payments are often (though not always) fixed.

Arrange automatic payments for every card or loan. Credit scores are extraordinarily sensitive to whether you pay your bills on time, so don't let travel, a busy schedule or a simple brain cramp trash your scores. Most lenders will let you set up automatic payments that take an amount you specify—the minimum payment, a set dollar amount or the full balance—every month from your checking account.

To give you an idea of how much late payments and other credit mishaps can affect your score, I asked the FICO creators to show how far a score would drop after any of the following actions:

	Prior score: 680	Prior score: 780
	Score after credit mishap	
Maxed-out card	650–670	735–755
30-day late payment	600–620	670–690
Settling debt	615–635	655–675
Foreclosure	575–595	620–640
Bankruptcy	530–550	540–560

Source: FICO.

WHAT'S A CREDIT UNION?

A CREDIT UNION is a financial institution that's owned by its members—the people who have deposits there. Unlike banks, credit unions are not-for-profit entities, and they typically offer lower fees and better interest rates. Most credit union accounts are insured by the National Credit Union Share Insurance Fund, which, like bank FDIC insurance, is backed by the full faith and credit of the U.S. government. Virtually everyone in the United States can join a credit union; to find one, visit the National Credit Union Administration's Web site (www.ncua.gov).

The better the score, the more points you could lose. A single skipped payment, for example, could clip 90 to 110 points off the 780 score.

Don't let disputes go to collections. Being stubborn can cost you. Yes, your insurance should have covered that bill; no, you shouldn't have to pay for a broadband connection that doesn't work. But if you let a commonplace problem like these escalate, your account will be turned over to collections and become a big black mark on your credit reports. Pay under protest and get your revenge in small claims court. (Don't get sued yourself, though: lawsuits and judgments are another major stain on your credit reports.)

Pay down and spread out your debt. More than a third of your FICO score depends on how much of your available credit you're using—your so-called credit utilization. The FICO formula likes to see big gaps between your balances (whether you pay them off each month or not) and your limits, especially on credit cards. (You're rewarded for paying down installment debt such as mortgages and auto loans, but your scores improve much more dramatically when you pay down revolving debt such as credit cards.) The scoring formula measures both your overall credit utilization (your total balances versus total limits) as well as your credit utilization on each card. So it's better to have small balances on several cards than a big balance on one card.

A balance may not be what you think. You have to worry about your credit utilization ratio even if you pay your balances in full each month. The balance that's reported to the credit bureaus is typically the one on your last statement, not the balance that's left over after you pay your bill. So if you charge $9,000 on a $10,000 card, it's going to look like you're using 90 percent of your limit (which is really, really bad), even though you paid off the balance in full when you got the bill.

Shoot for 10 percent. The less of your available credit you use, the more FICO rewards you. Keeping your credit utilization below 30 percent on your cards is good; getting it below 10 percent is even better. If you regularly use more, ask for a higher limit, spread your charges out on more than one card or make two payments every month—one just before your monthly statement closing date to lower the balance reported to the credit bureaus and a second one just before the due date to avoid late fees.

But don't let your cards gather dust. Overloading your cards is a bad thing for your scores, but so is not using them at all. The scoring formula prefers to see accounts that are being actively used rather than sitting on a shelf. Even a little activity is better than no activity.

Push back against lower limits. If you can't get the issuer to reverse its decision, try to move your balance elsewhere. If you've got high balances that you can't pay down quickly, consider transferring the debt to a personal installment loan from your local bank or credit union. The interest rate you'll pay is typically higher—10 to 15 percent for people with good credit, up to 22 percent for those with fair credit—but the scoring formula treats installment loan balances more kindly than the same debt on credit cards.

Consider moving debt off your credit reports entirely. You can make debt disappear from your credit reports, and thus credit-scoring calculations, by paying it off with a loan from a friend, family member or retirement plan. If you're tempted to tap your retirement account, though, let me be clear: I am not a fan of 401(k) loans. Lose your job, and any unpaid balance can quickly become a tax nightmare. If you can't pay back what you owe quickly, it typically becomes an inadvertent withdrawal, triggering income taxes and penalties that usually equal one-quarter to one-half the outstanding loan. Borrowing from your retirement to pay your cards is an especially bad idea if your finances are on the edge, because credit card debt can be erased in bankruptcy; 401(k) loans can't.

Play the home equity card cautiously. Moving a credit card balance to a home equity loan or line of credit may improve your scores but put you at greater overall financial risk. If you fail to pay the bill, you could lose your home. Also, as with a 401(k) loan, you're turning unsecured debt that could be wiped out through bankruptcy into secured debt that typically can't.

Don't close accounts or let them be closed. Closing accounts can't help your scores and might hurt them. Yet many issuers these days are slamming shut inactive cards rather than continuing to carry these unprofitable accounts. If you've got cards you haven't used in a while, take them out for dinner or a movie and pay the balance promptly. Better yet, use them to charge a regular expense, such as your electric bill, and arrange for automatic payments.

Apply for credit sparingly. Applications for credit don't ding your scores as much as some people fear; typically, you lose 5 points or less. But when every point counts, such as when you're in the market for a mortgage or a car loan, you don't want to squander any of your scores. Wait to apply for any other credit until you've secured the loan you want.

The lower your scores, the longer it will take to crawl your way back up the FICO scale. But progress is possible, and anyone can hit the 740 mark in time by using credit consistently and responsibly.

WHEN YOU FIND IT IMPOSSIBLE TO SAVE

In the last chapter, you read about how hard it is to balance your budget and save money when your overhead expenses are out of control. Reining those in is a key to getting your finances on track.

But the real secret to building wealth is even simpler than that.

Two economics professors, Steven Venti of Dartmouth and David Wise of Harvard, studied the issue of income versus wealth for the National Bureau of Economic Research using Social Security lifetime earnings and net income assessments for 3,992 households whose heads were near retirement age.

Here's what they found:

There's a huge variation in wealth at every income level. Many low-income families have a net worth close to, or even below, zero. But the same is true of many high-income families.

INSIDER TERMS

Net worth: A measure of financial wealth of an individual, household or company that typically subtracts total debts from total assets. Negative net worth is when debts exceed assets.

Income alone doesn't explain wealth disparities. Some of the lowest-earning households had managed to accumulate significant wealth. In fact, the economists determined that income differences explain just 5 percent of the wealth dispersion.

Life happens. What the researchers called chance events—inheritances, medical bills, marital status, number of children—affected wealth as well, but not nearly as much as you'd think. The economists concluded that chance events explained about 4 percent of the dispersion.

Investment choices matter, but not that much. How you invest your savings affects your return; the safer your choices, the lower your general returns, and vice versa. But investment strategies explained only about 8 percent of the variations in wealth accumulation.

In other words, the vast majority of the differences in wealth had nothing to do with income, chance events or investment choices. What did explain who accumulates wealth and who doesn't? Venti and Wise concluded it was this: *how much the families chose to save.* Those who made it a priority to save built wealth, regardless of their income level, individual circumstances or choice of investments.

I think about this study anytime I hear from someone who believes a big infusion of money—a fat raise, a lottery win, an inheritance—would solve their financial problems. The reality is that most people blow through extra money pretty quickly. Lump sums are usually gone within months, and a raise or other increase in income is quickly met with an increase in lifestyle costs. The people who actually get ahead over time are the ones who make a decision to save and stick to it. And you can start with pretty small amounts.

GETTING OFF THE PAYCHECK-TO-PAYCHECK MERRY-GO-ROUND

All it takes is $500 to get started.

Wendi was living pretty much paycheck to paycheck when she read one of my columns telling people they need $500 in the bank. That's enough to avoid bounce fees, steer clear of payday lenders and cover most minor emergencies so you don't have to add to your credit card debt.

"I decided it was solid advice and trimmed my spending that month and saved $500," Wendi wrote me. "Realizing how much money I wasted, I saved another $500 the next month, and so on."

Some months she saved even more. Unexpected dental work and a car repair, events that would have stressed her out in the past, didn't derail her.

"I now have $12,000 in savings I am using as a down payment on my first house, something I never thought would be possible for me on my own," Wendi wrote from Riverside, California. "Thank you. You changed the way I looked at my money and spending, and improved the quality of my life."

A $500 pad is something that just about everyone can scrape together with enough determination. And if you're not used to having savings, it can change your life. It may not seem like much, but $500 will cover a good chunk of the real emergencies that come your way, from car repairs to insurance deductibles to replacing an appliance that breaks down. Even if an unexpected expense is higher than $500, you'll at least reduce the amount you need to scrape up from other sources.

Here are some ideas for accumulating the initial $500:

- **Use your tax refund.** The typical refund check is more than $2,000, so most people will have enough to fund their cushion in one fell swoop. If you're not getting a refund or it's already spent, though, you still have plenty of options.
- **Try a "buy nothing" month.** Several dozen posters on the Your Money message board at MSN Money have tried this experiment, and many are surprised at the amounts of cash they're saving by buying only necessities for a single month.

If you bring your lunch and snacks to work, don't eat out and avoid shopping for thirty days, you may find you can make a good deal of progress toward your $500 goal.

- **Sell stuff.** Try yard sales, consignment stores and online auction sites such as eBay or classified sites like Craigslist. Sell your books on Half.com or Amazon.com. Make sure to put the cash you raise into savings immediately, or you will spend it.
- **Save your change.** Several readers tell of saving hundreds of dollars over the course of a year, even making a game of it with their children.
- **Review your bills.** If you haven't already, go through your regular bills and see what you can trim. Dropping premium TV channels or doing without pay TV entirely for a while could produce significant savings. Phone bills are often rife with extras that can be cut, including call waiting or pricey voice-mail systems, or you might be able to drop the line altogether and just use your cell. Or if you have high-speed Internet access, consider switching to digital phone service or an Internet calling service such as Vonage or Skype to save even more. Once you've trimmed, channel the extra savings into your bank account. If you save $10 on your phone bill, for example, put that much into savings each month.
- **Make your savings automatic.** Setting up a regular electronic transfer from your checking to your savings account is much better than making the transfers manually. If you have to make the decision to save every month, you'll probably decide to do something else with the money. If the decision is made for you, it's more likely to stick.

U.S. HOUSEHOLDS WITH LESS THAN $500 IN THE BANK

Age group	Percentage
Under 35	34.5%
35–44	25.1%
45–54	22.1%

Age group	Percentage
55–64	19.0%
65–74	18.8%
75 and over	14.9%

Source: Federal Reserve Board's 2004 Survey of Consumer Finances.

Many people who live paycheck to paycheck have trouble maintaining an emergency fund because they're vague about what constitutes an emergency. Essentially, it's an event that puts your livelihood or your family's safety at risk.

The television dying, for example, is not an emergency. The furnace dying is. A car repair may or may not be an emergency, depending on whether you have alternate transportation. If you can't get to work any

SAFETY FIRST

PEOPLE OFTEN ASK how they can get a better return on their emergency savings. As one man put it, "I want to make sure this money is working as hard as it can for me." Sorry, but when it comes to emergency savings, you don't want your money working hard; you want it sitting in a rocking chair, there for you when you need it.

That means keeping your funds in an FDIC-insured bank account. Other investments have a risk of loss. Even money market mutual funds, once considered a safe haven for money, aren't guaranteed to return every dollar you put in. (The risk may be minimal, but during the financial crisis one of the oldest money market funds did "break the buck," or return less than investors put in, and the federal government had to step in to ensure other funds didn't lose money.)

The good news is that you don't need to settle for lousy interest rates. Rates offered by online banks typically rival and even beat those offered by money market funds. These banks are FDIC insured, just like their brick-and-mortar cousins, and your money will be available quickly when you need it.

other way, then getting the car fixed justifies raiding your emergency fund. If you can take the bus for a while, it doesn't.

Regular, predictable expenses are not emergencies. Neither are gift-giving occasions such as weddings, holidays and birthdays.

Getting clear about what a real emergency is, and making rules about when you can touch your savings and when you can't, can help you build your fund faster and keep it intact for when you really need it.

WHY YOU NEED MULTIPLE INCOME STREAMS

Losing your job is a frightening, humbling experience. Losing your job in a recession can be a nightmare.

At one point in the recession, there were six unemployed people for every available job opening. The median length of unemployment shot from two and a half months in December 2008 to five months by December 2009. The number of long-term unemployed—people who had been looking for work for seven months or more—soared from 2.6 million to 6.1 million.

The idea of lifetime job security died a long time ago. Few of us stay with a single employer for more than a few years (typical employee tenure, or how long workers stay in their jobs, is about four years, according to the U.S. Bureau of Labor Statistics). But until the Great Recession, a lot of young workers were used to the idea that they would be calling the shots—that if a paycheck ended it was because they left one job for another (usually heading for one with a bigger check). Too young to remember the 10 percent unemployment rates of the early 1980s, they were caught horribly unprepared for the idea that a job might end and that it might take half a year or more to find the next one.

They discovered that one of the biggest gambles people take in their financial life isn't related to how they invest, how much insurance they have or any of the other topics that come up when risk is discussed. *The biggest risk is having all your income come from a single source.*

This isn't just an issue for individuals, by the way. Business owners are constantly being warned about becoming too dependent on one or two major customers. Consultants urge entrepreneurs to constantly seek out and develop new income streams so that their business's fate isn't irretrievably tied to that of a client's.

If only people working for a paycheck got the same coaching and advice! Well, you're getting it here and now. Even if you expect to work full-time for someone else for the rest of your career, you need to learn a few entrepreneurial skills and develop more than one source of income in your life. In good times, multiple income streams can help you pay down debt, build wealth and save for fun stuff like vacations. In bad times, multiple income streams can be a lifeline that saves you from bankruptcy or even turns into your next job.

Some people create multiple income streams by making substantial investments. They buy commercial or rental property, for example, or purchase a franchise business to run. But you don't need to invest a fortune to start a lucrative sideline.

On occasion, I poll the posters on MSN's Your Money message board to see what they do to raise extra money. All the work listed here are things you can do before or after a regular workday, available in most areas and not speculative—no big up-front outlays required. Some of the jobs require special skills, but most could be done by anyone who's willing.

Obviously, not every idea will work for everyone, but you should find at least a few options that could work for you or at least get you thinking about the possibilities.

Administrative Assistant

Leaner staffs mean plenty of workplaces don't have anyone to help with administrative tasks like filing or making photocopies. One woman made photocopies for a university department chair while serving as a teacher's assistant for another professor. "At least around here, a lot of people have too much paper-pushing to do it all themselves, but it's not enough work to warrant a full-time assistant," she wrote. "Thus, a few hours of my time a week gives them some breathing room and gives me some extra cash. But you have to ask around. No one advertises a 3-hour-per-week photocopying job."

Artist

One woman painted murals for children's rooms, while a man drew cartoons and caricatures at parties. Theme parks and other tourist attractions often employ caricaturists. As an alternative, you could set up a booth at a community fair to get started.

Auction Seller

More than a million people make at least a part-time income selling stuff online at auction sites such as eBay. One mother said she started selling her kids' discarded toys and clothes, then moved on to trolling thrift stores and yard sales for items she could resell. "Some things that I've always been successful with are old 'vintage' concert T-shirts, sports team clothing, designer brand purses, and collectibles like figurines or commemorative plates," she said.

Bartender

One man called this time-honored way to garner tips and new best friends a "part-time job sent from heaven. Great money, and in these times socializing and alcohol are a good escape."

Blackjack Dealer

One poster attended a local casino's free, six-week course to learn how to be a blackjack dealer, then accepted a weekend job there. "It was tiring since I had to work 9 p.m. to 5 a.m. (especially on Fridays after working till 5 p.m., and then doing this) but it was good money," he wrote. "With tips it was around $17 to $18 an hour."

Blogger

Most bloggers don't write for the money—which is a good thing, since the vast majority make less than $100 a month from their sites. A lucky handful, though, develop enough of a following that their income from ads and referrals is significant; some even make enough to leave their day jobs. If you're a decent writer, an expert in a certain area and passionate about your topic, you could make some money this way. If you're interested, start with ProBlogger.com.

Bookseller

Selling stuff on eBay or Craigslist is a moneymaker for many, but some specialize in reselling one thing: books. There are a number of sites that facilitate used-book sales, including Amazon.com, Half.com and Cash 4Books.net. Yard sales, thrift stores and friends-of-the-library sales offer low-cost books you can resell.

Cleaner

Office buildings need folks to tidy up nights and weekends after the occupants have gone home. Or start your own home cleaning service: "I charge $20 an hour (with a four-hour monthly minimum). I make my own cleaning products, so very little overhead (other than gas for the car). This will clear me a minimum of $160 this month."

Coach

Shaping young athletes can be a profitable sideline for someone with flexible hours and coaching skills, said one man who coaches high school track and field. "I am self-employed so I have the flexibility to be at practice at 3:30 every day," he wrote. "I am also considering coaching basketball in the winter for one of the local schools as well. Total compensation for these two seasons would be $4,000 to $5,000 per year, depending on the school."

Computer Whiz

The limits are dictated only by your skills. You could help regular people troubleshoot their PCs or set up networks for local businesses. One woman wrote, "I used to develop/maintain a company Web site for about $12/$13 an hour as a part-time thing on the side. It was convenient because I could do it from home in the evening or the weekends."

Convention Center Worker

These venues need plenty of part-time bodies during conventions and other events.

One person signed up for occasional work serving ice cream and wrote: "So far I've worked during a basketball game, a wrestling tournament and a concert. They call me with available dates and I pick and choose the dates I want, depending on my full-time job and things going on at home. It's fun and exciting."

Crafter

A number of Your Money posters have turned crafting hobbies into profitable sidelines. Several crafters sell their wares on Etsy.com, a site that connects artists and crafters with a sizable audience of buyers.

Editor/Writer

Not everyone can write a coherent paragraph. If you can wrestle sentences into shape, you might be able to earn extra money helping those who are less skilled. One writer, who lives in a university town in the Midwest, makes extra money editing dissertations and other writing projects. Many writers find jobs through sites such as Elance.com, which allows scribes to bid on article-writing projects.

Handyman

If you've got the skills and the tools, you can help people with the tasks they can't do—or can't get around to doing. "I do little things like sealing the roof for leaks, mending the fence, doing brake and easy maintenance needs on cars for other people," one person wrote. "These jobs usually take from 1 to 3 hours, and I estimate I make about $25 to $40 cash an hour."

Lawn Service Provider

One man said his income from his lawn-mowing service is only restricted by his lack of time. "Currently I only have two clients but that nets me $190 a month from about mid-March through October," he wrote. "If I had more time (already work a full-time job and part-time job) I would wash windows and clean gutters. There is good money to be made doing those things."

Music Teacher

If you can play an instrument and have the patience to teach others, you may be able to offer music lessons after school or on weekends. One part-time musician charged $15 for each half-hour session while making additional extra money playing for weddings and parties.

Odd Jobber

Craigslist is connecting people who are just willing to work hard with folks who need help. One man offered his services for $10 an hour, and has helped people move, done landscaping chores and cleaned out houses after people moved or died.

Another couple has found nearly two dozen ways to make money:

"We sell industrial scrap metal (up to $300+ a month), mow lawns, haul landscaping materials, deliver and remove furniture, deliver appliances, replace window screens, change locksets, clean storage sheds/garages, pick up decent furniture on the street and sell to college kids, sell other curbside finds on Craigslist, buy, sell and trade video games, repair/upgrade computers, assemble patio furniture, assemble/tear down swing sets, rake leaves, write résumés, fix old bikes for resale, clean gutters, repair fences, install toilets, whatever."

Organizer

Helping others unclutter and organize their homes and offices is a full-time profession for many (for more information on this career field, visit the National Association of Professional Organizers). Many get started by working for friends or neighbors, but you can also contact professionals such as accountants, attorneys and conservators to see whether their clients may need help.

Paper Deliverer

Yes, some folks still receive their news via dead trees. It's not a bad gig if you're an early riser, says one woman, who says she makes an extra $400 a month for an hour a day of work. Check with your local newspapers (including "shoppers," those free newspapers that get tossed up on your porch) to see who's hiring.

Pet Services Provider

Dog-walking, pet-sitting and even poop-scooping services are flexible jobs for animal lovers. Contact local vets and pet-supply stores to see if they'll let you put up a flyer.

Pizza Deliverer

This was one of my many part-time jobs in college, and one that was reasonably lucrative, thanks to tips. As one man wrote, "I delivered pizzas for Papa John's and ended up really enjoying it. I worked from 5 p.m. to 10 p.m. five days a week.... I ended up making anywhere from $300 to $450 a week between the tips and the pay. On my best night I earned $110 in tips."

Professional Shopper

Help the time-pressed, or the clueless, get through their shopping lists. "Seriously, you'd be stunned how many guys will pay you to buy their wives or girlfriends lingerie, or order flowers for their Grandma," one woman wrote. "I've even had women pay for an hour consultation on what to buy their new mother-in-law for Christmas or their father-in-law for Father's Day. You can make even more if you offer to take care of shipping for out-of-state gifts. Admittedly, it's sheer laziness on their part, but I charged $20 plus mileage (with a nominal $5 wrapping charge)."

Referee

Another way to employ sports skills is by playing umpire or referee. One couple works for the local parks department one night a week. He's an umpire and she's a scorekeeper; together they make $32 a game, for three or four games. Another man referees soccer games and says it's a sideline to consider for those who are "good with children, relatively fit and confident."

"You can start by going to your local soccer club and asking if they need a referee, and if they offer a club-certified referee class," he wrote. "Otherwise, you have to get FIFA certified, which costs less than $100, and you are good to go."

Seamstress

Those who sew reported making several hundred dollars a month with their skills.

One woman taught sewing and sewed for others while her kids were growing up and recently started slipcovers for extra money. Another seamstress drums up business by dropping into stores in outlet malls and asking whether there are any clothes in need of repair.

"There always are. I look them over with the manager, jot down what's required to bring them up to snuff, giving a quote for the work," she wrote. "I take them home with me and bring them back in a few days' time. It's unusual that one sweep through the malls doesn't net a couple hundred bucks."

Teacher

Not all teaching jobs require degrees and credentials. If you have a skill or a craft you can teach, you may find opportunities to offer seminars or workshops at community colleges, adult education centers or senior centers. Some of these gigs don't even require you to leave your house. One woman found a moonlighting post teaching online for a local university. "I can teach my classes in the evenings and on the weekends," she wrote, "from the comfort of my couch!"

This list is just to get you started thinking about the possibilities. If you have a particular skill or passion, you may be able to turn it into a lucrative sideline. And even if you don't make a fortune with your first attempt, you can learn from the experience and continue fine-tuning your plan to create multiple income streams.

Furthermore, sideline businesses have tax advantages. You can deduct legitimate business expenses, including supplies, mileage, equipment and a home office, on your tax returns, and put a portion of your profits into a simplified employee pension (SEP) or other retirement accounts. Consult a tax pro for details.

HOW TO SURVIVE A CRISIS

All your planning and preparation will be put to the test if you lose your job or suffer another big financial setback like a disabling illness or injury. Having lots of financial flexibility will help, but the decisions you make in the first few days and weeks can have a profound effect on your ability to ride out the storm.

So you should:

Conserve your cash. Paying down debt is generally a good idea—until your income is threatened. Then cash becomes king. If you've been making extra payments on your mortgage or student loans, redirect that money into savings. Pay the minimums on your debt and get deferments on any loans that offer them. Most utilities and telephone companies offer "lifeline" or low-cost service for people with low incomes; check their Web sites to see if you qualify.

Identify potential sources of income. You may need to step up your efforts on your side business or help a stay-at-home partner return to work. If you're disabled, you may have benefits through your job that can replace some of your income. If you've lost your job, *apply for unemployment benefits right away.* Some people worry that applying for unemployment will affect their credit (it won't) or that jobless benefits are some kind of welfare (they're not; your employer paid into the system on your behalf and you should get what is coming to you). The earlier you apply, the earlier you'll get your first check. Most states have a two- or three-week waiting period based on when you file, not when you lost your job. Now, unemployment benefits are typically available only to workers who lost their jobs through no fault of their own. You generally can't get benefits if you were fired for cause or voluntarily quit your job. If the facts are in dispute, though, go ahead and file; you can always argue your case, and you'll have a chance to appeal if your state's unemployment office decides against you.

Track your spending. You no longer have the luxury of not knowing where your money is going. Keep track of every cent, at least for now.

Don't tap your retirement funds if you can avoid it. It can be tempting to raid these pots of money, but the financial repercussions are so serious that you should avoid such withdrawals if at all possible.

Not only will you lose one-quarter to one-half of the withdrawal to taxes and penalties, but you lose forever the tax-deferred returns you could have earned. A $10,000 withdrawal now from your individual retirement account or 401(k) means $109,000 less for your retirement, assuming the money would grow at an average 8 percent annual rate for thirty years.

It's an especially bad idea to use retirement money to pay credit card bills. In a worst-case scenario, your credit card debt can be wiped out in bankruptcy court, while your retirement funds would be protected from creditors.

You also should be cautious about raiding retirement funds to pay for a mortgage on a house you may not be able to afford. If you're worried you'll lose your house, contact a HUD-approved housing counselor (www.hud.gov) to review and discuss your options.

Be wary, too, of taking loans against your retirement accounts. While you can't really borrow against IRAs and Roth IRAs—any money not returned to the account within sixty days is considered a withdrawal—many 401(k)s and 403(b)s allow you to borrow up to 50 percent of your account balance.

These loans come with a big risk: if you lose your job and can't pay the money back quickly, the balance becomes an inadvertent withdrawal.

Get your priorities straight. List your bills and other spending in order of importance. The items at the bottom of the list should be pretty easy to trim. You also should find savings by cutting back on big-ticket items such as groceries, dining out, utilities and transportation.

You should have another list: the "If Things Really Get Bad" list. Tops should be holding on to the roof over your head (the mortgage or rent), keeping the lights on (utilities) and ensuring you have transportation to get to job interviews (car payments and insurance). At the bottom should be your unsecured debts—credit cards, student loans and other personal debt that paid for stuff that can't be repossessed.

Any payment you skip can affect your credit scores, but some bills have bigger consequences than others. Knowing the potential fallout can help you prioritize.

Debt	Time when real trouble starts	Fallout
Mortgage	90 to 120 days late	Foreclosure, loss of home
Auto loan	1 day late (although many lenders wait 60 days)	Repossession, loss of car, potential for collection of unpaid debt
Student loans	270 days late	Wage garnishment,* tax-refund seizure
Tax debt	Depends on amount and on aggressiveness of collector	Wage garnishment, property or bank account seizure
Credit cards	180 days late	Account "charged off" and sent to collections
Child support	Depends on amount and on aggressiveness of collector	Lawsuit, wage garnishment, jail

* Wage garnishment is when a portion of your paycheck is seized to pay creditors.

If you have to choose which bills to pay, your list will remind you what's really a priority. Skipping credit card payments may result in a ding on your credit and phone calls from creditors, but skipping mortgage payments could leave you homeless.

When it comes to specific types of lenders, here's what you should know:

Mortgage lenders. If you don't pay, your lender can foreclose—a process that can take as little as three months (although most lenders wait for you to miss two or three payments before starting foreclosure proceedings). The further along the foreclosure process gets, the more you'll have to cough up in fees and collection costs to get your house back.

You may qualify for forbearance or mortgage modification programs to help get you through a bad patch. If your cash crunch will be short term, it makes a lot of sense to contact your lender to request help as soon as you know you might miss a payment. If you have no idea when your financial prospects will improve, contact a HUD-approved housing counselor to discuss your options (you'll find links at www.hud.gov) and read attorney Stephen Elias's excellent book, *The Foreclosure Survival Guide*.

Auto lenders. You can lose your car if you're even a day late with your payment, although it usually takes a month or two for the lender to call the repo man. But, like mortgage lenders, some auto lenders are willing to work with you if you (a) contact them early and (b) are in a temporary cash crunch that's about to be resolved.

Of course, if you don't need the car to get to work and you owe less than it's worth, selling it is often a great strategy to reduce your bills and free up some cash.

Unfortunately, many borrowers in your situation need the car, owe more than it's worth, or both. The options are grim:

- You can sell the car, but if you owe more than it's worth, you'll usually have to come up with the extra cash to get the lender to release the lien on the vehicle.
- You can arrange for a voluntary repossession, but that trashes your credit as much as an involuntary one, and the lender can still come after you for any unpaid debt.
- You can try to hide the car from the repo team. Good luck with that.

Student lenders. Finally, some good news: federal student loans have plenty of options to help you if you run into financial trouble. You typically can ask for forbearance or deferrals that allow you to skip payments for a total of three years. If you've already used up those opportunities, ask about income-sensitive, income-based or graduated repayment plans. If you can't make those payments, your loan typically won't be placed in default status until 270 days, or about nine months, have elapsed. Even then, you often can "rehabilitate" your loan with a series of on-time payments that will eventually erase the negative effects on your credit. Unfortunately, private student loans are far less flexible, but you still should call the lender as soon as you run into financial trouble to see what can be worked out.

Tax debt. The IRS and other taxing authorities often can offer you an installment plan; you also might try, with a tax pro's help, making an "offer in compromise" to settle your debt. Tax agencies have plenty of ways to get their money if you try to hide from them, including wage garnishment, liens on your property or bank accounts and seizure of your refund checks, so they're another creditor you don't want to avoid.

Credit card companies and other "unsecured" lenders. "Unsecured" means your borrowing isn't attached to an asset, like a house or a car. Credit cards, medical bills and personal loans are considered unsecured debt. It usually takes about six months of skipped payments for an unsecured lender to "charge off" your account and place it in collections. A "charge-off" is an accounting term that means the lender has given up on trying to get its money; it doesn't mean you no longer owe the debt. The account is either turned over to an in-house collector or sold or assigned to a third-party collector.

You have the legal right to ask collection agencies to stop calling you; that request must be put in writing. But some collection agencies respond to such letters by taking you to court, where they could win a judgment against you and (in most states) take up to 25 percent of your after-tax pay with a wage garnishment. It may be in your best interest to put off that day of reckoning.

Gerri Detweiler, a respected consumer advocate and debt expert, now recommends people talk to collectors even if they can't pay. You don't need to explain every financial hardship you've faced that led up to your current situation—in fact, the less said, the better, says Detweiler, who runs a helpful site called DebtCollectionAnswers.com. Explaining too much simply gives the collector more ammunition to use against you, but not responding at all can lead to a lawsuit.

"You can say, 'I've lost my job,' or, 'My income has been cut,' and 'I can't pay you right now. I'll get back in touch with you as soon as I get a job,'" Detweiler recommends.

Child support. Debtors' prisons are a thing of the past, but one of the few debts that can still land you in jail is a refusal to pay child support. Before you wind up behind bars, though, you're likely to face a lot of other unpleasant consequences, including wage garnishment, liens against your property, loss of any professional licenses and loss of your driver's license.

If you owe back child support, the best course is usually to pay as much as you can and try to make up the missed payments as quickly as you can. You may be able to forestall more serious action against you by showing you're making a good-faith effort. Or you may need to consult an attorney. If your financial circumstances have dramatically worsened, you can ask the court to modify your child support order.

WHEN YOU NEED MONEY FAST

This chapter has a lot of information—too much, perhaps, to take in all at once. So here's a cheat sheet on where to look when you need money fast, in rough order of preference.

1. RAISE CASH FIRST. TAP MONEY FROM:

- Your savings accounts
- A second job
- Selling unneeded items
- Cashing in an unneeded life insurance policy
- Selling nonretirement investments

2. THEN USE YOUR CREDIT. LOOK TO BORROW FROM:

- Home equity lines
- Credit cards
- Workplace retirement accounts (see warning on page 56)
- Friends and family
- Cash-value life insurance policies—these are policies that have an investment component that builds up over time, as opposed to term insurance, which has a death benefit but no cash value
- Brokerage accounts that offer margin loans, which allow you to borrow against the value of your investments (warning: if the investments you're borrowing against drop in value, the brokerage could seize and sell them to pay off the loan)

3. WHATEVER YOU DO, DON'T:

- Withdraw money from retirement funds
- Use a payday lender
- Take money from children's custodial accounts (UTMAs, UGMAs), since the money is legally theirs

ACTION STEPS

Building financial flexibility takes time, but it's an achievable goal for almost everyone. Here's what you need to do:

- If you have no emergency savings, build up a $500 pad.
- Make sure you're on track saving for retirement and have paid off troublesome debt, such as credit cards, before you start to further build your emergency fund.
- Build your access to credit. Review your credit reports and dispute any serious errors. Consider having two or three major credit cards. Open a home equity line of credit if you have sufficient equity in your home and can keep your hands off the money.
- Shoot for cash savings plus access to credit that equals twelve months' worth of must-have living expenses. Build up your cash savings over time to at least three months' worth of must-have living expenses.
- Create multiple income streams to reduce your dependence on a single income source.
- Have a plan for surviving a crisis, including conserving cash, suspending extra debt payments, slashing expenses and identifying alternate sources of income.

Pay Off Debt the Smart Way

THE OLD-SCHOOL RULES:
All debt is bad. Pay it off as fast as possible.

THE BUBBLE ECONOMY RULES:
Don't worry about paying off debt.
You have better things to do with your money.

THE NEW RULES:
Pay off toxic debt and use "good" debt to get ahead.

Like many people in their twenties, Christine struggled with debt—student loan debt, auto loan debt, credit card debt.

The credit card debt was the most frustrating, Christine said. She had stopped using the cards and so wasn't adding to her burden, but her monthly payments didn't seem to make a dent in what she owed. After we talked a bit, the problem became obvious: she was treating all her debt the same. In particular, she was making substantial extra payments on her low-rate student loans, which didn't leave much left over to pay off the credit card debt. Christine didn't realize that all debt is not created equal, and the differences were the key to getting a handle on her finances.

OUR TROUBLED HISTORY WITH DEBT

The generation that lived through the Depression learned what it meant to be burned by debt.

Back in the 1920s and into the 1930s, mortgages to buy homes were often short-term, interest-only loans that required the principal to be paid off or refinanced after five years. Refinancing was easy until the Depression cratered incomes and killed thousands of banks. Families who bought their piece of the American Dream using a mortgage could, and did, find themselves suddenly homeless.

The horror of mass foreclosures branded a generation with a real distrust, even hatred, of debt. While mortgages got better—the thirty-year, fixed-rate loan that was created in the mid-1930s—fear of debt prompted many to rush to pay these loans off as quickly as possible and celebrate their accomplishment with mortgage-burning parties.

INSIDER TERMS

Foreclosure: A legal process that allows a lender to repossess the collateral for a loan, typically a home or other piece of property, after a borrower has fallen behind on payments. In some states, lenders must go to court to start the process (known as a judicial foreclosure). In other states, lenders don't have to go to court; these nonjudicial foreclosures can happen more quickly.

What a difference a few decades makes. By the turn of this century, that degree of paranoia about debt was hard to find. Instead, an unprecedented explosion in the availability of consumer credit led a whole generation to believe that if they could afford the monthly payments, they could afford to buy whatever they wanted—no matter the ultimate cost in interest or in their overall financial well-being.

The inevitable result: millions of families became vulnerable to any setback; bankruptcies and foreclosures soared. But once again, we risk learning the wrong message. It's not that all debt is bad—far from it. Some debts are toxic and worth the effort to pay off fast. Other debts shouldn't cause you to lose a single night's sleep—in fact, you should delay paying them off whenever possible. Knowing the difference and crafting a plan to pay off your most pressing debts is essential for financial health.

INSIDER TERMS

Bankruptcy: Bankruptcy is a federal court procedure set up to help individuals and businesses eliminate debt or repay it over time. Bankruptcies for individuals are typically either Chapter 7 "liquidation" cases, in which the borrower asks the court to wipe out most unsecured debts, or Chapter 13 "repayment plan" cases, where the borrower attempts to repay creditors over three to five years.

THE GOOD, THE BAD AND THE NEUTRAL: HOW TO CATEGORIZE YOUR DEBTS

To start your debt payoff plan, you need to know what you owe. Go through your bills and pull copies of your credit reports (get free access annually at AnnualCreditReport.com) to make sure you don't miss any accounts.

DON'T FORGET TO INCLUDE:

- Credit cards
- Store cards
- Gas cards
- Personal loans
- Retirement plan loans
- Life insurance loans
- Federal student loans
- Private student loans
- Mortgages
- Home equity loans or lines of credit
- Business loans
- Auto loans
- Boat loans
- Other vehicle loans
- Medical debt
- Debt consolidation loans
- Collection accounts
- Payday loans
- Pawnshop loans
- Title loans
- Overdraft balances

For each debt, you'll need to note whom you owe, how much you owe, the current interest rate and the minimum payment. You can typically find the interest rate of a loan on your monthly statement or by calling your lender to ask. Calculating interest rates for payday advances and overdraft balances is tougher, but you can figure your annualized interest rate is in the triple digits.

The next step is dividing your debt into three piles:

1. Good debt is debt that helps you get ahead in your financial life. An affordable mortgage, for example, allows you to buy a home that will appreciate in value over time. Federal student loans in moderation can help you boost your lifetime earnings potential. A loan for your small business can help you invest in new equipment that can increase your revenues. These loans have other things in common: the interest rates are often low and typically tax deductible, further reducing the costs of carrying this debt. You'll want to pay this debt off eventually, but not until you've vanquished higher-priority debt.

2. Toxic debt comes with high or variable interest rates and includes credit card debt, payday loans, car title loans and pawnshop loans. This debt doesn't help you get ahead. Instead, it's a leech on your finances, draining away money in interest payments and leaving you vulnerable to bankruptcy.

3. Neutral debt falls in between good and toxic debt. Neutral debt typically has low, fixed interest rates and payments, which keeps it out of the "toxic" category, but it doesn't really help you grow your wealth, either. Examples include low-rate car loans, personal loans, debt consolidation loans and retirement plan loans. In an ideal world, you wouldn't have taken on this debt. Borrowing to buy something that loses value, like a car, isn't the savviest financial move. Neither is running up the debt that caused you to get the consolidation or personal loan. Retirement plan loans have their own risks, since if you lose your job, the loan can turn into an inadvertent withdrawal. If the debt has a relatively low rate, however, you can leave it alone while you pay off your toxic debt.

Categorizing debt can be tricky. It's entirely possible to overdose on what would otherwise be good debt. A mortgage you can't afford, for example, won't get you ahead—it will drain your wealth and may lead to foreclosure. Similarly, a retirement plan loan can jump from neutral debt to toxic debt if you lose your job and can't pay the money back quickly.

Some other debts that you should take special care in categorizing include:

Home equity borrowing. This might seem to be good debt—after all, it's essentially another mortgage on your house. But too often this money is frivolously spent—on vacations, cars and expensive home improvements that add little value to the home. Instead of growing your wealth, this borrowing drains it.

Also, much home equity borrowing is done on variable-rate lines of credit. Because you're paying only interest in the first ten years of the loan, the initial low payments can deceive you about how affordable this debt really is. While home equity lines of credit may not be toxic debt, you may want to make paying off your line a top priority after your credit card and other high-rate debts are paid.

The other way to borrow against your house is using a fixed-rate home equity loan. These installment loans have fixed payments designed to pay off the loan over time (usually over twenty years). Although the interest is tax deductible, the rate you pay is typically a few points higher than what you'd pay for a conventional mortgage. So this debt should probably land in your "neutral" pile, rather than be classified as "good" debt.

Medical debt. If you've worked out an affordable repayment plan with a hospital or other provider, you can classify it as neutral debt. If you've signed up for a high-interest loan or provider-supplied credit card to pay it off, it probably belongs under toxic debt.

Private student loans. Too often, people don't draw a sharp enough distinction between federal and private student loans. Both can help you increase your income, which can make them seem like good debt, but private loans often have higher interest rates than federal loans, and those rates are variable. Furthermore, there are strict limits on how much federal student loan debt you can take on, making it harder to overdose on this borrowing. By contrast, there's virtually no limit to how much private student loan debt you can get—and that has left far too many graduates drowning in unpayable loans.

Leah is one of them. She has more than $200,000 in student loans, the vast majority from private lenders, that she can't pay.

"I have pretty much exhausted my options as far as deferments, graduated repayment schedules, etc. etc.," she wrote. "It's so bad that a woman at my student loan company told me today I was never going to be able to buy anything!"

Leah was hoping she could get some relief through bankruptcy court, but the reality is that student loan debt typically can't be erased. Lenders got the laws changed so that only the most desperate hardship cases—the permanently disabled, for example—have any hope of getting their student loan debt wiped out.

Hopefully, your situation isn't so desperate, but you'll still want to place private student loans at the top of the neutral debt pile or the bottom of the toxic pile—something to be paid off immediately after your nondeductible credit card debt, payday loans and other bad debt.

Understanding the differences among types of debt helped Christine realize that she should suspend the extra payments she was making on her low-rate, tax-deductible federal student loans and throw that money instead at her toxic credit card debt. Instead of running in place, she could actually start getting ahead.

Once you've categorized your debts, you're ready for the next step, which is making sure you're paying the lowest possible rates.

HOW TO LOWER RATES ON YOUR DEBT

Way too many people pay way too much for their debt. Sometimes they're the victims of unethical loan officers, who put them in higher-rate mortgages or car loans than they deserve. Other times they use high-cost lenders, such as payday loan outfits, when other less-expensive options are available. Or they carry credit card debt at rates that are two or three times what they might qualify for elsewhere.

Too often, people don't realize a better deal could be theirs for the asking. And lower interest rates can help you get out of debt much, much faster. Here are three areas to consider.

Student Loans

If you have federal student loans, consider consolidating them into one loan and choosing the longest possible repayment term. Instead of the usual ten-year term, you may be able to choose a repayment term of up to thirty years, depending on how much money you owe.

Amount owed	Maximum term
Less than $7,500	10 years
$7,500 to $9,999	12 years
$10,000 to $19,999	15 years
$20,000 to $39,999	20 years
$40,000 to $59,000	25 years
$60,000 or more	30 years

Source: FinAid.org.

Why would you opt to stay in debt longer? Because federal student loans tend to be pretty cheap money, and they come with a number of repayment options that makes this extremely flexible debt. If you lose your job or suffer another financial setback, for example, you can get your payments lowered or even skip payments for a time without ruining your credit (if you're approved for a deferral or forbearance).

By choosing the longest-possible repayment period, you can lower your monthly payments to free up cash to pay off more troublesome debt. Once that debt is vanquished and your other financial bases are covered, you can always start making extra payments toward your student loans if you want.

Some people, believe it or not, opt not to. One of my readers had federal student loans from the days before rates were fixed, and watched with glee as those rates steadily plunged. He consolidated his loans and fixed the rate at about 3 percent. He figured that between the tax deduction on his interest and the historic inflation rate (which is a little over 3 percent), he was essentially being paid to carry this debt. "I'm not paying it off one second faster than I have to," he crowed.

Another thing to consider: once you pay off student debt, that money is essentially gone. It's not like paying down a credit card or line of credit, where every dollar you pay typically frees up another dollar of credit that can be used in an emergency. So before you accelerate pay-

SHOULD YOU DEFER STUDENT LOANS TO PAY HIGHER-RATE DEBT?

IF MONEY IS EXTREMELY TIGHT, you may be able to temporarily suspend your student loan payments with deferments or forbearance. You might be tempted to seek such a break so you can throw more money at your more troublesome debts. But remember that these suspensions have time limits, and if you use them up they might not be available to you if you suffer a layoff or other setback. Also, interest on the loans typically continues to accrue, so your loan balances will grow over time if you don't make minimum payments. You're usually better off saving your deferments and forbearance for when you really need them.

ments on federal student loans, make sure you've optimized your financial flexibility with a fat emergency fund and sufficient access to other credit.

If you have a low income and a lot of federal student loan debt, there's something else you should consider: loan forgiveness. The best deal is for people working in public service jobs. They can get their remaining debt erased after ten years of on-time payments. Eligible jobs include:

- All government jobs, whether federal, state or local
- Public education and public health care
- Military service
- Police and fire departments
- Social work
- Public and school libraries
- Public-interest legal services
- Education in high-need areas
- Nonprofit, tax-exempt 401(c)3 organizations

To qualify, borrowers need to be in the federal Direct Loan Program and make their payments using income-based repayment, income contingent repayment, standard repayment or a combination of these repayment plans.

The best approach, says financial aid expert Mark Kantrowitz, is for borrowers to obtain a federal Direct Consolidation Loan and choose the income-based repayment option, to maximize the debt that will eventually be forgiven.

If you're not in public service, you still don't have to pay your federal student loans forever. The income-based repayment option requires payments for twenty-five years. After that, the remaining debt is forgiven. For more details on these and other forgiveness programs, visit Kantrowitz's site, FinAid.org.

If you have private student loans, you don't have forgiveness options or many of the other features that make federal student loans attractive. Consolidating private student loans won't lock in your rate, unfortunately, and choosing a longer loan term may just leave you exposed to future interest rate increases when what you should really be focusing on is paying off this debt.

Consolidating does have the advantage of giving you a single loan payment, however, and you may be able to get a better rate if your credit scores have improved significantly since you took out the loans. (Unlike federal loans, private loans consider your credit history when setting rates.)

As of this writing, only a few private lenders are offering private student loan consolidation. For a list, visit www.finaid.org/loans/privateconsolidation.phtml.

Home Loans

Back in the old days, when refinancing was expensive, interest rates had to drop a percentage point or two before swapping your current loan for another, lower-rate one became worthwhile. These days, the costs are lower, which means the old rules no longer apply and you have to be ready to do some math.

INSIDER TERMS

Refinance: When you refinance, you replace an existing debt with another loan that has different terms. People typically refinance mortgages to lock in a lower interest rate, reduce their monthly payments or shorten the time they remain in debt. Refinancing always comes with a cost, although some lenders hide their fees by adding the costs to the loan amount or offering a higher interest rate than their competitors.

The key figures you need to know are the costs of refinancing and how much the new loan will lower your payments. Then you figure the break-even period—how long it will take for the lower payments to offset your costs. If the refinance costs you $2,500, for example, and lowers your payment by $200, your break-even point will be a little over twelve months.

There are some who say you should go for the refinance if you don't expect to move before the break-even point occurs. I'd suggest a more conservative rule of thumb: consider a refinance if the break-even point is two years or less.

Life is uncertain, and the uncertainty grows over time. It's harder to know where you'll be five years from now than two years from now. Furthermore, as you know, money has an opportunity cost. An investment that pays off in two years is more valuable, typically, than one that takes five years.

Before you submit any application for a refinance, though, there are other things to consider:

- **Not every homeowner can refinance.** Lending standards are tighter than they were a few years ago, and you may not be able to refinance if your credit scores aren't good, your income has plunged or you don't have sufficient equity in your home. Talk to a loan officer about prevailing standards before you submit an application.

- **Not every homeowner should refinance.** Obviously, it doesn't make sense if you're about to move soon, but you also may not realize any savings if you're already twenty years into a thirty-year loan, for example. By that point, most of your payment is going toward principal, not interest, so refinancing could just increase your costs in the long run. Also:

- **Thirty-year loans aren't for everyone.** Refinancing typically means restarting the clock on your mortgage. That's fine if you're relatively young—it's good debt and relatively cheap, after all—but it may not be a good idea if you're closing in on retirement or if you're determined to be debt free. You may want to consider a twenty- or fifteen-year loan instead.

- **Savings matter only if you put them to good use.** If you're refinancing to lower your payments, make sure you won't fritter away the extra cash. The money you free up should go straight to paying down your other debt.

Credit Card Debt

Until the credit crunch, the standard advice was to "call your issuer and ask for a lower rate." After all, the worst your issuer could do was say no, right?

That tactic often worked before the financial crisis. Once the recession hit, though, some issuers apparently decided that merely asking for a lower rate was a sign the caller was in financial trouble. Instead of considering the requests, these issuers responded to such calls by jacking up people's rates, lowering their credit limits and even closing their accounts.

This is what happened to Ronnie, who called his issuer to see if he could get a lower rate "to make some headway on my credit card debt." Instead, his call triggered a review of his account.

"Making this call turned out to be costly," he wrote. "They were not willing to help me out with a lower rate or reduced payments. In fact . . .

they took away $20,000 of available credit!!! Which in turn raises my [credit utilization] ratio and thus hurts my scores. The rep said I had too much available credit considering my income."

Other readers who suffered similar fates wanted to know if these abrupt moves, particularly when made in response to a phone call for help, are legal. Unfortunately, yes. Card issuers do have new restrictions on when they can raise your rate, since the credit card reform law effectively prohibits raising rates on existing balances unless you're sixty days or more late with your payments. But credit card companies can still raise your rate going forward, and there are no restrictions on their ability to lower your credit limits or close your account if they want to.

All of which means you need a new, more nuanced game plan. First, you need to know your FICO credit scores. These are the scores used by most lenders to determine your creditworthiness. Buy at least one of your scores from MyFICO.com so you know where you stand. Your game plan will be based on those scores:

FICO of 740 or above. Your scores are excellent, and credit card issuers will fight to get your business. That gives you plenty of leverage to get a lower rate, if yours isn't already rock-bottom. Collect credit card and balance transfer offers you get in the mail, or check out sites such as CardRatings.com, Bankrate.com and CreditCards.com. Then call and ask your issuers to match the rates you're seeing in these offers. If the phone rep balks, tell him or her you want to close your account. That usually gets you transferred to the loss retention department, which is often more flexible than the frontline reps. You probably don't want to actually close the account, since that could hurt your prime credit scores, but if you don't get what you want you can easily transfer your balance using one of the offers you've found.

FICO of 700 or above. You're still considered a low-risk customer, but you'll have somewhat less bargaining power than someone with better scores. You can follow the script above, but focus on collecting offers for people in your credit-scoring band so you have a realistic idea of what you can request (of all the sites, CreditCards.com makes this the clearest, breaking down offers by credit score quality).

FICO below 700. The lower your score, the higher your risk and the less leverage you have to get a better deal, so you'll probably need to consider other options. If your current issuer won't lower your rate, you may be able to do one or more of the following:

Use a balance transfer offer. The higher your scores, the more offers you're likely to find, but you still have to do some math to find the best one. Fees for these deals usually increase the debt you're transferring by 3 to 5 percent, so the interest rate break needs to be big enough and last long enough to offset the fee.

Check out personal loans. These are typically fixed-rate loans that allow you to pay off debt over three years. You'll find them at most banks, although your local credit union may offer the best rates and be more flexible about the credit scores needed to qualify.

Consider peer-to-peer loans. Sites such as Prosper or Lending Club also offer three-year, fixed-rate loans, using money raised from individuals willing to lend—hence the "peer-to-peer" moniker. The individuals lending money submit "bids" of the interest rate they're willing to accept, based on your credit scores and other history. Although results vary, you may be able to swing a better deal here than at your bank or credit union.

Use home equity or retirement plan loans with care. You may be able to lower your interest rates by using these loans to pay off other debts, but you're also putting your wealth at considerable risk, as we covered in the previous chapter.

CRAFT YOUR PLAN TO GET (MOSTLY) OUT OF DEBT

Now that you've sorted your debts, start with your toxic pile and identify the highest-priority debt. The idea is to make minimum payments on all your other debts so you can put every dollar possible toward paying off your most toxic debts. Once your highest-priority debt is paid off, you take the same payment and apply it to your next-highest-priority debt.

Normally, you would first tackle any payday loans, car title loans, pawnshop loans or unpaid bounce fees at your bank. The interest rates on these debts are effectively in the triple digits, so you'll want to dispatch them first. Once the triple-digit debt is gone, your next target will typically be the credit card with the highest interest rate.

THERE ARE SOME EXCEPTIONS, THOUGH.
YOU MAY WANT TO:

- Target maxed-out credit cards. If you have a card that's at or near its limit, consider paying that down first, even if it has a favorable interest rate. Maxing out your cards can trigger higher rates on any new balances and torpedo your credit scores. How far you should pay it down isn't an exact science, but in general you'll want to get your balances below 75 percent of your limits.

- Pay off a small bill if you need a quick win. If you're really overwhelmed by your debts, knocking out at least one bill can give you the motivation to keep going.
- Consider accelerating a retirement plan loan if your job is at risk. Retirement loans typically have low, fixed rates, which means they needn't be a priority—unless your job is shaky. As we've covered, most plans require you to pay back 401(k) and other retirement plans quickly after you leave your employer, or the balance you owe becomes a withdrawal and triggers a fat tax bill.

Finding a way to earn extra money can really help you speed up your debt repayment efforts. Wanda was an attorney by day, but picked up an evening job as a package loader for a delivery service. The three hours a night of physical work helped her keep in shape, and the extra money, combined with cuts in spending, helped her family pay off half of their $49,000 credit card bill in just thirteen months.

Before you send any extra money to a creditor, though, you'll want to road test your plan to make sure it will work the way you hope. You can find debt reduction calculators all over the Web. I like the downloadable spreadsheet Debt Reduction Calculator for Excel at http://download.cnet.com because it allows you to choose different approaches, such as paying your lowest-balance debt first or tackling your highest-rate debt. You can try out different scenarios so you can see how a few more dollars, or a different repayment order, would affect how soon you'd be out of debt.

If you can come up with a plan that eradicates your debt within five years—a plan you think you can stick to—then you're ready for the next step: setting up your repayment plan.

If, on the other hand, your toxic debt would take you much more than five years to pay off, you might want to consider your alternatives. Why five years? That's as long as you would have to remain on a repayment plan with a Chapter 13 bankruptcy; after that, most remaining unsecured debt, such as credit cards and medical bills, would be erased. If you qualified for a Chapter 7 bankruptcy, your debt might be erased in a few months without a repayment plan.

Chapter 7 Bankruptcy	
Primary purpose	Eliminates most unsecured debts.
Typically used when . . .	You have few assets.
Advantages	Wipes out credit card balances, medical bills and most other unsecured debt. Keeps collectors at bay. Is fast—most cases are completed and debts are eliminated within a few months.
Disadvantages	Not everyone can file for Chapter 7—if your income is above the median for your area, you may be forced to file Chapter 13. Your credit scores are damaged. You will damage the credit of anyone who has cosigned with you on a loan.
Chapter 13 Bankruptcy	
Primary purpose	Creates a repayment plan.
Typically used when . . .	You have assets such as home equity that you want to keep.
Advantages	Allows you to keep most property while giving you more time to pay off debt. You're protected from creditors during the three- to five-year period it would take to complete the repayment plan. You can keep most of your property and your remaining debts are eliminated after completing the repayment plan.
Disadvantages	The failure rate is high—most people (as many as two out of three) don't complete their repayment plans or get a discharge of their remaining debts. Takes a long time: three to five years. Prolongs the damage to your credit scores, since they can't begin to recover until your repayment plan is completed.

My experience is that many people who are deeply in debt are also deeply in denial. They are so determined to avoid bankruptcy that they grasp for any other solution, even when there really isn't one.

Sally contacted me because she couldn't make the minimum payments on her credit cards. She wanted me to recommend a debt consolidation loan, but her credit scores were too low to qualify and a loan wouldn't have helped her anyway, because her debts were so vast and her income was so limited. I encouraged her to contact both a legitimate credit counseling agency and a bankruptcy attorney. When she protested, again, that she didn't want to file for bankruptcy, I told her the truth: "You may not have any choice."

INSIDER TERMS

Credit counseling agency: The primary mission of a legitimate credit counseling agency is to help people avoid bankruptcy by repaying their credit card bills through a debt management plan (DMP). Credit counseling agencies may also offer budgeting classes and housing counseling, among other services. Legitimate credit counselors do not offer debt consolidation loans or debt settlement (offering creditors pennies on the dollar to settle old debts). The credit counseling industry was overrun by scam artists and other bad characters in the 1990s, but the IRS has cleaned up the industry considerably by yanking nonprofit status away from many companies. Still, it's buyer beware, so carefully vet any credit counselor before signing up.

The five-year payoff guideline forces people to look at how long it would take them to pay off their debt and compare that to the relief that may be available in bankruptcy court. Many people simply wait too long to file, continuing to pay debts that would be erased in bankruptcy court.

You may still decide to continue with your debt-payoff plans, even if they will take longer than five years. But if it will take ten years or twenty years or a lifetime, I'd urge you to reconsider. You may be creating a voluntary debtor's prison, when it's time to acknowledge past mistakes, find a solution and move on.

IS BANKRUPTCY YOUR BEST OPTION?

There's a widespread delusion in the United States that people rush to bankruptcy court when they could easily pay their bills, but the reality is far different. Bankruptcy experts will tell you most people wait far too long to file, struggling to pay debts that are simply too overwhelming. These debtors often deplete their retirement funds or home equity, resources that would have been protected from creditors in bankruptcy court, in their futile efforts to stay afloat.

Some people believe, erroneously, that they wouldn't be able to file for bankruptcy. It's true that filing has gotten tougher and more expensive since Congress passed a bankruptcy reform law that took effect in 2005. If your income is above the median for your area, you may be required to file the Chapter 13 repayment plan I mentioned, rather than be able to wipe out many of your debts in a Chapter 7 liquidation.

Most people who file, however, are allowed to go through with a Chapter 7 liquidation, which erases credit card and medical debts.

Either way, the impact on your credit scores will be profound. As you saw in the previous chapter, bankruptcy typically reduces fair-to-good credit scores to the mid-500s on the 300 to 850 FICO scale. If your scores were low to start with, bankruptcy will drive them even lower. Those low scores will make getting any credit tough for at least a couple of years.

You may not need to file for bankruptcy, of course. If you can't pay your way out of debt within five years, you first should consider talking to a legitimate credit counselor, one affiliated with the National Foundation for Credit Counseling (www.nfcc.org). If you qualify, you could be put on a debt management plan that would reduce or even eliminate the interest rates on your cards. You would make one payment each month to the credit counseling agency, and it would distribute the money to your credit card companies.

DMPs don't hurt your credit scores—they're considered a neutral factor in the FICO scoring formula—but your creditors may report you as late for a few months, since you're not paying what you originally owed, and that can hurt your scores.

That's why you should try to work out a payment plan on your own if you can; if you can't, you can take comfort in the fact that the damage your scores suffer when you're in a DMP would be less dramatic than what would happen in a bankruptcy filing.

Of course, bankruptcy might still be the best option for you, since it would allow you to wipe out debt, have protection from aggressive creditors and get a fresh start. Since credit counseling is designed to help people avoid bankruptcy, your credit counselor may not tell you if you'd be better off filing. So to understand all your options, you also should talk to an experienced bankruptcy attorney. You can get referrals from your state's bar association or the National Association of Consumer Bankruptcy Attorneys (www.nacba.org). Many bankruptcy attorneys offer a free or discounted initial session to discuss your situation.

If you decide to file, don't drag your heels. Procrastination just leaves you vulnerable to creditor lawsuits. Here's what to do:

1. Get your paperwork together. A partial list of what you should bring to your attorney would include:

- Sixty days' worth of pay stubs (you eventually may need to provide more to prove your income for the six months prior to filing)
- The last two months of bank statements
- Tax returns for the previous two years
- Statements for all brokerage and retirement accounts, including IRAs, Roth IRAs and 401(k)s
- Your most recent bills
- Any collection letters you've received or other correspondence about your debts
- Any current loan contracts (for homes, cars, etc.)
- Any lease contracts (for apartments, cars, etc.)
- Any home appraisals or tax assessments related to your home or other real estate you own
- Any paperwork related to past bankruptcies
- Any legal papers you've received, including but not limited to lawsuits, judgments, wage garnishments, divorce decrees, court orders and child support orders
- Proof of your identity, such as a driver's license or Social Security card

2. Stop paying debts that are likely to be erased. Discuss this with your attorney, but typically it makes little sense to continue paying debts that will be erased in bankruptcy, such as credit cards, medical bills and payday loans.

3. Start saving. Bankruptcy is expensive. A Chapter 7 typically costs $1,500 or more, including filing fees and your attorney's bills. A Chapter 13 may cost twice as much. You may be able to raise the cash if you stop paying your soon-to-be-discharged debts.

4. Stop using your credit cards. As soon as you know you're going to file, cut up the cards. "If you use a credit card that you don't intend to pay back," says Henry Sommer, a past president of the

National Association of Consumer Bankruptcy Attorneys, "that's considered fraud." In particular, don't take out cash advances or buy luxury items if bankruptcy is even a possibility, because those actions can scuttle your filing and get you charged with fraud.

5. Move your cash if necessary. If you owe money to a bank or credit union, it could try to seize any cash you have on deposit there once notified of your bankruptcy. So before you file, withdraw any money you have there and move it to a bank or credit union where you don't owe anything.

6. Don't buy anything major. You typically can't protect any asset purchased within ninety days of a bankruptcy filing, so don't buy a car or property or anything else of real value.

7. Don't give away money, property or assets. In fact, don't make any financial moves without consulting your attorney once you know you're going to file. Paying back a loan to a friend or transferring assets to a relative could be considered fraud.

8. Complete the required credit counseling. Before you can file for bankruptcy, you must complete a one-hour credit counseling session with an agency approved by the U.S. Department of Justice. The cost is typically $50, although the agency must waive the fee if you can't afford it. Make sure you get a certificate showing you've completed this counseling, as it will be required for your bankruptcy filing.

DEBT PAYOFF STRATEGIES TO AVOID

Whatever you do, don't fall for companies that seem to offer an easy solution to your debt problems. They may promise a lower-cost loan or offer to settle your debts for pennies on the dollar, but they won't deliver.

Too many debt settlement and debt consolidation firms are outright scams, and even the ones that don't disappear with your money may not resolve your debts and could end up costing you more in the long run.

These outfits feed on desperation. Debt consolidators might charge big up-front fees and then fail to deliver a loan, or give you one with higher interest rates than what you're already paying. Another common tactic is to make your payments look affordable by stretching out the loan term so that you wind up staying in debt far longer, and paying far more interest, than if you'd just paid off your bills on your own.

Debt settlement firms, meanwhile, have been multiplying like mushrooms after a rain. The idea is that you stop paying your bills and instead save up your payments until the debt settlement company can convince your creditors to accept a lump sum that is less than what you owe.

Sometimes it works—but there are many, many ways this can go horribly wrong. The debt settlement company could simply disappear with your money, or it could fail to negotiate effectively on your behalf. You could get sued by your creditors for not paying your bills and have your wages garnished or your bank account seized. Your credit scores will be trashed. Even if a settlement is successful, you'll face an income tax bill for any unpaid debt.

SO KEEP IN MIND:

- If you're interested in a debt consolidation loan, visit a local credit union for the best rates and terms.
- If you think debt settlement might be a better alternative than bankruptcy, first visit a bankruptcy attorney for a consultation. If it's a choice between Chapter 13 and debt settlement, discuss which might be better in your case. Then, if you decide you want to go the debt settlement route, ask the attorney for a referral to a reputable company (of which there are mighty few).

IMPLEMENTING YOUR PLAN

If your situation isn't dire and you can pay off your debts in five years on your own, then put your plan in place. An online bill payment system can allow you to set up your payments and quickly transfer extra funds where you want them to go. Remember:

- Stop charging. If you absolutely need to use plastic (for business travel, for example), use a card that you can pay off in full when the bill comes.
- Find a community for support. Debt repayment takes time, and the support of others in the same situation can keep you going. There are plenty of blogs and message boards that can cheer you on. One of my readers, Jane, read articles on saving and frugality every day to stay inspired. "I meditate daily about money, and am using the power of positive intentions and lots of other fun techniques about creating what I want

in my life," Jane wrote. "Learning about money has also taught me a lot about myself, and has highlighted behavior patterns that I am changing." A single mom with three kids, Jane paid off $3,000 of her debt in six months.

- Look for ways to bring in extra money. Jane shares her large house with two roommates (in addition to her three children). She also picked up two additional part-time jobs to supplement her main income as a physical trainer.
- Review your minimums monthly. Credit card minimums can change if your interest rate changes. Even if your rate stays the same, your minimum may gradually drop over time if you don't add to your debt. Lower minimums on your lower-priority debts mean you can send more money to your top-priority debt. Consider automatic debits, which allow the credit card companies to take the correct minimum payment monthly from your checking account.
- Every little bit counts. Continue to look for little expenses you can trim, and set up transfers so the saved money is applied to your debt.
- So do the big bits. Apply at least half of any windfall (tax rebate, refund check, inheritance or bonus) to your highest-priority debts. These big chunks will cut the time you stay in debt.

After your toxic debt is dispatched, you may want to switch to other priorities, such as building up your emergency fund and saving more for retirement. When those bases are covered, you can start working on your neutral debt and then your good debt.

Is there light at the end of the tunnel? Absolutely. Listen to what one of my readers, Martin, has to say:

"I am a 26-year-old male, and 3.5 years ago when I graduated college, my inexperience with handling money became quickly apparent. After I started my first job, I got in over my head and struggled to pay for just the basics each month. I had a car payment I couldn't afford, a rent bill that was nearly 30 percent of my take-home income, and credit card debt that was racking up faster than I could pay it off. After reading your articles and advice almost daily on MSN and applying them, I slowly began turning my financial situation around. I moved in with a roommate, traded my car in and paid cash for an old Honda, and slowly pulled myself out of credit card debt and began saving religiously, and focused on building my career and increasing my income. As a result of all of this, I closed on my first home today—and have only 'good' debt to my name (and plenty in savings). I couldn't have done this without your advice. I have built confidence in my financial decision making based on the skills you teach in your articles. Keep up the great work!"

DEBT PAYOFF AND YOUR CREDIT

There's a persistent and mostly unfounded myth that paying off debt will hurt your credit scores.

In fact, the opposite is true. Paying down debt typically helps your credit scores, because it widens the gap between the balances you owe and your credit limits or the amount you originally borrowed.

You'll usually see the most dramatic improvement in your scores when you pay down credit card debt, since the scoring formula is particularly sensitive to balances on your revolving credit lines.

But paying down installment debt helps, too, since you're widening the gap between what you owe and what you originally borrowed.

There is one downside to paying off installment debt. Once the loan is paid and the account closed, it can disappear from your credit reports; if it does, it's no longer helping your scores.

The good news is that you can continue to maintain excellent credit scores without an installment loan on your reports as long as you actively use other credit, such as credit cards. But remember, there's no reason to carry a balance. Simply use the card lightly and pay the bill off in full each month, and your scores should continue to shine.

ARE WE LESS WORTHY?

Compared to previous generations, we have a lot more debt—and a lot more trouble paying that debt. By every measure, from household debt loads to bankruptcy rates, debt is a much bigger problem than in the past. You might be tempted to conclude that earlier generations were better able to handle temptation or had higher moral standards about repaying the debt they accumulated.

But the reality is that until recently, people had far fewer opportunities to get into serious debt.

Consider consumer credit. A housewife might have an account with the butcher and the local grocer that she (or her husband) would pay off once a month. Another popular option was layaway, where she might select an outfit or a special toy for her children and make regular payments until the item was paid off and she could take it home. In the 1950s, the family might have added a travel-and-entertainment charge card to their wallet, particularly if the husband was a well-paid executive, but the bill still had to be paid in full each month.

Open-ended lines of credit were rare until the introduction of the general-purpose credit card in the 1960s. These cards allowed people make purchases and then carry a balance from month to month, if they chose.

Credit cards spread relatively quickly. By 1977, 38 percent of U.S. households had at least one credit card. Thirty years later, that proportion had grown to 80 percent, and those households typically had four or five different cards.

Credit card issuers were emboldened by two developments:

- **The FICO credit scoring system.** Introduced in the mid-1980s, credit bureau–based FICO scores allowed lenders to better predict the risk that a borrower would default—and to change their interest rates and terms based on those risks.
- **Loan securitization.** Issuers began packaging up debt into securities that could be sold off to investors. These securities sales raised money that could in turn be used to extend more credit to borrowers, while shifting the risk of losses from the issuing bank to investors.

As a result, credit card issuers began offering cards to more and more people, including those with more troubled credit histories. To lure new customers, issuers began offering low introductory "teaser" rates; to keep existing customers, they regularly bumped up credit limits and lowered minimum payments. In some cases, minimum payments dropped so low that the borrower wasn't repaying any principal, meaning that even if she stopped spending, she would never get out of debt.

Lenders worried less and less about whether people could afford the debt they were taking on. The idea was that they would make profits enough to offset the risks of default.

A similar loosening of standards occurred with other forms of debt. In the 1980s, for example, auto loans were typically two, three or four years long and required a down payment. By 2007, 80 percent of all auto loans stretched longer than four years and one in four new-car purchases involved negative equity—not only weren't the buyers making a down payment, but they were transferring over unpaid debt from a previous vehicle. Like credit card debt, most auto loans were packaged and sold to investors, shifting the risk of default away from the lender.

Down payment requirements disappeared from many mortgage deals, as well, and the nature of home loans changed dramatically. Instead of the thirty-year, fixed-rate loan that was standard until the 1980s, borrowers could choose adjustable-rate loans, hybrid loans (fixed for a few years before becoming variable), interest-only loans and loans with variable payments that sometimes didn't cover all the interest owed, let alone touch the principal (often called "option ARMs" or "pick-a-pay" mortgages).

Once-strict guidelines about how much a homebuyer could borrow went out the window. Instead of limiting mortgage expenses to 28 percent of income, some lenders approved mortgage payments that ate up 50 percent or more of a buyer's earnings. And the amount borrowed was often based on the *initial* low payments the nontraditional loans offered— not the much higher payments that would be required once the teaser period ended.

Past troubles with handling credit stopped being a barrier to borrowing, as well. Lenders simply assessed a higher interest rate for those with lower scores. Lenders relied so heavily on credit scores and loan securitization that once-important criteria such as income, assets and other debts also faded in importance. At the peak of the lending boom, some mortgage companies simply accepted your word about how much you made and owned. Deception was so widespread in these so-called "stated income, stated asset" loans that they came to be known as "liars' loans."

All these loans—liars' loans, poor credit loans, exotic loans with untraditional payback schemes—were in huge demand on Wall Street. Investors prized them for their higher returns and clamored for more. Lenders tried to keep up with the demand by giving brokers and loan officers financial incentives to steer borrowers into riskier options.

That's right—your friendly neighborhood banker or broker was paid more if you opted for a riskier mortgage over a conventional loan. Borrowers were told "only an idiot gets a thirty-year, fixed-rate mortgage these days"—and encouraged to use one of these alternatives to buy their dream home.

As a result, at the peak of the lending boom in 2005, borrowers with credit scores good enough to qualify for conventional financing got more than half of the subprime mortgages that were securitized and sold to investors, according to an analysis by First American LoanPerformance for the *Wall Street Journal*. By the end of 2006, that proportion had grown to 61 percent. So people with good credit were paying more for loans than they needed to, in large part because the more exotic loans were more profitable for Wall Street firms.

Lenders' excesses came back to haunt them. Defaults and foreclosures started to climb. Insurance contracts and investment derivatives based on these faulty loans caused Wall Street firms to suffer massive losses, requiring bailouts, takeovers and bankruptcy filings. Credit markets virtually shut down, cutting lenders off from money to lend and businesses from capital needed to pay expenses. For a few scary months in 2008, the entire financial system was at risk.

Our economy edged away from the brink, and lenders trimmed their sails considerably. Mortgage lenders once again required down payments, decent credit scores and proof of income. Auto loans became harder for the less-creditworthy to secure. Credit card issuers cut total available lines of credit from $5 trillion to about half that while raising rates on millions of customers. Lenders' caution is likely to persist—at least until the next boom.

But even now, it's still easy to get in over your head, particularly if you have good credit. Negative-equity auto loans are still abundant. Credit card issuers continue to brawl over prime customers, and you can qualify for multiple credit cards with limits that exceed your annual income. While 100 percent financing has all but disappeared, you can still buy a home with as little as 3.5 percent down with no requirement that you have any other savings once the deal closes.

So the moral of this story is that we as individuals need to put our own limits on how much we borrow. Unlike previous generations, we can't count on lenders to set those limits for us.

ACTION STEPS
To pay off debt the smart way, here's what you should do:

- Divide your debt into three piles: good, neutral and toxic.
- Get lower rates on your debt where possible.
- Prioritize your toxic debts and pay those off first.
- Don't rush to pay off low-rate, tax-deductible debts including mortgages and federal student loans. Consider consolidating federal student loans into the longest-available loan if you need to free up money to pay down more expensive debts.

Don't Avoid Risk . . .
Embrace It—but Sensibly

THE OLD-SCHOOL RULES:
Don't gamble in the stock market with money you can't afford to lose.

THE BUBBLE ECONOMY RULES:
There's no real risk if you stay diversified and invest for the long term.

THE NEW RULES:
Risk is part of life. While you can't avoid it, you can make sure the risks you're taking are appropriate for your goals.

Until the crash of 2008, most investors had been through what amounted to minor setbacks. Yes, the tech crash of 2000 was awful, but overall stocks recovered fairly quickly. The downturn after the 9/11 attacks was scary for a while, but we bounced back from that, too. Even the October 1987 crash, when the Dow Jones Industrial Average lost 22 percent in a single day, turned out to be a rather short-term setback.

So, few of today's investors really understood that the market could wipe out huge chunks of their wealth and not promptly give it back.

In fact, the drop was so steep and prolonged that many people started talking about the "lost decade" of investing, saying investors were no better off at the end of the "aughts" (the period from 2000 to 2009) than they were at the beginning.

The thing is, anyone who's studied stock market history knows there have been plenty of prior periods that brought investors to their knees—

most notably the 1929 crash and subsequent Depression, but there were drops of 30 percent or more that started in 1903, 1907, 1917, 1919, 1937, 1962, 1968 and 1973. In fact, the bulk of the 1970s was a terrible time for stock market investors as equities dropped and languished for years.

Yet even in the worst years, investors eventually prevailed if they simply stuck it out. Even those who jumped in right before the 1929 crash would eventually have realized significant gains. According to Ibbotson Associates, an investment research firm, there has never been a period in modern investing history when stocks earned less than an 8 percent average annual return over thirty years.

Index	Average annualized return of 30-year periods	Median annualized return of 30-year periods	Frequency of return greater than 10%	Frequency of return greater than 0%	Best 30-year period	Worst 30-year period
S&P 500 total return	11.30%	10.90%	81.50%	100%	13.70% (1975–2004)	8.50% (1929–1958)
S&P 500 inflation-adjusted total return	7.10%	7.10%	5.60%	100%	10.60% (1932–1961)	4.40% (1965–1994)

Source: T. Rowe Price and Morningstar/Ibbotson.

When losses are so deep, however, emotions often overcome reason.

Many of those who lived through the Great Depression, for example, became risk averse. Some were so scarred by the economic cataclysm that they refused to use banks again after losing their savings in the days before the FDIC insured deposits. Others swore off stock market investing, missing the subsequent recovery and a lifetime of potential gains. (Investors who jumped in during the depths of the Depression, 1932–1939, saw some of the best long-term gains: average annual returns of 12 to 13 percent. Even after inflation, these investors saw a real 9 to 10 percent return on their money.)

You don't want to repeat those mistakes. The crash of 2008 and the Great Recession will forever shape you and the ways you approach investing. But if you learn the right lessons from this experience—that you can't hide from risk, but you can understand and manage it—you'll ultimately get ahead.

WHY THERE'S NO SUCH THING AS A SAFE INVESTMENT

You can always tell the people who are new to investing. They're the ones who want to know which investments will keep their money safe while guaranteeing the highest returns.

Sorry, my dear, but you can't have it both ways. If you want safety, you give up returns. If you want better returns, you have to take some risks. Before we go any further, though, we need to explore this idea of "safety" or "riskless investing." Because there's really no such thing.

There *are* a few places where you can put your money without fear of losing your principal. One is in a bank account insured by the FDIC or a credit union account insured by the National Credit Union Share Insurance Fund, which, like the FDIC, is backed by the full faith and credit of the U.S. government. As long as your balance is under the insurance limit, you'll get your money back even if the financial institution fails.

Another is Treasury securities, which are essentially bonds the U.S. government sells to fund its operations. There's little risk of Uncle Sam going out of business.

But these supersafe investments aren't exactly risk free. If you buy a Treasury bond and interest rates go up, the value of your bond drops. If you have to sell the bond before it matures (a 10-year bond matures ten years after it's issued, for example), you may lose money.

INSIDER TERMS

Inflation: A rise in the general level of prices for goods and services. Inflation erodes the value of money over time, which is bad for savers but good for borrowers, who can pay back debt with cheaper dollars.

Perhaps the bigger risk, though, is that of inflation. Supersafe investments tend to have very low returns compared to other available investments. Most of the time, once inflation and taxes are factored in, you're losing ground over time. Even a moderate rate of inflation such as 3 percent will cut the value of a dollar almost in half in twenty years. So if your investments aren't even keeping up with inflation, you'll have less buying power in the future than you have now.

And most of us need our money to do a lot better than keep up with inflation. Why? Because someday we will be old.

WHY YOU NEED STOCKS IN YOUR PORTFOLIO

The young have a hard time imagining being old. The old have a hard time imagining how time could have flown so quickly.

So every time I hear twenty-somethings suggest that they're not likely to live to retirement age, or that they have plenty of time ahead of them to save for it, I have to answer: yes, you are, and no, you don't.

It boils down to math: life expectancy math and the miracle of compound returns. Let's take life expectancies first.

At birth, a male's life expectancy in the United States is about seventy-five years and a female's is nearly eighty. Those expectancies inch up over time; the longer you live, in other words, the longer you're expected to go on doing so.

Age	Remaining life expectancy	
	Male	Female
At birth	74.81	79.95
10	65.53	70.58
20	55.87	60.74
30	46.60	51.03
40	37.30	41.45
50	28.49	32.24
60	20.42	23.53
70	13.30	15.69
80	7.62	9.16

Source: Social Security Administration.

You may think you're some kind of exception, but odds are you're not. Consider:

- Out of 100,000 live births, 79,061 males and 87,051 females live to age sixty-five, according to the Social Security Administration's actuarial tables. In percentage terms, 79 percent and 87 percent are synonymous with "the vast majority."

- By age seventy-five, 60 percent of males and nearly 73 percent of females are still alive.
- Sixty percent of women are still alive at eighty, while the percentage of still-kicking men drops below half after age seventy-eight.
- More than half the women are still alive at age eighty-three.

In short, the chances are excellent you'll survive until the traditional retirement age and many years beyond.

You probably won't be able to work until you drop, even if you were willing to do so. The typical retirement age is now around sixty-two, and more than 40 percent of those who stop working before age sixty-five do so at least somewhat involuntarily, according to the Employee Benefit Research Institute (EBRI). They get laid off or have health problems or need to take care of someone who does. The older you get, the more likely you'll have to stop working.

A fifteen- or twenty-year retirement is a long span to cover without regular paychecks, and you may need to provide for an even longer period. If you have a college degree, for example, you're expected to have a longer-than-average life. Good health, good habits and good genes extend your life expectancy as well. Search for the Life Expectancy Calculator at http://money.msn.com to get a customized estimate.

How much you should save to cover your expected time without paychecks is something we'll cover in an upcoming chapter. Suffice it to say: it will be a lot.

Social Security will provide only a fraction of the money you're likely to need. The maximum check you could get from Social Security in 2009 was $2,323. The average check was closer to $1,100 (about $1,900 for a couple).

And as everybody knows, the Social Security system is in trouble. During the recession, the system started paying out more in taxes than it collected in benefits. By 2037, its reserves are expected to be depleted and there will be money enough to pay just 76 percent of the promised benefits.

Something has to be done, but so far, Congress hasn't been willing to do anything. The longer it takes lawmakers to address the problem, the more drastic the fixes that will be needed.

My view is that Congress probably won't abandon the safety-net nature of Social Security, so benefits for low-income workers will be preserved. It's the folks who make more that are likely to experience the brunt of any changes, including higher taxes and lower benefits.

In short, the farther you are from retirement and the more money you make, the more you should discount any promised check from Social Security.

If you're like most workers, you also can't rely on a fat pension. Traditional pensions, which offer a guaranteed check in retirement for as long as you live, are offered by fewer companies these days. Governments still tend to offer pensions, but the growing cost of this benefit is triggering some backlash among taxpayers. Even if you have a sweet pension now, your benefits going forward are at risk of being cut.

So that means that if you want to have a decent retirement, you'll almost certainly have to save for it. And reaching your goal will be dramatically easier if you let the stock market help you.

Simply put, a stock is a piece of ownership in a company. Companies issue shares of stock to raise money; investors buy the shares hoping to share in the company's growth (through rising stock prices). Many companies also distribute a portion of their profits to shareholders in the form of dividends.

If a company's earnings grow, its stock price will typically grow, too. But stock prices can rise and fall independently of a company's intrinsic value. The dot-com boom is a good illustration: investors piled into technology stocks with no earnings on the conviction that these companies had sparkling futures—when many, in fact, did not, and those that did couldn't possibly create enough earnings to justify their lofty stock prices.

Over time, the stock market does a pretty good job of assigning value to companies—rewarding those that consistently create profits, punishing those that don't—but that doesn't mean there can't be some serious aberrations in the short run.

One way to cushion your portfolio against those aberrations is to buy bonds as well as stocks. Investing in a company's bonds makes you one of the company's creditors—you're lending the company money for its operations.

Companies aren't the only entities that issue bonds. The U.S. government issues Treasury bonds. States, cities and institutions can issue bonds as well. A bond is essentially an IOU issued in return for the money you agree to lend by buying the bond, usually at a set interest rate with interest payments made twice a year or so.

A bond's value over time may rise and fall depending on prevailing interest rates. The value of a bond moves in the opposite direction of interest rates. If interest rates rise after the bond is issued, for example, the bond will fall in value. After all, who wants an old bond paying 5 percent when the new ones pay 7 percent? To entice someone else to buy, you'd have to drop the price of the bond to compensate. Similarly, if rates fall, older, higher-yielding bonds will become more valuable.

The rate you get also depends on the strength of the issuing entity's finances—the shakier its financial footing, the higher the rate it has to offer to attract investors. If a company does go out of business, its bondholders are usually among the creditors that may get some part of their investment returned. That's in sharp contrast to stockholders, whose investment is usually wiped out.

But as you know, safety and return are inversely linked. While bonds often outperform stocks in times of economic turmoil, over the long run returns from bond investments are typically lower than those offered by stocks.

Let's say you're trying for a $1 million nest egg. If you start at age twenty-five and assume an 8 percent average annual return—a reasonable assumption, given a diversified portfolio that's heavily weighted toward stocks—you would need to set aside about $287 a month.

If you invested only in bonds, though, your expected return would be closer to 5 percent. In that case, you'd need to put aside $655 a month to get to $1 million at age sixty-five.

Sticking to supersafe options? If you can eke out a 3 percent return, you'd need to save over $1,000 a month to hit the same goal.

The later you start, the more you have to shovel into your retirement accounts to reach your target number. With just twenty years to retirement, you'd have to put $3,000 a month into supersafe investments, compared to $1,700 into the stock-heavy portfolio.

The tough fact is that most people simply don't have enough spare cash lying around to fund their retirement if they use only low-return investment options. They need to take more risk to get to their goals. Not only have stocks offered better returns than any other investment over time, but stocks consistently outpaced inflation by 4 percentage points or more.

(By the way, you don't have to buy stocks or bonds directly to get their benefits. You can, and most often should, invest by buying mutual funds. A mutual fund is basically a basket of investments—usually stocks, bonds, cash investments or some combination of these. A mutual fund offers far more diversification than most individuals could manage on their own, typically investing in hundreds or thousands of different securities. Mutual funds also offer professional management of the underlying investments.)

You still might be skeptical about the reliability of stock market returns, given the recent unpleasantness on Wall Street and all the moaning about the "lost decade" for the stock market. It seems as if lots of people took risk and got no returns for their trouble.

It's true that if you'd invested $10,000 in a broad-market mutual fund such as Vanguard Total Stock Market Index, which is designed to mimic the return of all stocks, at the beginning of the decade, you'd have just $9,875 of that money at the end. Adjusted for inflation, your investment would be worth about $7,860. Ouch.

But most of us don't invest a single lump sum and let it sit. Instead, we contribute smaller amounts over time, which gives us the chance to benefit from any downturns (we're buying on sale) as well as the upswings. If you'd invested $500 a month in the Vanguard stock fund over that same decade, in fact, you'd have $66,729 at the end—a bit more than your $60,000 in contributions.

And if you invested the smart way, diversifying with bonds and international stocks in addition to U.S. stocks, you'd have done even better. Bonds happened to be consistent earners over that decade. Most categories of bonds returned an average annualized return of 6 percent or better. International stocks had a much more mixed run during the same time period but still ended the decade with an overall gain.

So a $500 monthly investment divided among the Vanguard Total Stock Fund (50 percent), the Vanguard Total International Stock Index (10 percent) and the Vanguard Total Bond Fund (40 percent) and rebalanced yearly would have been worth $75,916.

Since you can't really avoid risk, and you probably need to take some, the key is to be smart about what risks you take and how you manage them. Unfortunately, too many people in recent years weren't smart. Some were do-it-yourselfers who thought they knew what they were doing, until they learned otherwise. Others relied on advisers who were really just salespeople in disguise, with incentives to sell them the "hot" investment of the moment and no background in comprehensive financial planning. Either way, they got burned.

Particularly sad were the folks who were just inches from retirement, or who had recently retired, thinking they were set. Many had overdosed on stocks without realizing it until it was too late. Here are just some of the myths that came around to bite people:

Myth #1: "The risk of stocks goes away if you hold them long enough." This myth stems from the fact that the stock market does tend to bounce back over time. But any individual stock can drop in value to zero (if the company goes bankrupt, for example). Even the most respected company can lose market share and value over time. Furthermore, you can, and will, experience big swings in the value of even the most diversified stock market portfolio. There's no such thing as a riskless stock or a riskless stock portfolio.

Myth #2: "Asset allocation eliminates risk." Diversifying your portfolio among different asset classes (U.S. stocks of big, medium and small companies; international stocks; international bonds; U.S. corporate and government bonds; and cash) can help you reduce the risk of losing money, since these different investments usually don't move in the same direction at the same time. When stocks are doing poorly, bonds usually do well. But sometimes, as in the 2008 crash, everything goes into the toilet at once (well, everything but Treasuries; investors piled into those seeking relative safety and drove up their value). These cataclysms don't last forever, of course, but it can be pretty scary to watch everything in your portfolio plunge at once.

Myth #3: "I'm young [or risk tolerant, or a long-term investor]. I don't need bonds." I imagine there are a lot fewer people holding this delusion than there were before the crash. Theoretically, if you have thirty years or more until your goal and an iron stomach, you can ride out the ups and downs of the stock market without the cushioning benefits of cash or bonds. Most people, though, don't have nearly enough intestinal fortitude to watch the value of their portfolio drop by more than half (the Dow Jones Industrial Average, a key market measure, dropped 54 percent between its October 9, 2007, peak and its March 9, 2009, low). At some point, probably the worst point, they'll want to throw in the towel—and they will, of course, miss the subsequent upturn.

Even if you did have the stomach, you might not have the time. The real roadkills of the 2008 crash were the folks who had just retired or were just about to retire and whose portfolios were too heavily weighted toward stocks. The problem with retiring in a bear market, when stocks are losing value, is that you're siphoning money from a shrinking pool, which dramatically increases the chances you'll run out of cash before you run out of life. The money you take out isn't there to earn returns when the market bounces back, so you run a real risk of not being able to recover from a bad start.

Phil learned that lesson during an earlier bear market. He had retired at fifty-five with a $1.5 million retirement fund and plenty of confidence his best years were ahead. Seven years later, after the 2000–2001 bear market hit, the California resident was down to $300,000 and feeling he was "running out of money and options."

Phil was a poster boy for almost everything that can go wrong in retirement, from a bear market early on, to a withdrawal rate that proved unsustainable, to questionable financial advice that kept him invested in risky assets even as his portfolio plunged. "My financial adviser didn't deliver in providing me with a secure retirement income," Phil wrote me in an e-mail. "He kept telling me that the market would come back. Well, it hasn't in my case."

Phil had been withdrawing close to $30,000 a year for his retirement—certainly not an exorbitant sum, but because his portfolio was so heavily weighted toward stocks and because stocks fell so dramatically, his nest egg wasn't able to recover. By the time he wrote me, his "sustainable" rate of withdrawal—a rate that minimized the chances he would run out of money—was just $1,000 a month.

You might take Phil's situation to mean that retirees should bail on stocks entirely, but that would be learning the wrong lesson. To understand why, though, we have to delve a bit into financial planning history.

Until the mid-1990s, calculating sustainable withdrawal rates was pretty much a guessing game. Many planners simply picked a figure somewhere below the expected rate of return on a portfolio. If the planner figured the client would earn an 11 percent average annual return, for example, he would subtract 3 percent or so for the inflation rate and allow an 8 percent annual withdrawal rate, or perhaps slightly less if he were a conservative type.

That seemed a little too off-the-cuff for Bill Bengen, a financial planner in El Cajon, California. Bengen knew that there was no such thing as an "average" market. Some years are way up, others are way down and sometimes the market goes sideways for a long, long while. Bengen suspected that withdrawal rates that seemed reasonable when based on averages would turn out to be too high when faced with real market conditions.

Bengen's research, using model portfolios and subjecting them to historic market conditions, proved his suspicions to be correct.

Depending on the portfolio's mix of stocks and bonds, Bengen found that even a 5 percent withdrawal rate—adjusted each subsequent year for the inflation rate—could cause someone to run out of money in twenty years. A 3 percent withdrawal rate from a balanced portfolio almost never did. His influential findings were published in a four-part series for the *Journal of Financial Planning* starting in 1994 and have become the basis for financial planning practice today.

Bengen also found that having a portfolio that was too heavily weighted in bonds was usually *worse* than one that went overboard with stocks—in other words, it was more likely to run out of money at most withdrawal rates. Bengen helped reinforce the idea that even risk-averse retirees should have at least 50 percent of their money in stocks in order to get enough long-term growth to overcome inflation and other portfolio killers.

Mutual fund giant T. Rowe Price later added to our understanding of sustainable withdrawal rates by building on Bengen's work and using computer simulations known as Monte Carlo simulations to determine the likelihood various portfolios would run out of money.

INSIDER TERMS

Monte Carlo simulation: A computer-aided technique used in financial planning to predict the probability of meeting specific goals, such as retirement, in the future. Sets of financial variables—such as interest rates, inflation and investment returns—are combined over and over again, in hundreds or thousands of different ways, to compute these probabilities.

CHANCES OF SUCCESS

The chart below estimates the chances that a given type of portfolio won't run out of money over a thirty-year retirement period depending on initial withdrawal rates and the investor's asset allocation.

Initial withdrawal	Stock/bond mix			
	80/20	**60/40**	**40/60**	**20/80**
7%	28%	19%	7%	1%
6%	45%	38%	24%	7%
5%	65%	63%	57%	40%
4%	84%	87%	89%	89%

Source: T. Rowe Price.

If your withdrawal rate starts at 4 percent and adjusts thereafter to the rate of inflation, you have a better than 80 percent chance of not outliving your money, regardless of your portfolio mix. If your withdrawal rate rises, though, the chances of your running out of money climb, too—and the likelihood of disaster increases with how much money you have in bonds. At a 6 percent withdrawal rate, for example, the chances of your portfolio successfully outliving you are just 45 percent, with 80 percent of your portfolio in stocks and 20 percent in bonds. The chances fall to just 7 percent if the proportions are reversed and you hold mostly bonds. We'll discuss this issue more in the chapter on retirement, including the importance of picking the right withdrawal rate and how to cope with bear markets. For right now, though, it's important to realize that unless you retire with a whole lot of money, stock market risk is probably something you'll be managing for your whole life.

HOW TO FIGURE OUT YOUR ASSET ALLOCATION

You can geek out on the subject of asset allocation, if you want to.

Some people—amateur investors and professional advisers alike—really get into nudging their portfolios this way and that, trying to squeeze out a little more return or ratchet down volatility a notch. (Volatility basically means the swings in the value of your portfolio.) They'll experiment with a little more exposure to foreign stocks here, or selling off some junk bonds there, searching for just the right mix.

The rest of us have lives.

It's not that I begrudge you this hobby, if that's what you like to do. But you can create a good portfolio that gives you decent returns with a lot less work. You can:

Turn your asset allocation over to a financial planner. A financial planning pro can take a lot of the guesswork out of asset allocation, creating a customized mix for you based on your time horizon (how long until you'll need the money) and risk tolerance (how much volatility you can stomach). Now, not everyone who calls himself a "financial adviser" or a "financial planner" knows what he's doing, since anyone can use those titles—there are no experience, education or ethics requirements, unfortunately. But if you look for a fee-only planner who is either a certified financial planner (CFP) or a certified public accountant/personal financial specialist (CPA/PFS), you'll probably be in good hands. You can get referrals to fee-only planners from the National Association of Personal Financial Advisors (www.napfa.org) or from the Garrett Planning Network (www.garrettplanningnetwork .com). You can find a CPA/PFS via the American Institute of Certified Public Accountants (http://pfp.aicpa.org).

Get advice from your brokerage or 401(k) or mutual fund company. Vanguard, for example, offers its investors access to CFPs who can advise them about asset allocation. If you have $500,000 or more invested, you can access Vanguard's professional asset management services. Many other big investment companies also offer advice for a fee (usually a few hundred bucks, although you could pay more or less, depending on how much you have invested with the firm). As above, you'll want to make sure you're getting advice from someone with a comprehensive background in financial planning. If the person offering advice is just a salesperson (a broker or anyone else earning commissions based on what you buy), look for more independent counsel.

Use an electronic adviser. Financial Engines (www.financial engines.com) and ESPlanner (www.esplanner.com) are two online resources that can give you detailed, specific advice not only about your asset allocation but about which investments you should pick. Of the two, Financial Engines is more user-friendly, but ESPlanner is more exhaustive (giving advice about spending, saving and insurance targets as well as asset allocation) and allows you to factor in more variables.

The cost is around $150 a year for ESPlanner and $160 for Financial Engines.

With these options, your job isn't over once you've decided on your ideal asset allocation and your specific investments. You'll need to revisit your portfolio at least once a year to "rebalance," or return to your target asset allocation. Otherwise, you could end up taking too much risk.

Let's say your target asset allocation is 50 percent U.S. stocks, 10 percent international stocks and 40 percent bonds. If international stocks do particularly well for a while, they might grow to 20 percent or even 30 percent of your portfolio. If they subsequently crash—and what goes up in a hurry often does the same in reverse—your portfolio will take a much bigger hit than if you'd returned to your original allocation by selling off some of your international stocks and buying U.S. stocks and bonds instead.

Sound like a lot of work? In that case, you could:

Choose a balanced fund, asset allocation fund or "lifestyle" fund. These funds differ somewhat in approach, but the idea is the same: to do most of the work for you. Balanced funds have been around the longest, and they typically invest 60 percent of their assets in U.S. stocks and 40 percent in U.S. bonds. Asset allocation funds usually add foreign stocks and sometimes foreign bonds into the mix, and they may adjust their allocations "tactically" to try to take advantage of changing markets. Lifestyle funds, like asset allocation funds, tend to invest in a broader array of asset classes but typically keep the mix fairly fixed, although you're often given a choice of mixes—one lifestyle fund might be branded a "conservative" mix, another "moderate" and a third "aggressive," for example. Whatever the approach, these funds promise to stick to it and will rebalance when their asset allocations stray from the intended targets.

Pick a target-date maturity fund. With names like "Outlook 2020" and "Target Retirement 2045," the funds promise to take *all* the muss and fuss out of retirement investing. You simply pick the fund with a date close to your expected retirement (or other long-term goal) and let the fund's managers take care of the rest. Not only do they distribute your contributions around a broad spectrum of stocks, bonds and cash, but they rebalance those allocations over time so that your mix *gets more conservative as your goal approaches.* (As you learned before, this is Retirement Investing 101: you want a bigger chunk of your money in bonds and cash as you approach your last day of work, since you'll have less opportunity to make up any losses.)

These so-called target funds, or targeted funds, have really taken off in recent years and are available at most brokerages, mutual fund companies and 401(k) providers. The big problem with target-date maturity funds is that there's nothing really standardized about them. Their "glide paths" can differ sharply: one might start out invested 80 percent in stocks and drop over time to just a 20 percent allocation by the target date; another might start out at 70 percent and slide to 30 percent.

The funds' investment philosophies can differ tremendously as well. Vanguard, known for its low-cost approach to investing, puts your money into index funds that try to match rather than beat the market. T. Rowe Price and Fidelity have more faith in their fund managers' ability to pick winning stocks, and thus they take a more active approach to choosing investments.

Furthermore, target funds notoriously failed to protect those close to retirement during the 2008 crash. Because every asset class except Treasuries and cash plunged at once, the average 2010 target fund fell 36 percent between October 2007 and March 2009. Some funds that had been goosing returns with riskier strategies exploded even more spectacularly: Oppenheimer Transition 2010 lost more than half its value during that bear market, while AllianceBernstein's 2010 target fund plunged 47 percent.

So target-date funds aren't quite the buy-and-forget option they're often marketing as being. They're probably most appropriate for new, nervous investors who otherwise might be tempted to sit on the investing sidelines and for those who are many years from retirement and realize they're too busy to handhold their portfolios. But as you get closer to retirement, you'll need to take a more active approach to your money regardless of how you invest initially—which we'll discuss in the retirement chapter.

IF YOU STILL WANT TO EXPLORE TARGET-DATE MATURITY FUNDS AS AN OPTION, HERE ARE SOME ADDITIONAL FACTORS TO CONSIDER:

- **Watch the fees.** In any "fund of funds" arrangement, annual expenses can quickly get out of hand if you're paying chunks of change for all the underlying funds plus another layer for management of the larger portfolio. This isn't a major concern at the lower-cost shops like Vanguard, Fidelity and T. Rowe Price, but it is definitely an issue at full-service brokerages.

- **Monitor performance.** If your target fund takes an active management approach, you'll need to at least occasionally monitor your fund against appropriate benchmarks to make sure the underlying funds' quality isn't slipping. (Index funds give you the assurance that you'll never do significantly worse than the market, although you'll never do significantly better, either.)
- **Don't pay a load.** Speaking of brokerages, the idea of paying a sales charge, or "load," for one of these funds is particularly egregious. The only time forking over 5 percent of your principal makes any sense is if you're getting expert help in putting your portfolio together. Since the fund does the asset allocation for you, the salesperson isn't doing much to earn your money.
- **Watch the taxes.** Even with low-turnover index funds, you'll have some tax issues with a targeted maturity portfolio. The occasional rebalancing is likely to throw off taxable capital gains distributions. Targeted funds are probably best held in tax-deferred accounts.

WHY INDEX FUNDS ARE AN INVESTOR'S BEST BET

If you want to know why investor Warren Buffett is such a big deal, the answer is pretty simple. The "Oracle of Omaha" has consistently achieved above-average market returns.

Lots of investors beat the market occasionally, but very, very few manage to sustain their runs. And most investors fail miserably when they try. They trade too much, hold on to losers, chase "hot" stocks and generally lose their shirts. I'm not just talking about amateur investors here. Professional money managers have the same dismal record. Most consistently fail to beat the market averages over time. And it's pretty much impossible to predict in advance which active managers will achieve this rare feat.

That isn't going to stop some of you from trying, I know. Some of you are gamblers, and others are lured by the idea that people who are smarter or faster or savvier than the herd can make outsize returns on Wall Street. If that's your bent, I'd advise you to steer clear of anyone who wants to sell you an expensive "trading system" or "secret" knowledge about the market. Stick with the real winners, like my MSN colleague Jim Jubak (www.jubakspicks.com), who write extensively about the markets and whose techniques and advise are up front, transparent and accessible to anyone with Internet access or a library card.

Being an active investor is a lot of work, I'll warn you. You'll have to do extensive research, monitor your investments carefully and be disciplined about when you buy and sell. You will pay more as well: active management simply costs more in trading commissions, fees and taxes. I think most of us are better off acknowledging that we don't want to do all this work, particularly when the odds are so stacked against us. Fortunately, there is a better way: index funds.

Index funds are mutual funds designed to mimic the return of a market index. S&P 500 index funds, for example, invest in the stocks that make up the Standard & Poor 500 market index. Other index funds may invest in narrower or broader swaths of the market (such as "small company" index funds or "total market" stock or bond funds). If there's an index measuring a market, there's probably an index fund to go with it.

All mutual funds charge ongoing fees to pay for their operations, but index funds typically charge much less. (A fund's expense ratio is figured by dividing its assets by those costs, which typically include management fees and administrative costs and may include marketing expenses, known as 12b-1 fees. The expense ratio doesn't include sales charges, or "loads," which are an additional fee that you might pay if you buy the fund through a brokerage.) With an index fund, you're not paying more for an active manager's trades or supposed expertise. You eliminate the risk that you've picked the "wrong" manager or investments. You get the return the market gets, pure and simple.

Letting go of the idea that you must—or even can—beat the market is enormously liberating. Instead, you're investing in the productivity of a huge number of companies and people. Over time, this productivity will grow and increase the value of your investment. And you will keep most of that investment, instead of giving one-third or more of it to Wall Street.

And yes, the toll those fees and commissions would take on your investments is really that bad. Let's say you invest $5,000 a year for forty years. If you manage an 8 percent average annual return, your nest egg would eventually be worth nearly $1.3 million. If fees, trading costs and taxes nick just 1 percentage point off that return, your portfolio would be worth just under $1 million. If costs trim 2 percentage points from your return, you would be left with just under $775,000.

There's no such thing as an investment option that's entirely free, of course, but some of the index funds out there get pretty darn close. While the average expense ratio for a no-load (no-commission) large-company mutual fund is close to 1 percent, Vanguard's S&P 500 Index Fund charges one-fifth of that (.19 percent). You can wind up paying expense ratios of over 2 percent for some brokerage-sold funds.

If you really want to dig into the whys and wherefores of index investing, I highly recommend *The Little Book of Common Sense Investing* by John Bogle. Bogle is the founder of Vanguard funds and considered the father of index investing.

Or you can take the word of the world's greatest investor. Warren Buffett himself has repeatedly said that most investors should stick to low-cost index funds.

"A very low-cost index is going to beat a majority of the amateur-managed money or professionally managed money," Buffett told a press conference in 2007, a day after the annual shareholder meeting for Berkshire Hathaway, Buffett's insurance and investment company.

By the way, neither Buffett nor Bogle is a big fan of a more recent innovation: exchange-traded funds (ETFs). Like mutual funds, ETFs invest in a basket of stocks or bonds, usually (but not always) mimicking an investment index. Unlike mutual funds, though, ETFs can be traded throughout the day.

It's this ability to trade that concerns the big Bs. They worry that the average investor will be too tempted to speculate with ETFs instead of taking the more buy-and-hold approach. Furthermore, ETFs don't always closely track their benchmarks. On a volatile trading day, like the "flash crash" in 2010 when the stock market briefly fell 1,000 points, the big financial institutions that normally guarantee smooth trading of ETFs couldn't handle the wild price swings and many ETFs fell far more than the value of their underlying investments.

If you're planning on investing a big chunk of money at once and can resist the temptation to trade, though, you should still investigate ETFs. They typically have lower expense ratios even than index funds, although you may have to pay a trading commission to buy them (which is why they're typically better for lump-sum purchases than ongoing investments).

HOW TO KEEP YOUR HEAD WHEN ALL ABOUT YOU ARE LOSING THEIRS—IN GOOD TIMES AND BAD

On October 6, 2008, CNN published a poll that showed more than half of Americans thought another depression was "very" (21 percent) or "somewhat" (38 percent) likely.

At that point, of course, our economy had suffered some real body blows. In the days leading up to the poll, the financial crisis that started with the subprime mortgage meltdown had accelerated with breathtaking speed.

A month earlier, the federal government had taken over mortgage behemoths Fannie Mae and Freddie Mac and started its bailout of insurance giant American International Group (AIG). Then Merrill Lynch had been sold to Bank of America in a fire sale as Lehman Brothers melted down into bankruptcy. Washington Mutual was seized by the FDIC. Congress failed, and finally succeeded, in passing a $700 billion bailout bill.

The week immediately following the release of the CNN poll would be one of the worst on record for the stock market, as investors wondered if the crisis—which had by now spread to Europe and would soon stretch around the globe—could be contained.

It was in that environment that I told my readers they were overreacting.

I was as stunned as everyone else by the magnitude of what was happening. I believed a recession was coming and that it might be severe. But I didn't think we would return to a time when the official unemployment rate was 25 percent, bank failures wiped out the savings of millions and one-third of the nation was, in President Franklin D. Roosevelt's haunting words, "ill-housed, ill-clad and ill-nourished."

That twelve-year period of economic disruption and widespread poverty was unprecedented in our nation's history, and from it sprang many of the safety nets that protect us today, including FDIC insurance, Social Security, unemployment insurance and food stamps.

Furthermore, the actions of the nation's financial and political leaders—however flawed and easily second-guessed—were informed by that disaster. Federal Reserve chief Ben Bernanke closely studied the Depression, and he knew that one of the reasons economic conditions became so abysmal is that the government didn't act quickly enough and in fact pursued exactly the wrong policies by allowing institutions to fail and tightening the money supply.

The various bailouts left a lot to be desired—so much money was doled out with so little supervision. But the fact that it was done averted the much-worse crisis we might have experienced otherwise.

Not everyone wanted to hear that message, of course. There were an awful lot of talking heads spouting an awful lot of nonsense in those days. Some panicked, others despaired and a few seemed absolutely delighted to assure us that we were headed for our doom. The patter continued for months, even after it was obvious that the recession's hold was waning.

In a way, this overreaction was the flip side of the bubble-years mania that kept insisting "things are different this time."

During the bubble, real estate prices soared at historically unprecedented rates, yet the cheerleaders insisted all was well—values were sound and prices had higher to climb, they said. Lending practices made less and less sense, but Wall Streeters assured us their computer models accounted for all risks and that everything would be fine. The stock market roared on even as early signs of a recession showed in falling earnings and a nascent credit crunch, and the pundits told us all was good.

When the herd is pounding away in one direction, it's awfully hard to pull up and go a different way. But many times in your financial life, that's exactly what you'll need to do.

During the boom, the smart, contrary action was to limit borrowing, be skeptical of huge price run-ups and prepare for bad times. During the crash, the smart, contrary action was not to panic.

Whether you're faced with a personal setback such as a job loss, a run-of-the-mill economic downturn or a once-in-a-lifetime cataclysm, having a plan and implementing it can keep you from giving in to fear. That plan includes:

Staying invested in stocks. The problem with getting out of the market is that you won't know when to get back in. Markets usually turn around well before the actual economy starts improving, and they typically advance so rapidly that people who aren't already invested miss most of the gains. That was certainly the case in 2009. After hitting a low in March 2009, the markets surged by 60 percent by the end of the year.

Paying attention to your asset allocation. The nattering nabobs pointed to the "failure" of diversification, since everything except Treasuries and cash plummeted at once. But this synchronized performance was temporary, and some of the most-beaten-down sectors bounced back the strongest. "Rebalancing is critical during these periods," leading financial planner Ross Levin told his clients in a quarterly newsletter published during the crisis. "By systematically rebalancing, you are forcing yourself to buy low."

Levin admitted that even he was scared when the market hit its bottom that March. What if everything he'd been telling his clients about staying invested was so much hooey, and that it really was different this time? The experience underscored for him the importance of "putting your own oxygen mask on first"—that is, staying calm and sticking to the plan you worked out in advance, rather than panicking and abruptly changing course.

ACTION STEPS

To be a smarter investor, remember these tips:

- Diversify, diversify, diversify. A mixed portfolio of stocks, bonds and cash is the best choice for most investors and most investment goals. Include foreign as well as U.S. stocks, big companies as well as small ones, corporate as well as government bonds.
- Create your target asset allocation for each investment goal. Rebalance at least once a year so you stay on target, or use funds that do the allocating and rebalancing for you.
- Research the costs. Morningstar.com keeps track of expense ratios for mutual funds and exchange-traded funds. If you're paying much more than 1 percent annually for your funds, look for cheaper options.
- Stick to your plan in times of market turmoil. Don't let fear (or greed) stampede you into actions you'll later regret.

Your Home Is Not a Piggy Bank— Preserve Its Equity

THE OLD-SCHOOL RULES:

You should stretch to buy a house and pay off the mortgage as quickly as possible.

THE BUBBLE ECONOMY RULES:

Buy as much house as your lender will allow; don't worry about paying down your mortgage; remodel for maximum resale; keep trading up.

THE NEW RULES:

Buy less house than you can afford; pay down your loan the smart way; remodel with cash; don't move if you can help it.

The advice that you should stretch to buy a home actually made sense for many, many years. In the 1970s and 1980s, the average worker could count on steadily rising paychecks that would shrink the relative size of a payment on a thirty-year, fixed-rate loan (which is how most people bought their homes). Even after adjusting for inflation, most people experienced real increases in income over time. As their incomes rose, many even decided to pay off their loans early, a decision that made sense when interest rates were high.

Many families also had a built-in backup plan. Single-income families were more common, so if the breadwinner lost a job, the other spouse could go to work to save the house. It wasn't like today, when there's often no one on the sidelines and many families need both partners' paychecks to make the mortgage payment.

Also, a much bigger proportion of the workforce was covered by traditional, defined-benefit pensions thirty years ago, which means they didn't have to save massive amounts of money on their own to have a decent retirement.

Another big difference: lending standards. Back then, it was pretty tough to get a mortgage for more than you could really afford. Lenders were pretty conservative about who got money, and how much, in the days before credit scoring, loan securitization and adjustable-rate mortgages allowed them to offload risk.

Clearly, the world has changed a lot since then.

One of the most dramatic changes has been in earnings. The steady growth in wages started to collapse at the end of the 1990s. Median incomes actually shrank for several years and still hadn't fully recovered a decade later. What's more, income volatility increased. That means big swings in workers' income became more common, particularly for men and the less educated. One month, you're loading up on overtime; the next month, your hours are cut or you're out of a job. Many families could no longer count on steady income, let alone steady raises that might make paying a big loan easier over time.

The combination of stagnant wages and more volatility should have made homebuyers—and lenders—more conservative. But the lending industry began innovating all kinds of new loans that allowed people to "buy more house" than ever before. Old-school loans required borrowers to pay principal and interest with every payment, but the new loans allowed people to pay only the interest that was due—and sometimes, with the most dangerous mortgages, not even that. Option ARMs (or pick-a-pay mortgages) had a minimum payment option that didn't even cover all the interest owed; the difference between what you paid and the larger amount of interest you actually owed was tacked onto your mortgage balance, so that the amount you owed could balloon over time. The interest-only and minimum payment options weren't permanent— eventually the payment would skyrocket upward, so the larger payments would cover some of the principal owed. But people were qualified for loans based on the initial low payments, often with no assessment about whether they would be able to afford the higher payments to come.

Loosening lending standards fueled a spectacular run-up in home values in many areas. Before the bubble popped, home prices in the ten largest cities were growing at a 20 percent annual rate. Potential homebuyers worried they'd be priced out of their markets, and many used exotic mortgages so they could stretch to buy the homes they wanted— further fueling the bubble.

At the peak of the madness, lenders stopped making any effort to verify how much some borrowers made or owned. As a result, borrowers were getting approved for loans that were eight or nine times their incomes. (In your parents' day, a loan that was three times your income was considered big.) Some borrowers didn't understand the risk, while others were convinced by their lenders that they would be able to refinance to another, "safer" loan before their payments reset.

It all came to a crashing end, of course, when the housing bubble popped.

Home values started to fall, rather than rise, shocking people who thought real estate could only go up. (Those of us who have experienced regional real estate recessions knew better, but it's hard to convince people in the midst of a boom that it really *isn't* different this time, and that what goes up can come down.)

Millions had borrowed so much that they couldn't sell their homes even for what they owed on them. The notion that they could refinance to a better loan turned into a cruel joke as easy credit vanished along with their equity. The vicious cycle had begun. As people lost their homes, banks slashed prices to quickly shed themselves of these unwanted assets, which drove home values down still more.

The mortgage crisis's impact wasn't restricted to home values. The effect of souring loans was magnified on Wall Street by derivatives and credit default swaps that ostensibly were meant to manage risk, but ended up compounding it. The mortgage crisis led to a full-blown financial panic, which touched off the Great Recession—the biggest economic downturn in the United States since the Great Depression.

As layoffs mounted, more and more people found themselves in homes they could no longer afford. Instead of an investment and a ticket to wealth, their houses became albatrosses around their necks.

There were others, though, who came through the crisis relatively unscathed. Their homes may have lost value on paper, but they were still able to make their payments and even refinance to better deals when the crisis drove interest rates to generational lows. These homeowners understood a number of things that their worse-off neighbors didn't, including:

A home isn't really an investment. Homeownership *can* help you build wealth over time. Paying down a traditional mortgage is a kind of forced savings, and price appreciation, when it happens, can help you build equity. But the real return on your investment, once all the costs are considered, is likely to be paltry. Since real estate is never a sure thing and homeownership isn't for everyone in all circumstances, you have to make sure it's right for you, and that you do it right, before you plunge ahead.

It's smart to buy less home than you can actually afford. Limiting your mortgage payments to no more than 25 percent of your gross income gives you some wiggle room in uncertain times. Although lenders will let you borrow more, people whose homes eat more of their income tend to sacrifice other important financial goals, like saving for retirement, for their kids' education and for emergencies. Living closer to the edge, they have fewer resources to fall back on when things go wrong.

You must protect your equity. Your home equity is part of your long-term wealth. It shouldn't be squandered to pay for short-term expenses or purchases that lose value. It should be reserved for emergencies and for long-term goals. (Many people have funded comfortable retirements by selling appreciated homes, downsizing and living off the difference.)

A home is for the long term. In normal markets, it can take years for a home to appreciate enough to offset selling and moving costs. In bad markets, it can take a decade or more just to get back to even. Although you may need to move for a variety of reasons—job change, change in family status or a deteriorating neighborhood—you'll want to keep your moves to a minimum and pick homes where you expect to live for many, many years to come.

THE THREE WORST REASONS FOR BUYING A HOME

Before launching into how to buy a home, we should talk about whether you should. If any of the following is the primary reason you're buying a house, you should think again.

Bad reason #1: "It will be a good investment"

Maybe it will, maybe it won't. Before the real estate bubble, average home price appreciation barely outpaced inflation. (By contrast, in every thirty-year period since 1928, the stock market's average annual return has beaten inflation by at least 4 percentage points.) Average appreciation figures don't account for the carrying costs of owning a home—the points you paid to get your mortgage, the interest you pay on your loan and the costs of insurance premiums, property taxes, maintenance, repairs and home improvements.

Some people get lucky. They buy at the right time in a market that subsequently gets hot, and their houses don't demand too much upkeep. Or you could be like the reader whose basement flooded right after moving in, followed by a leak that required a $7,000 fix, followed by breakdowns in the septic system, air-conditioning and wiring. "By the time we moved 2 years later, we added up all the bills and came to a total of $36,000," she wrote.

Not every house is a black hole. As I said earlier, homeownership can help you build wealth as you pay down your mortgage and as home prices rise. In fact, homeowners are generally far wealthier than renters. In the Federal Reserve's latest Survey of Consumer Finances, homeowners had a median net worth of $234,200, compared to a measly $5,100 for renters. But it doesn't automatically follow that homeownership will make you rich, that every home purchase is a good investment or that it's the right choice for everyone in all circumstances.

Bad reason #2: "I'm tired of throwing away money on rent"

Renting often is cheaper than owning. In really expensive cities, such as New York and San Francisco, renting is so much cheaper that it's tough to make the case for becoming a homeowner. Buying in these markets often means settling for a much worse property or an awful commute, compared with what you can afford if you continue to rent.

You're not really throwing money away when you send a check to your landlord, anyway. You're exchanging it for a place to live. You're also getting flexibility and freedom—things you sacrifice when you buy a home. When you're a renter, it's the landlord, not you, who is generally responsible for maintenance, repairs and fixing the toilet that blows up in the middle of the night. If the neighborhood should start to slide or you get or lose a job, you can up and move, often with just a few weeks' notice.

It's true that you may have to deal with rising rents and recalcitrant landlords. Homeowners, however, are often stuck with rising taxes and maintenance costs, as well as recalcitrant neighbors. Moving is never fun, but moving when you own a home is an expensive, time-consuming process in the best of times. Finding a buyer can take months. Selling costs will eat up about 10 percent of your home's value, once you add agent commissions and moving expenses. If you're already "underwater" on your mortgage—owing more than the house is worth—you may wind up with a short sale or foreclosure on your record, which will trash your credit.

In other words, homeownership is more like marriage; renting is more like living together. Make sure you're ready to be wedded to a house before you propose to leave behind life as a renter.

Bad reason #3: "I need the tax deduction"

Tax deductions are nice, when you can get them, but they're no reason to take on a mortgage. That's because your write-off is limited by your tax bracket. If you're in the top federal tax bracket (with taxable income of $373,650 or more in 2010), every dollar you pay in mortgage interest saves you only thirty-five cents in taxes. Most people get even less because they're in the 25 percent tax bracket or lower. In other words, buying a house just for the mortgage break would be like giving somebody a buck just to get thirty-five cents or less in return.

And not every homeowner gets a tax deduction. Homes in many parts of the country aren't expensive enough for the interest deduction on the mortgage to be larger than the standard deduction taxpayers otherwise get. If you can't itemize, you don't get the break. Also, the amount of interest you pay typically declines over the life of the loan. So even if you get a write-off at the beginning of your mortgage, you may keep it for only a few years.

Property taxes are also deductible if you can itemize, but that's a whole different can of worms. These taxes are based on the assessed value of your home, and in most places their growth rate isn't capped. (California is one exception; by law, property assessments can increase no more than 2 percent each year.) If prices start to rise rapidly in your area, you could find yourself having to pay an increasingly unwieldy tax bill. Many older people on fixed incomes wind up having to sell their homes, priced out by their own property tax bills.

In any case, many of the real costs of owning a home aren't deductible. Uncle Sam won't give you a break for insurance, repairs or maintenance, for example, and those costs can really add up. If you fail to maintain your home properly, you'll pay even more when it comes time to sell. Many buyers won't even bid on a property that shows significant neglect. Even in hot markets (remember those?), buyers are likely to ask for expensive concessions to pay for the repairs you should have been doing all along.

So when should you buy a home? My standard answer has been the same over the years, regardless of whether the market was rising or falling. It's: "When you're ready." That means when you have a strong desire to own your own home, the timing is right for you, you can swing all the costs and you plan to stay put awhile.

That way you can ride out any downturns in the market and benefit from any appreciation while enjoying a nice and affordable home in the meantime.

IS YOUR HOME WORTH LESS? PROTEST YOUR PROPERTY TAX BILL

THE ONE SILVER LINING of the real estate downturn is that you may be able to get your property reassessed and lower your tax bill. You have to work for this break, though; your county tax assessor isn't likely to cut your bill otherwise. Your assessor's Web site may list deadlines for appealing assessments as well as forms and procedures for challenging your bill, or you may need to call and ask for this information. Typically, you'll need to collect recent sales information for five to ten comparable homes in your neighborhood. You can look these up at the assessor's office or hire a real estate agent or appraiser to do the work for you. You may need to schedule an informal meeting with the assessor, or you may simply be able to submit your case and wait for an answer. If the assessor balks, you may have to schedule a formal hearing to protest and make your case again. Much of the time, though, homeowners who appeal their assessments in declining markets get some kind of adjustment in their favor.

WHERE YOU LIVE CAN CREATE OR DESTROY WEALTH

You've heard the old saying that the three most important factors in real estate are location, location and location. You've probably also heard that it makes sense to buy the worst house in the best neighborhood you can afford, because you'll have the most opportunity for price appreciation.

That may be true, but the author of the seminal book *The Millionaire Next Door* cautions that buying into a pricey neighborhood can have unintended consequences for your finances—and for the finances of your *children*.

In his more recent book *Stop Acting Rich*, Thomas Stanley notes that our neighbors can exert a powerful influence on how much money we spend. The cars they drive, the vacations they take, the way they educate their children can set an unconscious "norm" for us, whether we can afford it or not. It's the old "keeping up with the Joneses" pressure, writ large.

Stanley notes that most of the millionaires he studied lived in neighborhoods that were "easy" to live in, meaning that their homes were affordable and that they tended to be nearer the top of the economic scale for their areas. They weren't constantly striving to keep up with the Joneses, because they *were* the Joneses.

Their place near the top of the neighborhood economic spectrum also influenced their children. People who felt that their families were generally better off than most of their neighbors were more likely to be wealth accumulators rather than spenders, Stanley found.

By contrast, people who felt their childhood neighbors were generally better off than their own families were less likely to be wealth accumulators in adulthood. Perhaps to make up for those childhood feelings of being "less than," they often spent heavily on the badges of wealth, such as expensive cars and watches, rather than saving and investing to accumulate wealth.

THE STARTER HOME MYTH

The introduction of the thirty-year, fixed-rate mortgage during the Great Depression gradually helped open the doors of homeownership to the majority of U.S. households. After World War II, the demand for homes skyrocketed as economic prosperity finally returned. The government expanded the availability of mortgages to help returning soldiers buy their first homes. Builders responded by constructing whole neighborhoods of smaller, mass-produced, affordable homes, with Levittown, New York, as their model.

The idea developed that young couples could start out with one of these "starter homes," featuring one or two bedrooms and a bath, then quickly move up to a larger "forever home" as their wealth (and family size) increased.

Millions of families did exactly that as rising wages made bigger mortgages more affordable and real estate appreciation built equity.

SHOULDN'T I PUT MY EQUITY TO WORK?

DURING THE BOOM, it was popular to tell homeowners that they shouldn't let their equity sit around "doing nothing." The folks doling out this advice were typically lenders that wanted to make money from home equity borrowing and promoters of various get-rich-quick schemes, who suggested people borrow against their homes to buy real estate or business franchises. As a result, many homeowners who once had substantial equity found themselves deeply underwater when real estate prices started to fall.

One would-be real estate mogul told me he used the equity in his California house during the boom to purchase several rental properties in Arizona and Nevada—two places that subsequently suffered even sharper downturns than the Golden State. At the time he told me this, the reader had already lost most of the rental properties to foreclosure and was in danger of losing his home.

Having home equity gives you flexibility. If you have to move or can't make the payments, you can always sell the house; if you don't have equity, your options are foreclosure or a short sale, both of which damage your credit scores. If you have equity, you can tap into it when you face a true emergency. And if you run short of money in retirement, you can downsize or use a reverse mortgage and live off your home's value. But none of these options is available to you if you've already squandered your equity. So the best course is often to leave it alone to "do nothing"—except be there when you need it.

But there were costs to this arrangement. Families may have spent years in less desirable housing than they could have rented, waiting for their chance to move up. They also incurred costs to sell and move that they wouldn't have faced had they simply waited to buy their forever house.

But the real disadvantages of settling for a starter home didn't become apparent for many until the housing meltdown that started in 2007. Families who had anticipating moving on to better quarters were now stuck. Particularly hard-hit were those who bought condos in overbuilt markets.

I tried to warn them. In 2004, I took a long look at the condo market and wrote: "This is the tech-stock bubble all over again." Condo developers were on overdrive, building hundreds of thousands of new units a year and converting billions of dollars' worth of apartment units into condos. But once-spectacular price increases had already started to slow, presaging the wipeout that was to come.

As in previous real estate recessions, condos were the first hit and likely will be the last to recover. That's because condos are the real estate world's consolation prize. They will never replace the single-family home as the real estate investment of choice because condos have too many drawbacks and too limited appeal for most borrowers. Many older units (and some of the new ones) suffer from shoddy construction, while condo conversions are basically apartments in drag, with all the noise and shared-space problems that plague rental units. Furthermore, many resident-run condo associations do a poor job keeping up with maintenance and repairs, with one out of three failing to keep enough money in the bank to pay for needed upkeep, according to Calabasas, California–based Association Reserves.

The recession made matters worse. As prices started to drop, those who couldn't sell their units for what they owed on their mortgages often decided to rent them out instead. At the same time, lenders were tightening restrictions on making mortgages to condo projects that were largely renter occupied. That made it harder for those who remained and wanted to sell or even refinance. The more values dropped, the more renters appeared and the more lenders refused to offer mortgages on the units. It was an exact replay of what happened in Southern California and Boston during their regional housing meltdowns, but it still caught many condo owners by surprise.

That's not to say you should never buy a condo or that you have to wait until you can afford your dream house before you buy a home. But you should never buy property expecting to move on in a few years. Make sure you would be comfortable with the quarters and the neighborhood for at least five years, and preferably ten, before you commit to a house.

WITH CONDOS IN PARTICULAR, YOU SHOULD:

- Read the codes and covenants. These outline what's allowed and what's not. Many restrictions are designed to preserve the complex's value, but you may find the lack of freedom stifling. Make sure you know what you're in for.

- Talk to other occupants. A high number of renters or complaints about the condo association should be red flags.
- Ask about the association's operating budget and reserve fund. Bad signs: more than 10 percent of owners are late paying their condo association fees, and more than 50 percent of maintenance liabilities aren't funded.

HOW TO BUY A HOME YOU CAN ACTUALLY AFFORD

During the housing boom, I warned readers not to let anyone involved in the home-buying transaction tell them how much house they could afford to buy. I pointed out that real estate agents, mortgage brokers and loan officers all had conflicts of interest, since they could profit more from larger transactions.

I got a lot of huffy e-mails from real estate agents insisting they would *never* encourage a client to buy more house than they could afford. I'm sure the agents' intentions were pure. But it's awfully tough for anyone who's not intimately involved in your finances to really know what you can afford. To do that, they would need to know, among other things:

- When you plan to retire and how much money you'll need to do so
- How many kids you plan to have and how you intend to educate them
- How many vacations you'll take and how expensive they will be
- What kind of cars you'll drive and how often you'll replace them

And on and on.

(By the way, I didn't hear much protesting from mortgage brokers and loan officers about my advice not to let them sway purchase decisions. Maybe they were feeling guilty about all the incentives they received to put people in riskier, more expensive loans.)

So how much *should* you spend on a house? The traditional way to calculate that is to add up all your income and make sure that your housing expenses, including mortgage payment, homeowners insurance and property taxes, don't exceed a certain amount of that total. The traditional limit, now used again by many lenders, is 28 percent of gross monthly income. Some financial advisers recommend capping your outlay at 25 percent; others suggest stretching to 33 percent or more.

These limits, by the way, apply only if you don't have a lot of other debt. Most lenders don't want more than 36 percent of your total income to go toward mortgage and other debt payments. If your total debt would push you over that figure, most lenders will reduce the size of the mortgage for which you qualify.

Here's how the varying limits translate. The figures assume you earn $45,000 a year and that you would pay $480 in homeowners insurance and $2,000 in property taxes annually. (In reality, those figures would fluctuate with the value of the home you buy.) This also assumes a thirty-year loan at 5.5 percent interest and a big enough down payment that you'll avoid private mortgage insurance (PMI).

HOW LARGE A MORTGAGE CAN $45,000 A YEAR GET YOU?

If share of income devoted to housing is:	The monthly cash requirement is:	Less: taxes and insurance . . .*	. . . leaves cash needed to pay the mortgage . . .	. . . and translates into this loan amount†
25%	$938	$207	$731	$128,745
28%	$1,050	$207	$843	$148,470
31%	$1,163	$207	$956	$168,372
33%	$1,238	$207	$1,031	$181,582

*Assumes $480 a year for insurance and $2,000 for taxes.
†Assumes a thirty-year, fixed-rate loan at 5.5% interest.

As you can see, the percentage of income used has a huge effect on how much house you can buy.

Most Internet mortgage calculators use the 28-percent-of-total-income figure. If you want to see how much mortgage you could afford under other scenarios, adjust your income by using the following multipliers:

INCOME CONVERTER TO MAKE ONLINE CALCULATORS WORK BETTER	
Share of your income* devoted to housing:	Multiply your income by:
25%	0.90
28%	1.00
31%	1.11
33%	1.18

* Gross income.

You can make the calculations more precise if you want, by figuring out how much you need to contribute to various goals, such as your retirement and your kids' college education.

Estimate how much your house is going to cost you in maintenance and repairs each year (figure about 1 percent to 3 percent of the home's total value annually, depending on its age and condition). Then see how much of your remaining income is eaten up by your housing costs (including insurance and taxes), and see how you feel about that.

All that math making your head hurt? Here's the short version: you'll probably be most comfortable using the 25 percent lid. You may want to go even lower if:

You plan to have children. Kids can be expensive—families with kids typically spend 10 to 15 percent more than childless households—and many couples discover they want to have the option of one partner staying home or working part-time once kids arrive. That's tough to do if you need every penny of both incomes to make ends meet. If you really want to be conservative, do your calculations based on the income you think you'll have after the first baby comes.

You have an expensive hobby, like travel. Most homeowners are willing to put their wanderlust on the back burner to buy more house. If that's not you, buy less house.

Your income varies considerably. Most American workers have variable incomes, thanks to the prevalence of overtime pay and bonuses (and, these days, pay cuts and reduced hours). If yours swings wildly from year to year, though, consider basing your calculations on your average earnings over several years or (even more conservative) on the minimum you expect to make.

You may think you can't possibly limit your housing expenses by that much, especially if homes cost a lot where you live. However, you can stretch further if:

You're absolutely debt free. No credit card debt, student loans or car payments—and none anticipated in the near future? You probably can handle a bigger nut.

You don't have to worry about retirement. Many teachers and civil servants have terrific pensions—so good that to be sure they'll be fine, they just have to throw a few bucks each year into an IRA or deferred-compensation plan.

You're pretty sure your income will climb steeply in coming years. Fresh out of law school and doing a few years in the public defender's office? If private practice is your goal and you don't want to wait to buy a home with the bigger income that's coming, stretching now can work out okay. But make sure you can live with the risk that things might not pan out the way you hope, and a big chunk of your income will continue to be devoted to your house.

HOW TO PICK A MORTGAGE

We refinanced our mortgage during the housing boom, when exotic home loans were in flower. Our lending officer pitched us some of the possibilities, including adjustable-rate loans, hybrid loans, interest-only loans and pick-a-pay or option ARMs. When we told him we were "thirty-year, fixed-rate" kind of people, he laughed. "So am I," he said. "I've always had thirty-year loans on my own house."

We do pay a price for being traditional. Adjustable-rate and hybrid loans typically start out with lower payments and can end up costing less in a falling-rate environment. But there are no surprises with a traditional thirty-year, fixed-rate mortgage. The payments stay the same as long as we have the loan. If rates drop, we can refinance (at a cost—more on that in a moment). If rates rise, we're protected.

Another fixed-rate option is the fifteen-year mortgage. These are immensely popular with people who want to own their homes free and clear as fast as possible, and the interest savings are truly impressive.

INTEREST PAID ON FIXED-RATE LOANS FOR A $300,000 MORTGAGE

	Interest rate	Monthly payment	Total interest paid
30-year loan	5.13%	$1,633	$288,045
15-year loan	4.38%	$2,276	$109,655

Wow, you may be thinking. Who in their right mind would choose to pay nearly three times the interest for a thirty-year loan?

A lot of us, actually.

You'll notice the loan payments on a fifteen-year mortgage are substantially higher. That means you'll either buy less house or accept a mortgage that takes a bigger bite of your budget. If you're self-employed or otherwise have a variable income, you may be more comfortable committing to the lower payment and then making extra principal payments when you can.

You also should strongly consider the thirty-year option if you have other, higher-rate debt to pay off. Paying a low-rate, tax-deductible mortgage off fast doesn't make much sense if you're carrying higher-rate debt like credit cards or auto loans.

How about adjustable and hybrid loans? These mortgages typically come with lower initial rates because you, rather than the lender, bear much of the "interest rate risk"—the possibility that interest rates will go up. If you have a one-year adjustable-rate mortgage (ARM), your rate and payment can change after the first year, and every year thereafter. With hybrid ARMs, your rate would be fixed for a certain period (typically three, five, seven or ten years) and then usually would adjust annually after that.

How much your rate and payments can rise depends on the terms of your loan, but typically the adjustments are limited to 1 or 2 percentage points each year, with a lifetime cap of 5 to 6 percentage points. So if you started with an initial monthly payment of $1,430 on a $300,000 loan, that could rise to over $2,500 in a few years if rates jumped sharply higher.

BEFORE YOU AGREE TO AN ADJUSTABLE-RATE MORTGAGE:

- Consider locking in the rate for at least as long as you plan to own the home. Plan to move in about seven years? Opt for a 7/1 ARM.
- Do the math and make sure you can afford the maximum payment. Life doesn't always go as planned. You may be in the home longer than you expect, and you don't want to be forced out by unaffordable payments.

Loan options that once allowed you to avoid paying down your principal initially—interest-only loans and pick-a-pay or option ARMs—have pretty much disappeared in the wake of the mortgage meltdown. They were first touted as a way for business owners and commissioned salespeople to manage their loans. Disciplined borrowers could pay only interest, or even less with option ARMs, when cash flow was tight and then make big principal payments at year's end, when bonuses or dividends were paid. Unfortunately, lenders started promoting these loans as a way to buy much more house. Borrowers were told they were foolish to pay down their principal because rising prices would build equity for them.

Of course, these loans turned out to be a truly horrible idea for many buyers. Ironically, the few people who might have been disciplined enough to use them properly were usually conservative enough to prefer traditional loans.

HOW TO GET THE BEST DEAL ON A MORTGAGE

I'm a pretty well-informed customer when it comes to getting a mortgage. And I still get surprised. On our last refinance, for example, I was delighted with the rate a major lender offered us and with its offer to let me lock in a better deal without extra costs if rates fell.

Well, already-low rates fell even further—except at the lender I was dealing with. The lender had received so many applications that it decided to "choke off" extra business by keeping its rates the same while competitors lowered theirs. We abandoned our application and went with another lender.

There are enough moving parts to a mortgage, and the market can change so rapidly, that I would need a whole 'nother book to cover the ins and outs. Before you apply, you would be smart to arm yourself with just such a book (I recommend Ilyce Glink's *Buy, Close, Move In!* as a good primer). But you can greatly increase your chances of getting a good loan if you:

Boost those credit scores. Getting a loan can be tough if your scores are below 620—and I would argue you're probably not ready for homeownership if your credit troubles are recent enough to give you such low scores. Spend some time repairing your finances, paying down your debt, saving for a down payment and otherwise living within your means before you splurge on a home. You'll start having more loan options once your FICO scores are above 660 and you'll get the best rates and terms if your scores are 740 and above.

Scrape together a decent down payment. No-down-payment loans used to be plentiful—no more. Now the Federal Housing Administration (FHA) requires at least a 3.5 percent down payment, and many other lenders want 10 percent or more. If you have at least a 20 percent down payment, you can skip the private mortgage insurance that can add $100 or more to your monthly payment.

Shop around. Mortgage lenders are always adjusting their deals, sometimes multiple times a day. To get truly apples-to-apples comparisons, you'll need to take a morning off and call at least half a dozen lenders on the same day to see what they're offering on the type of mortgage you want. Technically, lenders aren't required to disclose their charges in what's known as a "good faith estimate" until three days after you actually apply for a loan. But reputable lenders will be happy to disclose their costs if you ask. You will want to supply them with an idea of your FICO scores, down payment and how much you want to borrow to get the most accurate quote.

Compare not just the interest rate but the costs of the loan, including points you pay to get a lower rate (a point is 1 percent of the loan amount) and various fees the lender charges to get the loan. Don't buy the idea that there's such a thing as a "no-cost" mortgage or refinance. Loans always have costs, although they can be disguised as a higher rate or as fees that are added to your principal.

Which lenders should you call? If your local credit union offers mortgages, start there. Local banks may be competitive as well. Include at least a couple of the major lenders as well. As of this writing, Schwab Bank published a daily list of the biggest mortgage lenders and the interest rates they offered on various loans.

Consider more than one application. Applying for a mortgage can involve significant up-front costs. You'll typically have to pay for an appraisal and many lenders charge an additional fee just to apply. But applying to more than one company can be an antidote to "gotcha" pricing, where lenders try to sneak in fees or bait you with one rate before switching to another. When you're trying to close on a house or take advantage of falling rates to refinance, having a second application can help you ensure that your deal goes through.

WHEN TO REFINANCE YOUR HOME LOAN

The old rule used to be that you should consider refinancing when interest rates had dropped at least 2 percentage points from what you were paying. But that was back when refinancing costs were much higher than they are today. These days, you have to do more research—and more math.

The key figures to know are how much the new rate will lower your payment, and how much the refinance will cost you out of pocket. If a refinance lowers your payment by $200 a month and costs $2,500, your break-even point will be in the thirteenth month after you refinance.

You'll certainly want to be able to recoup the cost before you plan to move out of the house. But I would argue you probably want to cover your costs in no more thirty-six months, and preferably less than twenty-four months. That's because life is uncertain and plans change, and the money you shell out today for a refinance may be more valuable than the stream of savings you get in the more-distant future.

You also want to think about how much longer you'll be in debt. You don't want to keep replacing one thirty-year loan with another indefinitely—most people want to own their home free and clear by retirement age, and that's a worthy goal. You don't want to have to sweat about making a big mortgage payment when you're no longer working and living off Social Security and your investments.

Ideally, you'd replace your current mortgage with one that will have the home paid off in the same amount of time. If you're five years into a thirty-year loan, for example, you could look for a twenty-five-year version. (The rates on twenty-five-year loans are comparable to those on thirty-year loans; you'll get lower rates on twenty- and fifteen-year terms.) Or you could simply get another thirty-year loan and try to pay it off in twenty-five years with extra principal payments. (HSH's mortgage amortization calculator, at www.hsh.com, can help you figure out how much extra you would need to pay.)

Of course, you may be after a lower payment to free up money to pay off more troublesome debts, like credit cards. That's certainly fine. Once the other debt's gone and the rest of your financial ducks are in a row, though, you can focus on getting the mortgage retired.

You also need to look at the total costs of the loan over the long term. Even if you have a much shorter break-even point, for example, you could wind up paying more for a new loan if you're several years into your current loan or if you've made substantial extra payments on your mortgage.

One of my readers discovered he wouldn't be much better off refinancing his mortgage, even though he could get a much lower rate and lower his monthly payment.

In 1993, Desai got a thirty-year mortgage for $97,500 with a 6.75 percent fixed rate. Four years later, he began making $200 extra payments each month to pay down the principal. A few years after that, he looked into getting a fifteen-year mortgage on the remaining $68,000 balance for a lower rate of 5.5 percent, but discovered he would pay less over the long haul by keeping his current mortgage.

"If I do not refinance and continue to prepay $200 a month extra, I will be paying off my mortgage in 110 months," paying a total of $91,670, he said. If he refinanced and continued prepaying the mortgage, it would take longer to pay off the loan—117 months—and cost slightly less: $88,457. But add in the $2,600 costs of the refinance, and his pretax savings would be just $614. Desai has decided it's not worth the bother.

Stretching out your payments just makes matters worse. People who are twenty years into a thirty-year mortgage will find they can spend tens of thousands of dollars more over the long run if they refinance into another thirty-year mortgage. Once you're far into a loan, most of what you've got left to pay is principal anyway. You might just pay it off and get debt free.

HOW TO BUDGET FOR YOUR FIRST HOME

A dear friend bought her first house and called me to share the exciting news. Being who I am, I immediately suggested she put her $8,000 first-time buyer's tax credit into a savings account for home repairs and maintenance.

"Oh, I won't need that," she assured me. "The house has been inspected, and everything is fine."

If you're already a homeowner, you may have just groaned aloud. If you don't own a home yet, you need to know that a house can be an expensive proposition at best and ruinous at worst. The variety and scale of costs are often far more than first-time buyers can imagine.

Home inspections are an essential part of the process and can give you some idea of what lies ahead. A competent inspector can alert you to obvious problems and give an expected life span for a house's components, including the roof, siding, water heater, and heating and air-conditioning systems. Using the home inspection report, you can start to prioritize what needs fixing when and start saving for down-the-line expenses, such as replacing the roof. (One of the best ways I've found to estimate repair costs is to use Angie's List, a subscription site that includes member reviews of an array of services. I pick contractors with a lot of reviews and high ratings, then read the individual reviews, which usually include details of the job's scope and cost.) An inspector cannot, however, see through walls or predict every problem that could affect your home. You have to be prepared for surprises.

You do have some control over your budget. For many jobs, how much you'll spend on your home depends on the quality of materials you pick and how much of the work you can (or are willing) to do yourself. For example: a do-it-yourselfer can scrape, putty and paint a home's exterior for a few hundred bucks and the investment of a few summer weekends' worth of time, while hiring out the same job can set you back $5,000 or more.

But many jobs won't really have a do-it-yourself option. My experience has been that most big jobs—roof replacements, heating and air-conditioning replacements, pipe replacements—have a price tag somewhere between $3,000 and $6,000. My readers with bigger homes in harsher climates than ours (we live in California) report that their typical bills can be much higher—$10,000, $15,000, even $20,000 or more.

That's why I suggested my friend save her $8,000 tax credit. Ideally, every homeowner would have enough cash after closing to cover at least one big repair bill. You also need to set aside money for annual maintenance. If you don't take care of your house, minor problems can blossom into major repair bills. Good maintenance doesn't come cheap, however.

"You can expect to spend anywhere from a couple thousand dollars to more than $10,000 per year, depending on the size and condition of the house, on general maintenance," says real estate expert Ilyce Glink. "Some years it will be less and some more. Keeping up with the maintenance will be easier and less costly than if you wait for a small problem to grow exponentially bigger."

One of our neighbors had trouble with sinks and toilets that were slow to drain. She used plungers and chemicals, but put off calling a plumber or rooter service. The tree roots that were invading her sewer lines eventually grew big enough to break the pipes, which had to be replaced at a cost of more than $6,000.

Your maintenance costs will depend on the age, size and condition of your home, as well as the climate. These are some of the tasks you'll want to include:

- Conducting annual inspections of the heating, ventilation and air-conditioning systems
- Replacing those systems' filters once a month or as needed
- Inspecting the roof and flashing, repairing as needed
- Making annual chimney inspections
- Cleaning and repairing gutters
- Doing regular inspections of paint, caulk and masonry for deterioration
- Repainting the home and trim (every five to fifteen years, depending on climate and quality of materials)
- Maintaining the septic system (if you're not on a sewer system)

You can find more-detailed home maintenance checklists on the Web.

You should also budget for appliance replacements. Most household appliances have a useful life of somewhere between ten and fifteen years, according to *Consumer Reports*, although some, like trash compactors, tend to wear out faster.

And, once again, how much you'll pay can vary widely. You can buy a *Consumer Reports*–recommended range for as little as $500 or spend $10,000 on a luxury Viking unit. A $26 annual membership at ConsumerReports.org will give you access to the site's vast storehouse of reviews and estimated costs for various appliances so you can better plan for this expense.

Setting aside the money in advance to cover all these expenses is especially important now, when credit can be hard to come by. A few years ago, most buyers could instantly open a home equity line of credit to pay for repairs. These days, even buyers who put 20 percent down may have trouble tapping their equity.

If you do have sufficient equity, though, you should think about getting a home equity line to supplement whatever savings you're building. That's because disaster can strike before you're ready to pay for it. One reader had to cover a $15,000 repair bill after Hurricane Ike separated her roof from a wall, allowing six inches of water to pour into her living room. (You should know that many insurance policies require you to pay for any covered repairs and then submit the bills for reimbursement.)

"My insurance settlement did pay $13,000, but that came later," she wrote. "I had to pay cash up front, which is more and more reason to have an emergency fund if you live in a disaster-prone area like I did."

THE SMART WAY TO PAY DOWN YOUR MORTGAGE

One way to get a decent, guaranteed return is by paying off debt you've already incurred. If you're carrying credit card debt at 16 percent, for example, every dollar you pay off earns you an instant 16 percent return on your money. So shouldn't we be tackling all our debt, including our mortgages?

Not so fast. There are situations where paying down a mortgage makes sense, such as when you're approaching retirement or when reducing your principal will get you a much better deal on a mortgage refinance. But most people still have better things to do with their money than to pay down a low-rate debt that's often tax deductible to boot.

It's not that I don't understand the impulse to speed up the day that you own your home free and clear. There's something psychologically satisfying about knowing the bank can't take your castle. Besides, the numbers can seem pretty impressive. Let's say you have a thirty-year, $250,000 mortgage at 6 percent interest. Your monthly payments are $1,498.88.

BY PAYING AN EXTRA . . .

. . . $100 a month, you could save nearly $52,000 in future interest and pay off the loan four and a half years early.

. . . $250 a month, you could save nearly $100,000 in future interest and pay off the loan nine years early.

. . . $500 a month, you could save nearly $144,000 in future interest and pay off the loan almost 14 years early.

So who wouldn't go for that, right? Indeed, a March 2007 study coauthored by a Federal Reserve economist estimated that 16 percent of U.S. households pay extra on mortgages each year. But anyone who really understands money would realize the savings aren't all they're cracked up to be.

For one thing, mortgages tend to be some of the cheapest money you can get, and, as mentioned earlier, the interest is often deductible. If you're in the 25 percent federal tax bracket, that 6 percent interest rate may be costing you as little as 4.5 percent if you itemize and even less when you factor in state income taxes. (Your tax break depends on the amount of interest you pay and the total of your other itemized deductions.) Even if you don't get any tax break at all on your mortgage, though, the rate is still dirt cheap compared with that on most other loans.

Furthermore, those seemingly impressive interest savings are spread out over future years, when their value will be substantially eroded by inflation. Remember, a dollar twenty-five years from now probably will be worth less than fifty cents is today, given a 3.1 percent inflation rate.

A dollar invested today in a retirement plan, by contrast, will grow substantially—and retirement needs to be your top priority, as you'll learn in the next chapter. Contributions to a workplace retirement plan will get you a lot further ahead, for a variety of reasons:

- Although some employers dropped or trimmed company matches during the recession, most plans still offer some kind of matching funds, often equaling 50 percent of every dollar you put in up to 6 percent of your pay. If you're not contributing enough to at least get the full company match, you're leaving free money on the table (and missing out on an immediate 50 percent return).
- You save taxes on the money going in. Federal tax brackets range from 10 to 35 percent; there are also federal tax credits when lower-income workers make retirement contributions.

When the money comes out, you'll owe taxes, but most people's tax rates fall in retirement compared with the period when they're working.

- Over the long term your money can earn better returns in the market compared with paying off low-rate debt.

Even if you stick your money in a cash account, the up-front benefits of retirement plan contributions are compelling enough that you should opt to put money there rather than your mortgage. In fact, the Fed study found that households who prepay their mortgages blow more than $1.5 billion a year, or $400 per household, by accelerating their loan payments instead of contributing more to their retirement accounts.

The research found that at least 38 percent of those who were making extra payments on their mortgage were "making the wrong choice." Instead, these households would get back eleven to seventeen cents more on the dollar by putting the money into a workplace retirement plan such as a 401(k).

The study didn't mention Roth IRAs, but they're another account you should take advantage of if you possibly can. You don't get a tax break up front, but the money comes out tax free in retirement.

If you're already maxing out your retirement funds, though, your next step still shouldn't be making an extra mortgage payment. You need to look first at all your other debt. Chances are, if you have any, it's accruing at a higher interest rate than what you're paying on your home loan. That's especially true for credit card debt: it makes no sense to save less than 6 percent by prepaying a mortgage when you're paying more, probably much more, in nondeductible interest on your plastic.

What if you're free of other debt? You can start to tackle that mortgage, right? Not quite. There are other threats to your financial security you need to address, especially:

Financial inflexibility. As you read earlier, fewer than three in ten households have enough savings to withstand even three months of unemployment. Half say they live paycheck to paycheck at least some of the time, according to a survey commissioned by the Consumer Federation of America. Having an emergency fund equal to at least three months' expenses (plus access to a home equity line of credit) can make the difference between a rough patch and financial disaster; that should be your priority after saving for retirement and retiring high-rate debt.

Then there's the issue of:

Inadequate insurance. If you have people financially dependent on you—minor children or a spouse who needs your paycheck to pay the mortgage—you need life insurance and usually plenty of it. In addition, you need adequate health insurance, since medical bills are a factor in half of all bankruptcies. Also crucial: long-term disability insurance, which most Americans don't have.

Fewer than 30 percent of all workers have long-term coverage, according to the U.S. Bureau of Labor Statistics. Yet your chances of suffering a disabling accident or injury are pretty high: At age thirty, for example, you have more than a 50 percent chance of being disabled for three months or longer before you turn sixty-five, according to the Council for Disability Awareness. One in seven U.S. workers is disabled for five years or more. Wouldn't it be ironic if you skipped disability coverage to prepay your mortgage, then wound up losing your house? The bottom line: if you have access to long-term disability coverage at work, buy it.

Okay, so what if you're maxing out your 401(k) and Roth IRAs, sitting on a pile of emergency cash and insured up the yin-yang? I still wouldn't necessarily attack that mortgage. If you have kids, for instance, you might want to be tucking more away into a 529 college savings plan to make sure they aren't saddled with student loans, as too many young graduates are today. Again, assuming the money is invested prudently in a mix of stocks, bonds and cash, you should make a much better return than what you can get prepaying your mortgage, and the money is tax free when used for college.

Of course, you could pay down your mortgage, assuming you'll be able to tap that equity later to pay college bills. But that may be a gamble, because lenders are making it tougher to tap home equity as property values fall.

Some folks, of course, aren't dissuaded by counterarguments. They want those safe, guaranteed returns of paying down a mortgage. There is one large group of homeowners whose returns may not be safe or guaranteed, however: those who are already underwater.

If you owe more on your house than it's worth, you're at high risk of foreclosure if you lose your job or suffer some other financial setback that makes it hard to cover your payments. You can try paying down your mortgage faster to build up equity, but continually falling home prices will make it hard for you to gain any ground. What may happen instead is that you lose your house anyway, along with all that extra money you paid. (Prepaying a mortgage could reduce the amount you still owe in some states; consult a bankruptcy attorney for details if you're nearing the brink.)

A smarter choice typically is to build up your emergency fund instead. That extra cash could help you make payments in the future if your financial life goes south or help you get a fresh start if you wind up losing the house.

WHAT IF YOU'RE APPROACHING RETIREMENT? THEN, THE MATH CHANGES A BIT:

- The tax benefits of a mortgage are typically minimized by the time you hit retirement age. Plus, trying to make mortgage payments in retirement often means having to take more out of tax-deferred accounts than you otherwise might, which can make your tax situation worse.
- Furthermore, paying off your loan tends to substantially reduce your living expenses, which is a great benefit on a fixed income.

I'd still contribute the maximum you can to retirement accounts and make sure you have a fat emergency fund. But if you want to make extra mortgage payments to be debt free by retirement, that's not a bad choice. This may be the one situation where the price for peace of mind is actually pretty reasonable.

WHICH REMODELS MAKE SENSE— AND HOW TO PAY FOR THEM

The remodeling industry does not want you to read the next section. But you deserve to know the truth. And the truth is: remodeling is not an investment in your home.

Think about it:

- With a real investment, you commit your money and hope to make some kind of profit.
- With remodeling, you're all but guaranteed a loss.

Even at the real estate market's peak, most remodeling projects didn't pay for themselves. Homeowners typically recouped an average 86.6 percent of their costs at the peak of the real estate market in 2005, according to *Remodeling* magazine's Cost vs. Value Report—and that's only if homeowners sold within a year of finishing the work. Wait any longer, and your return will be less. That's because home-improvement projects start to get dated as soon as you finish them. Today's stainless steel is tomorrow's harvest gold, in other words.

As home prices plummeted, the average return on remodeling projects dropped to 63.8 percent. No improvement came close to paying for itself in 2009. Even projects with the best payoffs, such as new siding and minor kitchen remodels, typically resulted in a significant loss.

REMODELING COSTS RECOUPED, BY PROJECT AND YEAR		
	2005	**2009**
Upscale siding replacement	103.6%	83.6%
Bathroom remodel (midrange)	102.2%	71.0%
Minor kitchen remodel	98.5%	78.6%
Major kitchen remodel (midrange)	91.0%	72.1%
Major kitchen remodel (upscale)	84.8%	63.2%
Master suite addition (midrange)	82.4%	65.2%

Source: *Remodeling* magazine.

The home-improvement-as-investment myth, combined with easy credit, fueled an awful lot of irresponsible spending in the past few years. People thought it was okay to tap their home equity so they could ape the fancy kitchens and bathrooms they saw on HGTV, little realizing they were throwing away their wealth.

This is not to say you should never remodel your home. Appliances and surfaces wear out over time. You might want to improve an inefficient layout. Or perhaps the home's previous owners had awful taste. (One of my relatives, a serial remodeler, says most of what she does is tear out the "improvements" of past owners.)

Also, it might make more sense to remodel than to sell and buy another home. Swapping homes is *really* burning money, as you lose about 10 percent of your current house's value to real estate commissions, selling expenses and moving costs. If your home update would cost less than 10 percent of your home's value, or if you really love your current neighborhood, the improvement project might be worthwhile.

But you should view home improvements for what they are: consumption spending, not investing. Ideally, you should pay cash for consumption. The only time it makes sense to borrow money is when you're buying an asset that stands a chance of gaining value over time. Of course, the right project, carefully chosen and executed, can add *some* value to your house. If you plan to live in it for many years, you could consider financing 50 percent of the cost of any major improvements.

The 50 percent limit is just a rule of thumb. Because most projects are unlikely to recoup more than two-thirds of their costs and some will return less, it's smart to be conservative by saying only half the cost of your project will increase your home's value and thus can be financed. But if you're going to finance any part of the cost, make sure your improvement really does add value. That means you should:

- Beware any upgrade that makes your house bigger or fancier than most others in your neighborhood, as such remodels are unlikely to add much value.
- Be cautious about adding pools or spas, as they repel as many buyers as they attract in most markets (because of the hassle or because of the drowning risk with young children).
- Aim to please the crowd rather than indulging your personal tastes. Bold statements like brightly colored appliances won't be a hit with many buyers.

What if you can't finance the project you want, either because your credit or your home equity is shot? Then it's time to start saving cash and considering alternatives. Among the possibilities:

- Can you refurbish rather than remove? Refinishing or refacing cabinets is usually less expensive than replacing them. Reglazing tubs and sinks can extend their lives and save you thousands compared with a gut remodel.
- Can you rethink how you use space? Adding square footage may seem like a logical way to deal with a space crunch. But maybe you just need to ditch some clutter or re-purpose

a room. Never use your formal dining room? Maybe it could be your office or a guest bedroom instead.

- What can you do with a little paint? Paint is inexpensive and relatively easy to apply, and it can dramatically transform the look of a room.

Finally, if you're trying to sell your home, you clearly shouldn't sink money into a major remodel. But there are some low-cost fixes that real estate agents typically recommend as likely to return far more than they cost. Their advice:

- Lighten and brighten. Wash windows, remove heavy curtains, trim back branches and bushes that cover windows (free to do it yourself; $100 to $300 to hire window washers).
- Unclutter. Pack up one-third to one-half of your belongings and store them ($200 to $300 a month for off-site storage) to make rooms and closets look larger.
- Deep-clean. Scour your house from top to bottom ($200 to $300 for professionals; basically free if you do it yourself).
- Spruce up landscaping. Trim bushes and hedges, plant flowers, renew mulch ($300 to $400 for professionals; inexpensive if you do it yourself).
- Stage for effect. Rearrange furniture and décor to highlight positives and downplay negatives (costs can range from free, if you pick up a home-staging book at the library, to $500 and up for professional help).

WHAT IF YOU'RE UNDERWATER ON YOUR PROPERTY?

Many, if not most, foreclosures happen because borrowers can't afford their payments. But some people walk away from their mortgage simply because the home turned out to be a bad investment. These people believe (and they may be right) that the damage to their credit scores will heal before their home value rises enough to restore their equity.

Most of us would have trouble making that leap. Eight out of ten people, according to one study, believe homeowners have a moral obligation to pay their mortgages. But the same study indicates that people are more willing to default if they know someone who already has, which may be one reason why these so-called strategic defaults—nonpayment when the borrower apparently could afford to pay—seem to be on the rise.

If you're thinking of becoming one of them, remember that no one can predict the future of real estate values. Your neighborhood may take a decade or more to recover—or it may bounce back sooner. But you will have to live with the consequences of your actions. Since most of us feel that moral obligation, violating it would take a toll on our integrity—not to mention the toll another foreclosure takes on our neighborhood and community, driving down home values and even increasing crime rates as squatters move into abandoned homes.

The picture changes, though, if you're struggling to pay a mortgage on an underwater home. I see way too many people killing themselves trying to pay home loans that simply aren't affordable—and driving themselves even more crazy trying to get mortgage modifications from indifferent lenders.

That's not to say they shouldn't try. People who are having trouble paying their mortgage should contact a HUD-approved housing counselor (referrals at www.hud.gov) for a personal assessment of their situation and options. If a loan modification is an option, it should be pursued with the HUD counselor's help.

If, however, you can't convince your lender to modify your loan—and many people can't—then it may be time to let go of the house. Doing so would allow you to start over, and the damage to your credit isn't permanent, although there will be repercussions. Your options include:

A short sale. This is where you find a buyer and convince the lender to accept less than what you owe. Short sales take time and approval isn't guaranteed, but this is often the best option, if you can swing it. A short sale can damage your credit scores as much as a foreclosure would, but you'll spend less time in lenders' penalty box. Typically, you will be able to get another mortgage after two years, whereas those who go though foreclosure may have to wait as long as seven years to get another loan.

A deed in lieu of foreclosure. You ask the lender to take the property back. Again, the damage to your scores is similar to a foreclosure, but you may be able to get another loan within two years. One potential downside is that you have to move out—with a foreclosure, you could remain until you're kicked out, and save up the money you would otherwise be paying toward a mortgage or rent.

Foreclosure. In some areas, foreclosures take a year or more to complete. That's a lot of time to live rent free in your house before you have to leave. If you don't want to be a homeowner again for awhile, letting the lender take back the house may be the best of bad options.

It's important that you get an experienced attorney's advice before you decide, however. Many states allow lenders to sue borrowers for the difference between what the borrower owes and what the property eventually sells for. This is known as a deficiency judgment. Whether the lender actually pursues this option may depend on its own internal policies and how juicy a target you are—people with lots of nonretirement assets to seize may be more at risk than those living paycheck to paycheck. If you're thinking about walking away from a property, you need to discuss the implications with a bankruptcy attorney familiar with your state's laws and the common practices of lenders in your area.

What if the house that's underwater is a rental property? Many people scooped up second homes and even apartment buildings during the boom, hoping to become real estate moguls. Others held on to a previous home when they moved on to their next place. Some people did so even when the math didn't work—the rents they received didn't cover their costs—because they believed the property would appreciate.

If you own an underwater rental, here are the questions you need to ask yourself:

Does the property offer positive cash flow? If the rent you receive covers all your out-of-pocket costs—including mortgage, taxes, insurance, maintenance and repairs—then you really don't have a problem. You probably can afford to hang on until prices recover. If the cash flow situation isn't quite positive, but the tax breaks you get as a landlord offset your costs, you might still be all right keeping your rental, but talk to your tax pro to make sure you're not exaggerating the benefits. If your mortgage on the property isn't fixed, however, you'll need to reassess the situation if your payment adjusts higher. Many rentals that make financial sense when interest rates are low may no longer be such a smart investment if costs climb.

If the cash flow isn't positive, how long can you afford to bleed? Real estate is different from most other investments. If you buy a stock and it falls, you lose the difference between what you paid and what the shares are now worth. Real estate, on the other hand, can demand you keep shelling out money even after you've lost your shirt. For example, one of my readers had a rental property in Arizona that was costing her

$1,000 a month more than she could collect in rent. Values in the area had fallen sharply and it could be years before her investment was once again worth what she paid. She wasn't saving enough for retirement or emergencies and she was watching her net worth shrink every month as she tried to hang on to this property. If she were wealthy, had plenty of cash to burn and strongly believed in the future of real estate in this area, she might be able to justify hanging on to this money-sucking investment. As it was, this particular piece of real estate was driving her toward bankruptcy. The best of bad options would be to try to arrange a short sale for the property; if that couldn't be arranged, she likely would be better off in the long run letting the lender foreclose rather than trying to save a property that was rapidly bleeding her dry.

Can you stomach being a landlord? Many people found out, too late, that being a landlord demands a lot of work, a tough skin and a lot of risk. Finding good tenants can be hard, while vacancies and unexpected repairs can take a toll on your finances. If your property generates positive cash flow, you might just suck it up or hire a property management company to help you with the hassles (for a cut of the rents). If you're underwater and losing money, though, it might be time to admit you made a mistake. As mentioned earlier, it's essential that you get good legal advice before you decide on a course of action. You may be more vulnerable to a deficiency judgment because you're an investor, rather than a homeowner, and you need to understand the risks and realities before you proceed.

A FEW WORDS ABOUT REAL ESTATE GURUS

Ever since I started writing about personal finance, there have been real estate gurus who insisted there were secret ways and proven methods that only they could reveal to make a fortune buying and selling properties. To get this hidden knowledge, you had to sign up for expensive workshops and seminars. Some of these folks have a veneer of respectability and even get quoted in major media publications, which shows you that financial literacy is as much a problem for journalists as anyone else.

I thought perhaps the real estate meltdown would shut them up. It hasn't. Some shifted from touting zero-down investing to buying foreclosures, but they're still out there.

Clearly, smart real estate investing can produce wealth. But everything you need to know to get started is freely available, starting with books on property investing at your local library. You don't need to pay some charlatan thousands of dollars for his or her "secret" scheme. Furthermore, investing in real estate on a shoestring is dangerous. If you don't have a decent emergency fund, the first major repair or tenant vacancy can cause you to lose your property.

And being a landlord isn't for everyone. It takes a lot of work, people skills and tolerance for conflict.

By all means, investigate the possibilities if you're interested. But you can pretty much figure if an investment scheme is being touted in an airport ballroom, on the Internet or on late-night TV, the only one who'll make money is the one who's doing the touting.

ACTION STEPS

Here's how to handle a mortgage, protect your home equity and get the most out of home ownership:

- Remember that homeowning isn't for everyone. Make sure you can swing all the costs and are prepared to stay put for five to ten years before you purchase a home.
- Set your own limits on how much money to borrow to buy a home. House payments of no more than 25 percent of your gross income will allow you to save for other goals, such as retirement.
- Keep up with routine maintenance and repairs to stave off more expensive problems down the road.
- Being mortgage free by retirement age is a worthy goal. But make extra payments on your mortgage only after you're saving adequately for other goals and have paid off all other debt.
- Preserve your equity for emergencies and long-term goals. It's best to pay for renovations with cash, but you certainly shouldn't finance more than 50 percent of their cost.
- If you're struggling to pay your mortgage, make an appointment with a HUD-approved housing counselor to review your options. If you can't arrange a mortgage modification, you may need to consider a short sale or foreclosure.
- If foreclosure is a possibility, get good legal advice so you understand your risk of being sued by your lender.

Saving for Retirement Must Come First

THE OLD-SCHOOL RULES:

You can count on a good pension to get you through your golden years.

THE BUBBLE ECONOMY RULES:

Even if you don't save much, you can rely on stock market returns and rising home prices to fund your retirement.

THE NEW RULES:

Start saving early for retirement,
save as much as you can and don't stop.

Some myths have grown up around how previous generations handled retirement.

One of the most persistent myths is that people didn't live long enough for retirement to be a possibility. In reality, the life expectancy for a sixty-year-old at the turn of the last century—in 1900—was about twelve years for nonwhite males, fourteen years for white males and nonwhite females and fifteen years for white females. By the time Social Security was created during the Great Depression, life expectancies were a year or two longer.

That's certainly shorter than the twenty or more years of life today's sixty-year-olds can expect, but it's not as if Great-Grandfather Elwood worked until he keeled over on his sixty-fifth birthday.

What is true is that most seniors back then (57 percent of people age sixty-five and older in 1900, according to the Census Bureau) lived in multigenerational households—homes where there were at least two generations of adults. Grandma and Grandpa already either lived with their adult children and grandchildren or they moved in when they could no longer work or care for themselves.

Multigeneration households became less common as older people became healthier and more prosperous. Only 17 percent of people sixty-five and older, and just 12 percent of the overall population, lived in multigenerational households by 1980. Social Security provided a safety net against poverty, and Medicare, created in 1965, helped people sixty-five and older afford the medications and treatments that continued to extend their lives.

Another big retirement development was the spread of pension plans. These really began to take off during World War II, when employers were prohibited from raising wages in many cases and resorted to adding benefits to attract workers. The traditional pension promised steady paychecks in retirement that would last as long as the worker lived, and sometimes as long as his or her spouse lived. Unlike today's 401(k)s and IRAs, the traditional pension doesn't rely on worker contributions or investment skills.

WORKERS COVERED BY PENSIONS, 1940–2010	
Year	Percent covered
1940	15%
1950	25%
1960	41%
1970	45%
1980	46%
1990	43%
2000	39%
2010	37%

Source: Employee Benefit Research Institute.

But pensions didn't completely absolve workers in previous generations of the responsibility to save for their own retirements. For one thing, even at their peak in 1980, fewer than half of U.S. workers were ever covered by a pension plan. And even those who *were* covered didn't necessarily end up with generous checks. Pensions typically weren't designed to replace the majority of a worker's paycheck, and usually only those who stayed with a single employer or union for decades earned the maximum benefit. Most workers changed employers too often or didn't stay in their jobs long enough to get the best deal.

INCOME SOURCES FOR PEOPLE 65 AND OVER			
Source	1974	1998	2005
Social Security	42.0%	40.3%	40.1%
Pensions and annuities	14.0%	19.9%	19.3%
Assets (savings)	18.2%	20.4%	13.6%
Earnings	21.3%	18.2%	24.8%
Total median income (2005 dollars)	$12,074	$15,929	$15,422

Source: Employee Benefit Research Institute.

So for most working people, pensions have been at best a supplement to Social Security and their own savings, rather than a replacement for it.

And notice that we're not talking about princely sums here. The median per person income—half of the elderly had incomes below, and half above—was just $15,422 in 2005.

Of course, some people in our parents' and grandparents' generations enjoyed a much more comfortable retirement without having saved a small fortune. They may have benefited from especially generous pensions, particularly if they were union or government workers or spent thirty years or more with a large company. They may have cashed in on the value of appreciated homes and downsized so they could live off their equity. A few may even have inherited money.

You may be so lucky. But you probably won't be. Here's why:

Pension coverage will continue to dwindle. As desirable as they are, traditional pensions aren't making a comeback—they're just too expensive for today's lean-and-mean corporations to consider. Many old-line companies that once had pensions have frozen or discontinued them. Even public service workers who still have substantial pensions need to keep looking over their shoulders, since government employee benefits have become a target in many areas for taxpayer outrage. You can't lose the benefits you've already earned, either in the public or the private sector, but in the future your pension program could become much less generous as governments try to balance their budgets and taxpayers push back against what they see as overly liberal benefits.

Home values are a question mark. Housing prices are bouncing back in many areas of the country, but future appreciation may be slow. In any case, most people at retirement don't downsize or move—they opt to "age in place." You may be able to tap your equity through a reverse mortgage, although that's an expensive option that should be considered only if you haven't saved enough to cover your living expenses.

Your parents are spending your inheritance. Even if your folks are well off now, they may need every last dime to cover their living and medical expenses for the rest of their (probably long) lives. Mutual fund company Fidelity estimated that a couple who retired in 2010 at sixty-five would spend $250,000 just on out-of-pocket medical expenses—a sum that doesn't include nursing home or other custodial care.

INSIDER TERMS

Long-term care: A combination of services to help people with disabilities and chronic illnesses, including dementia. The medical services provided may be covered by health insurance or government programs, but custodial care—help with daily activities such as bathing, dressing, toileting, eating—typically are not.

AARP estimates 60 percent of people over sixty-five will need long-term care at some point in their lives, and it doesn't come cheap: currently a semiprivate room in a nursing home averages $198 a day, or about $6,000 a month, while home health aides average $21 an hour or $504 a day for round-the-clock care. These expenses, by the way, are typically not covered by Medicare, the government health program for seniors. If your parents don't have long-term care insurance, they'll be paying out of pocket until the money's gone and they can qualify for Medicaid, which is the government health program for the very poor.

All these costs are among the reasons that most people in this country never receive a dime of inheritance, and most of those who get anything receive less than $100,000. Yes, trillions of dollars will be inherited over the next few decades, but most of it will transfer within a relatively small number of vastly wealthy families.

So if you want a decent retirement, you're going to need to save to get there.

DOES SOCIAL SECURITY HAVE A FUTURE?

In 2010, a full six years earlier than expected, the Social Security Administration announced it was paying out more in benefits than it expected to collect in taxes.

Thanks to the recession, Social Security had been deluged by an unexpected surge in early retirement applications. Baby Boomers who lost their jobs opted for reduced benefits when they couldn't find work. At the same time, revenues dropped because higher unemployment meant fewer paychecks to tax.

Because of surpluses in previous years, Social Security isn't scheduled to actually "go broke" until 2037. At that point, the system will have only enough money to pay seventy-six cents for every dollar in benefits that has been promised. (The actual year the system goes bust, and the percentage of benefits that can be paid, has changed over time depending in large part on the economy. For the most recent estimates, check your latest Social Security benefit statement, which arrives in the mail about three months before your birthday each year.)

To make the system work, Congress will have to reduce benefits, increase taxes or, more likely, do both. There are no easy fixes here, despite rhetoric to the contrary. A 2010 report by the U.S. Senate's Special Committee on Aging outlined many of the options Congress could consider, such as:

- Trimming benefits for everyone by 3 to 5 percent, with a 5 percent reduction reducing the deficit by 30 percent. Alternately, reductions could be phased in over time and those with low lifetime earnings could be made exempt, which would protect the safety-net features but do less to fix the deficit.
- Raise the full retirement age from sixty-seven to sixty-eight, seventy or higher by indexing it to longevity. Each of these solutions would eliminate less than a third of the deficit.

- Increase the Social Security tax rate from 6.2 percent to 7.3 percent. This would eliminate the deficit if implemented immediately. If tax increases were phased in over time, the tax rate eventually would need to be raised to 8.2 percent.
- Eliminate or modify the Social Security tax cap. Currently workers pay into the Social Security system until their wages hit a certain cap, which in 2010 was $106,800. If that cap were eliminated, but earnings above that mark didn't count toward benefits, the shortfall would be eliminated. If higher earnings did count, about 95 percent of the deficit could be wiped out.
- Decrease the cost-of-living adjustment. Reducing this inflation adjustment by 1 percent would eliminate 78 percent of the deficit. Cutting it by half a percent would reduce the deficit by 40 percent.
- Invest some of the tax proceeds. Investing 15 percent of the trust fund assets in the stock market could lower the deficit by 14 percent, assuming stocks grew by 9.4 percent a year. Investing 40 percent could reduce the deficit by one-third. If the investments didn't perform as well as expected, the reduction in the deficit would be less.

All of these solutions would be unpopular, and some of them wildly so. The longer Congress delays on crafting a solution, though, the more drastic that solution may need to be. Social Security itself is too popular a program to imagine Congress bailing on it entirely, but it could easily turn into more of a safety net for the very poor, with the rest of us facing steep benefit cuts.

With so much uncertainty, you would be smart to discount the future value of Social Security in your retirement projections. The longer you are from retirement and the higher your earnings, the bigger the discount you may want to apply. If you're in your thirties and earning an average income, for example, you may want to count on getting only half the benefit currently promised. If you're the same age and making six figures, you may want to discount the possibility of Social Security checks entirely.

HOW MUCH YOU REALLY NEED TO SAVE

If you're like most people, you have more demands on your money than you have money. You may be overwhelmed by debt, or struggling from paycheck to paycheck. You may be worried about how to pay off your student loans or save for your children's education. You may have heard some pundit insist that emergency funds should be your top priority, or getting out of debt. You probably know you should be saving for retirement, but surely that can wait.

Except it can't. Even a modest retirement is likely to cost a small fortune, and the only way most of us will get there is by getting time to work for us rather than against us.

That means making retirement our top financial priority. We need to start saving early and keep going, no matter what. Even a short gap of a few years in our retirement contributions can shave 30 percent or more from our ultimate nest egg.

Let's say Jeanne starts saving for retirement starting in her first year out of college. For simplicity's sake, we'll assume she contributes $4,000 a year between ages twenty-two and sixty-five and earns an 8 percent annual return. Her nest egg on retirement is worth $1.3 million.

Her twin, Joanne, puts off saving for retirement until she's twenty-seven, but then saves $4,000 a year, just like her sister. Her nest egg at retirement: $881,263, or 32 percent less. If she waits ten years to start, her final tally is even lower: $536,854, or less than half of what her sister accumulates.

Some people put off saving for retirement, believing that other goals are more important and that they can make up for lost time later. But that's really, really tough to do. To compensate for her late start, Joanne would have to more than double her retirement contributions—to $9,700—to match her sister's final nest egg. If you did get a late start or you can't contribute as much as you want or you suffer an investment setback, you may be tempted to throw in the towel. But anything you put aside will help you move closer to your goal of a comfortable retirement.

BEFORE WE GO ANY FURTHER, THERE ARE TWO THINGS YOU NEED TO KNOW:

- No one can tell you precisely how much you'll need for retirement.
- You still have to make an educated guess.

An exact retirement estimate would require the answer to too many things that can't be known in advance, including how long you'll live, how healthy you'll be, what setbacks or windfalls you'll encounter, how your investments will perform and the rate of inflation, among many, many other factors.

But people who at least make a stab at estimating their retirement needs tend to save more than those who don't, according to studies by the Employee Benefit Research Institute. And you don't want to find out, after it's far too late, that you could have had a much better retirement if you'd just boosted your 401(k) contributions a couple of percentage points.

A good place to start is one of the many retirement calculators available for free on the Internet. For starters, try the Ballpark E$timate at Choose to Save (www.choosetosave.org/ballpark).

Another good, simple option is the Retirement Planner at MSN Money (http://moneycentral.msn.com/retire/planner.aspx).

If you want a retirement planner with more complexity—one that allows you to add in an expected inheritance or a future home downsize, for example—the calculator that's built into Quicken personal finance software is a good option.

Any retirement planner is going to require that you guess a little—or a lot. Another problem is that many simple calculators don't use state-of-the-art methods.

For example, many calculators use only static returns. But assuming your investments will return 8 percent, 9 percent or any other static figure year in and year out is old school because it doesn't reflect reality—nobody gets a steady return every year. Some years they're way up, others they may be way down.

Financial planners today typically use Monte Carlo simulations, a statistical technique that factors in real-world performance to calculate thousands of possible results for a given portfolio. With these simulations, you can learn your probability of success—the chances that your portfolio and your financial plan will provide enough money for retirement.

There's also a serious debate in the financial planning community about whether typical retirement calculations overestimate retirement spending.

The default assumption is that you'll need 70 percent to 80 percent of your current gross income to retire. Although some financial planners argue that replacement rate is too low—and it may be if you have expensive hobbies, like travel—others have more recently contended that such percentages may be too high because they don't reflect the fact that many people's spending drops as they age.

In fact, the U.S. Department of Labor's Consumer Expenditure Survey shows significant spending declines in every major category except health care as people age.

WHAT WE SPEND, BY AGE				
Item	45–54 years	55–64 years	65–74 years	75 years and older
Average annual expenditures	$61,179	$54,783	$41,433	$31,692
Food	$7,696	$6,357	$5,338	$3,935
Housing	$19,562	$17,611	$13,845	$12,035
Apparel and services	$2,228	$1,622	$1,381	$755
Transportation	$10,691	$9,377	$6,740	$4,392
Health care	$2,930	$3,825	$4,779	$4,413
Entertainment	$3,297	$3,036	$2,418	$1,349
Personal care	$736	$630	$559	$456
Education	$2,012	$867	$345	$192
Miscellaneous	$957	$1,316	$659	$507
Cash contributions	$2,152	$2,163	$2,033	$2,291
Insurance and pensions	$7,853	$6,943	$2,616	$1,003

Source: Consumer Expenditure Survey 2008, U.S. Department of Labor.

The drop in spending appears voluntary, according to financial planner Ty Bernicke, who studied the data, because household wealth continues to climb with age. One theory is that a vigorous period of early retirement is often followed by less spending as people's energy and interests wane and they stick closer to home.

The idea that people don't have to plan for ever-increasing income needs, however, could have profound effects on their retirement plans.

Bernicke, who is among those arguing that planners may be encouraging people to oversave, uses the example of a couple who wants to retire at age fifty-five with an $800,000 nest egg earning an average of 8 percent a year, with $60,000 of after-tax spending money the first year. Traditional retirement planning dictates that their spending needs would escalate to more than $145,000 a year by the time they died at age eighty-five. Except that they wouldn't make it that far, since their ever-increasing withdrawals would almost certainly deplete their savings by age eighty-one. To avoid running out of money, they either would have to retire seven years later or reduce their annual spending needs by an initial $12,000, or 20 percent.

Reverse the assumption that spending has to increase, though, and the couple can not only retire early but would leave heirs a substantial estate of more than $2 million, Bernicke said. Even if you just assume their spending stayed steady—the natural declines in spending offset by inflationary pressures—they could retire early without running out of cash, he said.

Many financial planners are wary about assuming spending will decline, since that removes a valuable "fudge factor" in their calculations, said Bob Veres, editor of the *Inside Information* newsletter for financial planners and author of *The Cutting Edge in Financial Services*.

"If something catastrophic happens (with traditional retirement planning), they still have the ability to reduce their spending," Veres notes. "If the planning is for reduced spending, then what happens if something significant happens? There is no elasticity."

But the idea that most calculators overestimate retirement spending rings true with Roger Ibbotson, a finance professor at the Yale School of Management and founder of the influential investment research firm Ibbotson Associates.

Consider this. Most calculators would say you need 80 percent of your gross (pretax) retirement income. But if you were saving 10 percent of your income when you retired, you already would have been living on 90 percent of your pay. Once you stopped working, you also would stop paying 7.65 percent of every paycheck to Social Security and Medicare, and your work-related costs—commuting, parking, lunches out, even dry cleaning—likely would decline dramatically.

Ibbotson believes trying to replace 80 percent of your net income, which he defines as your gross, pretax pay minus any retirement savings, is a more sensible goal for most people. He also wanted to create a system that employed the financial-planning world's sophisticated techniques, but that was simple enough that any consumer could use it.

With the help of two Ph.D. researchers at Ibbotson Associates and two financial planners from Kreitler Financial in New Haven, Connecticut, Ibbotson built what he thinks is a better mousetrap. Using Monte Carlo simulations and actuarial data about typical life spans, the researchers created charts that individuals can use to quickly look up their ideal savings rates based on their ages and incomes.

A warning here: if you're much over thirty-five and you haven't already saved a substantial sum for retirement, the suggested savings percentage is going to be scary—either a little scary or a lot scary, depending on how old you are and how much you've put aside.

IF YOU'RE STARTING FROM SCRATCH . . .

If you have no retirement savings to speak of, this is how much the Ibbotson study recommends you begin saving based on your gross income level.

Age	$20,000	$40,000	$60,000	$80,000	$100,000
25	5.8%	8.2%	10.0%	11.2%	N/A
30	7.0%	10.0%	11.8%	13.6%	N/A
35	8.6%	12.2%	14.6%	16.4%	17.6%
40	10.2%	14.8%	17.6%	19.8%	21.4%
45	12.4%	18.0%	21.4%	24.0%	26.2%
50	15.0%	22.0%	26.2%	29.8%	32.2%

If you already have some retirement savings, you can reduce the percentage you're saving. The calculator at http://tinyurl.com/4zfg74 can help you figure out by how much. You can download a pdf of the full charts, published in the *Journal of Financial Planning*, at http://tinyurl.com/26cw5j.

What Ibbotson's percentages reflect is the importance of an early start if you want to be assured of a comfortable retirement that starts at age sixty-five. "If you haven't started by age thirty-five or forty, it's really hard" to save enough to accumulate an adequate nest egg, Ibbotson says. "The longer you wait, the more you have to save" to make up for the delay.

In fact, the percentage of your income you must save if you start at age forty-five is typically more than twice what it would have been had you begun at age twenty-five, according to Ibbotson's charts. If you wait until age fifty-five, the percentage is often triple what it would have been had you started thirty years earlier. Someone in their midfifties who earned $80,000 a year, for example, would have to save more than one-third of their income—36.6 percent—to accumulate enough to retire at sixty-five.

ARE YOU ON TRACK?

These are the amounts the Ibbotson study recommends you have saved at various ages and income levels.

Age	$20,000	$40,000	$60,000	$80,000	$100,000	$120,000
40	$7,692	$21,824	$39,176	$58,674	$78,710	$103,038
45	$16,005	$45,408	$81,512	$122,082	$163,768	$214,387
50	$26,023	$73,831	$132,533	$198,497	$266,277	$348,581
55	$37,434	$106,207	$190,650	$285,540	$383,042	$501,436
60	$51,562	$146,292	$262,607	$393,310	$527,612	$690,691
65	$68,650	$194,775	$349,637	$523,658	$702,467	$919,594

To understand how to use this research in your retirement planning, you should understand the assumptions Ibbotson and his cohorts made, and how you might want to fine-tune the number you get. Among the assumptions:

Replacing 80 percent of net income will be enough for most people. Net income, as I mentioned earlier, is defined by Ibbotson as your gross income minus what you're saving for retirement. Some planners think you'll need far more; a few think you'll need less. My take:

80 percent of net income is probably enough to ensure a comfortable but not luxurious retirement. If you want to travel a lot, spend more lavishly or retire early, you'll need to save more.

Your postretirement medical care costs aren't included. This is a significant omission. As I noted above, Fidelity estimates that a couple retiring in 2010 would need a quarter million dollars to pay for out-of-pocket medical costs. The Center for Retirement Research at Boston College came up with numbers that are somewhat lower, but note that soaring medical costs mean a couple retiring in 2040 might need nearly half a million dollars.

WHAT A 65-YEAR-OLD RETIREE WILL NEED FOR FUTURE OUT-OF-POCKET HEALTH CARE EXPENSES

Retirement year	Born	Single	Couple
2010	1945	$102,966	$205,932
2020	1955	$141,752	$283,503
2030	1965	$188,899	$377,798
2040	1975	$245,767	$491,534

Source: Center for Retirement Research.

This is another reason to kick up your savings a percentage point or two.

Immediate annuities are a proxy for the sum you'll need. I think this is a pretty brilliant solution to the issue of life expectancy. Rather than guessing how long people might live, or asking them to guess, Ibbotson turned to the experts. Insurance companies that sell immediate annuities, which give people a lifelong stream of income in exchange for a lump-sum payment, are experts at managing the life-expectancy risk of large groups of people.

To figure out how much you'd need at age sixty-five, the researchers looked at the cost of an inflation-indexed immediate annuity with a lifetime payout that would replace 80 percent of your net income. The main problem with this approach is that the size of the checks you get depends on prevailing interest rates when you buy your immediate an-

INSIDER TERMS

Immediate annuity: An insurance contract that provides regularly scheduled payouts after the payment of a single, lump sum premium. Immediate annuities typically offer fixed payments, but immediate annuities that offer variable returns, with payments that rise and fall based on the performance of underlying investments in stocks, bonds and cash, are also available. Payouts from a fixed immediate annuity depend on a number of factors, including the recipient's age and health when payments start and prevailing interest rates.

nuity, and interest rates were pretty low when the research was done. If rates rise substantially, you'd get more bang for your investment buck and may not need to save as much.

There's no way to know in advance what interest rates may be like when you retire; just know that your nest egg may not need to be as big as Ibbotson indicates.

Social Security won't change. Obviously, the researchers are on shaky ground, but at this point they didn't have much choice. You may get your full, promised benefit if you're in the lower-earning brackets, say $40,000 and below, but the more you earn and the younger you are, the less you might want to expect from Social Security.

Ibbotson's approach doesn't allow you to adjust this input, so you may prefer to use another retirement calculator to adjust your savings rate if you want to reduce or eliminate your expected Social Security benefits from your calculations.

You'll get market returns. The charts used Monte Carlo simulations to come up with savings rates and nest eggs that have a 90 percent probability of success, meaning you'd have enough to live on without significant risk of running out of cash. But this approach assumes you'll at least match the market benchmarks, and most individuals don't. They trade too much, bet on "hot" investments that fall flat and let their emotions distort their investing.

Even if your portfolio is entirely made up of index funds, you're still paying at least some fees, however minimal, that ensure you'll underperform the market. If you trade frequently or use investments with sales loads or high annual fees, you're likely to fall even further behind. This is yet another reason to save at least 1 percent more than the indicated percentage (and to keep your investment expenses as low as possible).

In short, Ibbotson's guidelines are not the be-all and end-all of retirement calculations. But they're a good starting point.

What if you're way behind already, and can't see any way to catch up? Don't panic. You may be able to craft a decent retirement if you're willing to work past traditional retirement age. Even a part-time job for a few years can reduce the retirement fund you'll need.

Or you may be able to live on much less than you are now.

RETIRED BY FIFTY—WHAT IT REALLY TAKES

I mentioned the Bolons in the first chapter. They were the family of six who lived in high-cost Southern California and still managed to leave the nine-to-five grind in their early forties.

Now I'd like you to meet Fred Ecks, who bailed on the work world even earlier.

Ecks got his first full-time job at twenty-one after graduating from California Polytechnic State University with a degree in computer science. Not long afterward, he tried to figure out how much he would need to save to live on the interest of his investments, given the 8 percent or so that short-term government bonds could earn back then. The sum—$121,000—seemed impossibly huge at the time.

"It would take me 10 years to save that much. I'd be 34," he remembers thinking. That seemed impossibly old, "so I gave up."

Ecks eventually settled in to full-time work, got married and bought a house in Boulder, Colorado. He had a mortgage, credit card debt "and lots of toys," Ecks remembers. And he was getting "tired of being tired all of the time."

He was at a coffee shop when he heard a radio program about the book *Your Money or Your Life* (the same book that helped transform the Bolons' lives). He went next door to a bookstore and bought the tome, which he "devoured" over the next weekend. He became "a man with a mission" to save enough money so that he could say good-bye forever to paid work.

That was in 1994, when he was twenty-eight. Seven years later, at age thirty-five, he achieved his goal, although he says it's only recently that he's felt comfortable saying he's retired.

There were some bumps along the way. His wife didn't share his sense of mission, and they parted ways. He accepted a job at Sun Microsystems and moved back to California, living in his van in the company's parking lot for six months while he continued making payments on the Colorado house.

Eventually the home sold, and Ecks moved into the first of a series of shared apartments and rented rooms. In the notoriously high-cost Silicon Valley, he never paid more than $600 a month for shelter. When a friend totaled his van, he paid cash for a used Geo Metro to replace it. He ate out infrequently, cooked cheap meals at home and shopped for clothes and household goods at thrift stores.

The Sun Microsystems job paid well and had benefits, although Ecks never cracked the $100,000 annual pay mark. Still, he saved 50 percent of his gross income while still pursuing his passions, including learning to sail and traveling. He visited Mexico and Guatemala on a Green Tortoise bus and drove to Alaska, among other destinations.

He wanted more meaning in his work, though, so in 1999 he took a computer job with Greenpeace at the environmental organization's world headquarters in Amsterdam, Netherlands. Although his pay was less than one-third of what he'd been making at Sun, his cost of living was lower as well, and he still managed to save 25 percent of his income.

After a year or so, he was ready to come home. He convinced Greenpeace to let him work half-time in San Francisco. He then bought the "world's smallest condo"—a 307-square-foot space, about the size of a decent hotel room—in downtown San Francisco in 2001. He paid the $127,250 purchase price with a check.

By the end of that year, he was ready to say good-bye to paid work. He told Greenpeace to stop paying him even though he continued working four hours a day as a volunteer. He now had the ability to take off when he wanted, which he soon did by sailing to Mexico with a friend.

He'd also met a woman who shared his passion for simple living and financial independence. Ann Haebig says she's "always been frugal."

"Even in college I had in mind the idea of saving 'enough' and eventually quitting," says Haebig, who works as a database architect. "I didn't know how to make that goal real in any concrete way until I found *Your Money or Your Life* in 1999 or 2000. I started charting my progress in earnest then."

Eventually, Ecks sold the condo for $235,000, and the couple rented a house for a while before buying an old houseboat for $3,100. They had it towed to a marina in South San Francisco where Ecks could also moor his thirty-year-old, twenty-seven-foot sailboat. Berth rent and a live-aboard fee cost $600 a month. That was less than half of the $1,500 a month Ecks typically spends, a sum that's more than covered by his investments.

Recently, Ecks and Haebig moved back to Colorado to look for a house. The real estate recession that had devastated so many provided them with a buying opportunity to find a home where they could settle down, perhaps for the rest of their lives.

Ecks is concerned enough about the eroding power of inflation that

WHAT RAIDING YOUR RETIREMENT FUNDS WILL COST YOU

IT'S A RARE WEEK when someone doesn't ask me about tapping retirement funds early. Usually it's someone with a load of credit card bills who sees a 401(k) or IRA withdrawal as an "easy" way to get out of debt.

It's not. It's expensive and it's stupid. You'll pay penalties and taxes that typically equal one-quarter to one-half of any withdrawal, plus you lose the future tax-deferred returns that money could make. If you're thirty years from retirement, every $1,000 you withdraw will cost you $10,000 or more in retirement. If you're younger, the toll is twice as bad—a twenty-five-year-old would lose $20,000 for every $1,000 withdrawn.

Plus, many of the people asking these questions are at high risk of bankruptcy because they have so much debt. In bankruptcy, your unsecured debt can be wiped out or reduced, while your retirement funds would be protected from creditors. So using retirement funds to pay credit cards is, not to belabor the point, really, really dumb.

By the way, raiding or cashing out your retirement fund for any other purpose isn't smart, either—although way too many people do it. As many as half of workers who leave their jobs cash out their retirement funds when they go. They'll be poorer for it in retirement.

he keeps half of his portfolio in stock market investments (the other half is in Treasury bonds). But his experience, and that of many others who have embraced simple living, is that expenses actually go down over time as a person gets better at trimming costs.

In any case, Ecks said, the couple feels wealthy where it counts: in time and freedom.

"It's not what you have," he says. "It's how little you need."

As I wrote about the Bolons: voluntary simplicity isn't for everyone. But people do find ways to live on relatively little.

A third of people age sixty-five or over rely on Social Security for 90 percent or more of their incomes, the Social Security Administration says. For about one out of five people in that age group, or 22 percent, Social Security checks are the sole source of income. The average Social Security check is just over $1,000 a month.

If you don't want to live that close to the bone in retirement, then you need to get cracking on building up your retirement savings.

WHERE TO PUT YOUR SAVINGS

Now that you understand you need to save for retirement, and you have some idea of how much to save, another question looms—which account should you use? Most people can choose from a truly bewildering array of retirement accounts, all with different tax treatments, contribution limits and other rules and restrictions.

Here's what you need to know if you're a W-2 employee (someone who is employed by someone else):

Your 401(k) or 403(b) is a great foundation. Your contributions are tax deductible, and your gains grow, tax deferred, until you withdraw them in retirement. Most 401(k)s and 403(b)s also offer some kind of company match, which is essentially free money. You should contribute at least enough to get the full company match.

Some critics complain that fees are too high in some plans, and that can be particularly true in small-company plans administered by insurance companies. That's no reason to forgo a plan, since the tax and match benefits typically offset the costs, but you should push your employer to look for less expensive options. If you're part of a large-company plan, you often get access to investment options with far lower expenses than you'd encounter as an individual (retail) investor.

Because you get a tax break on your contributions, you'll face income taxes on your withdrawals. This is usually a pretty smart trade-

WHAT SHOULD I DO WITH MY OLD 401(K)?

IF YOU LEFT MONEY in a previous employer's retirement plan, you're not alone. About one-third of workers who leave their jobs don't bother to move their money, according to a Hewitt Associates study.

That's not necessarily a bad thing. Your account continues to grow, tax deferred. You also get more protection from creditors than if you roll the money into an IRA. (If you get sued or file for bankruptcy, your 401(k) accounts have unlimited protection, while IRAs are protected up to $1 million.)

But you do have other choices. Such as:

Rolling the money into your new employer's plan. Not all employers will accept these rollovers, but if you have this option and like the investment choices your new plan offers, this is often the best solution. You'll have fewer accounts to monitor, your account continues to have maximum protection against creditors and you may wind up paying less (see below).

Rolling it into an IRA. A rollover IRA would give you more freedom to choose your own investments—you wouldn't be limited to the plan's choices. You may, however, wind up paying more for this freedom, since the investment options available to retail investors are often more expensive than the extremely low-cost institutional funds provided in many large-company 401(k) plans. If your old plan isn't great and your new one doesn't accept rollovers, though, transferring your money to an IRA is often the best option. Any mutual fund company or brokerage will help you with the paperwork.

What you don't want to do is cash out your account. You'll trigger penalties and taxes that eat up one-quarter to one-half of your balance, plus you lose all the future tax-deferred returns the money could have earned.

off, since most people's tax brackets drop in retirement. In other words, you get an up-front break, when your tax bracket is higher, and you pay taxes at a future, lower rate. If your tax bracket turns out to be higher in retirement, the math may still work, because a bird in hand (a tax break today) is usually more valuable to us than two in the bush (taxes paid thirty years from now). The contribution limit for these plans was $16,500 in 2010, with people fifty and over allowed to put in an additional $5,500 in "catch-up" contributions.

Consider contributing to a Roth IRA if you're eligible. Financial planners increasingly emphasize the importance of having retirement money in different tax "buckets" (accounts that get different tax treatment) so that you can better control your tax bill when you're retired. Contributions to a Roth aren't deductible, but your withdrawals in retirement are tax free. Furthermore, you aren't *required* to make withdrawals; unlike most retirement plans, Roths don't force you to take money out after you turn seventy and a half. The benefits of a Roth are particularly strong if you're young (in your twenties and thirties) and the account has many years to grow; if you expect to be in the same or higher tax bracket in retirement; or if you're older and may want to pass the money along tax free to an heir. But you can't contribute to a Roth if your income exceeds certain limits. In 2010, the ability to contribute ends when your modified adjusted gross income is $120,000 or more if you're single or when it exceeds $176,000 if you're married. You can contribute to a Roth even if you're already contributing to a 401(k) or other workplace plan. The contribution limit in 2010 was $5,000, with people fifty and older allowed to contribute an additional $1,000.

When to fund a traditional IRA. If you don't have a workplace retirement plan, you can deduct your contributions to a traditional IRA. If you do have a plan at work, you can deduct your contributions if your income is below a certain amount. In 2010, deductibility for singles began to phase out at $56,000 and disappeared at $66,000. For married couples, the phaseout began at $89,000 and ended at $109,000.

If you do have a plan at work, that probably should be where you contribute the bulk of your retirement money, and you certainly should use it to get the full company match. If your workplace investment choices aren't great, though, you can open a traditional IRA at a brokerage or mutual fund company and choose from a far greater array of options.

As with a Roth, the contribution limit in 2010 was $5,000, with people fifty and older allowed to contribute an additional $1,000. Note: the contribution limit is for both types of accounts combined; if you contribute $3,000 to a Roth and you're under fifty, for example, you're only allowed to contribute $2,000 to a traditional IRA in the same year.

To contribute to a retirement plan, you typically have to have "earned income" (wages, salary, etc., rather than investment income). If you're working and your spouse isn't, however, you can contribute to a Roth or an IRA for him or her—in essence doubling the amount that you as a couple can save in these plans each year.

Think about a taxable account. With all the emphasis on deductions and tax deferral, you may be surprised to learn that many financial planners believe at least some of your retirement money should be in a regular old taxable brokerage or mutual fund account. Why? Because you control the tax bill. If you hold your investments a year or more, you qualify for favorable capital gains rates. You won't face early withdrawal penalties or minimum required withdrawals in retirement.

Exactly how you'll divide up your retirement contributions can depend on a number of factors. If you're in a low bracket now and expect to be in a higher one in retirement, for example, you might want to max out your Roth contributions. If your tax bills are killing you and you've got a good plan at work, you might want to max out there. If you want to hedge your bets, you might want to put money in a variety of different pots.

Let's say Jarrod is thirty and already makes $60,000 a year. He senses a bright future and above-average earnings ahead of him. His company will match 50 percent of the first 3 percent of his salary that he contributes to the 401(k), so he signs up to contribute 3 percent of each paycheck into the company plan. Then he sets up another transfer of $417 a month into a Roth IRA. He'll contribute $1,800 a year to the 401(k) and $5,000 to his Roth (which is pretty close to the 11.8 percent, or $7,080, Ibbotson's charts say he ought to contribute to his retirement). With his next raise, he may boost his 401(k) contributions or start a taxable brokerage account for additional retirement savings.

Maria, on the other hand, is forty and making $80,000 a year. She rents and is childless, and she cringes every time April 15 rolls around, since so much of her income gets taken in taxes with few deductions to offset the toll. She plans to move to a lower-tax area in retirement, so maximizing her tax breaks today is a top priority. She signs up to have 14 percent of her income, $11,200, deposited into her 403(b). An unexpected bonus: the contributions reduce her paychecks less than she anticipates. Since she's no longer paying federal and state income taxes on the money that's contributed to the plan, the actual reduction in her check is close to 10 percent.

AN INCENTIVE TO SAVE

THE FEDERAL TAX CODE provides a credit of up to $1,000 for those on a low income who can save. The "saver's credit" is available to singles with an adjusted gross income up to $27,750 and married couples with combined incomes up to $55,500 who contribute to a 401(k), 403(b), IRA or other retirement savings account. In other words, you can get a tax deduction for your contribution, plus money back in your refund.

To get the maximum credit of $1,000, you must contribute at least $2,000 to the account and have an adjusted gross income of $16,500 or less if single and $33,000 or less if married. But smaller contributions and contributions made by people with higher incomes—up to the limits noted above—can qualify for smaller credits.

If you use tax software such as TurboTax, the credit should be automatically calculated. If you use a tax preparer, make sure he or she knows about the saver's credit.

If you are self-employed—as a freelancer, a contractor or a small business owner—you have even more options for retirement savings, including SEPs, solo 401(k)s, profit-sharing plans, even old-fashioned defined benefit pension plans.

The simplest of these is the SEP, or simplified employee pension. You can contribute and deduct up to 20 percent of self-employment income (or 25 percent of your pay if you're an employee of your own corporation), up to a certain maximum ($49,000 in 2010). Setting one up is as easy as filling out a form at your favorite brokerage, bank or mutual fund company. Tax software will figure out your eligible contribution, or you can ask a tax pro.

Your other options tend to be more complicated, so you'll want to consult that tax professional before you proceed. The most complicated plan is the defined benefit pension, which can set you back a few thousand dollars to start up plus ongoing costs for an actuary and various filing requirements that also can run a few thousand bucks a year. If you're making a ton of money and want to put much of it aside for retirement, though, a defined benefit plan can make sense, since it allows much higher contributions—up to $195,000 in 2010.

Also, if you have employees, your plan typically must cover them as well. That's all the more reason to consult a small business tax pro about your options.

HOW TO SUPERCHARGE YOUR RETIREMENT SAVINGS

SAVE HALF OF EVERY RAISE. When you get a boost in pay, stop in at your human resources department and increase your 401(k) contribution by half that amount. A 3 percent raise would mean a 1.5 percent boost in your contribution rate. You'll still get a slightly bigger check and your retirement savings will be painlessly increased.

Put it on automatic. Set up an automatic transfer from your checking account to your IRA or other retirement account. Start small if you have to—$25 or $50 a month is better than nothing. You may be surprised how much you don't miss the money and how easy it is to save a bit more.

Use windfalls. You can't put your tax refund check or an inheritance directly into your 401(k). But you can increase your retirement contribution a bit and draw on your windfall to help you adjust to the reduction in your paycheck. Obviously, you'll want to continue saving at the greater rate once the windfall is exhausted, but hopefully by then you'll figure out other areas to cut back to make your budget balance. Or you can put the money directly into an account earmarked for retirement, such as an IRA or the taxable brokerage account mentioned earlier.

HOW TO CREATE A PENSION IF YOU DON'T HAVE ONE

Earlier in this chapter I mentioned immediate annuities, which are an insurance product you buy for a lump sum of cash that promises you a steady stream of payments.

If you don't have a pension, or your pension and Social Security won't pay your basic overhead expenses when you get to retirement age, you might want to consider buying an immediate annuity. That way, your living expenses will be covered regardless of how your investments perform after you retire.

(Immediate annuities are different from another insurance product, deferred annuities. Deferred annuities are typically sold as retirement savings accounts, allowing you to put away money during your working life to be withdrawn later. Many deferred annuities allow you to invest in accounts that are similar to mutual funds; these are known as variable annuities, since the returns you get and your ultimate nest egg may vary. Deferred annuities typically come with such high expenses that they should only be considered by people who have maxed out their other retirement savings options. Even then, consult with a fee-only financial planner before you buy.)

Immediate annuities allow you to offload investment risk to the insurance company. You don't have to worry about how the markets or your investments perform, since you're guaranteed a check. But you also don't benefit if the stock or bond markets outperform after you hand over your money.

And you do have to worry about the strength of the company you choose, since you're counting on their promise to pay. If your insurer fails, your account may be taken over by another company and your payments may continue with little or no disruption. If a buyer can't be found, however, you may wind up having to file a claim with a state guaranty fund. Every state has a guaranty fund that covers annuities, but typically only up to a value of $100,000.

Rating agencies such as A.M. Best, Fitch, Moody's and Standard & Poor's can help you gauge the financial strength of annuity providers, but once you pay your money, you're typically committed—you can't move your annuity if the company's financial health deteriorates.

The risks involved are among the reasons why financial planners generally recommend investing no more than 25 percent of your retirement funds in an annuity.

As one expert told Bankrate.com, "I don't think you should ever put all your eggs in one basket because you'll end up making an awful big omelet if something goes wrong."

Also, as mentioned earlier, the check you get depends in large part on prevailing interest rates. If rates happen to be low when you buy, that reduces your check. That's why many financial planners in recent years have urged their clients to wait to buy an annuity, or to split their annuity money into chunks so they can purchase annuities over several years to take advantage of rising rates.

Different insurers offer different payouts, which is why it pays to shop around. Start with Vanguard, considered one of the low-cost leaders in the field, and get some quotes as well from www.immediate annuities.com. Your payments also will vary based on your life expectancy, which is estimated based on your age and health, and the various options you choose.

If you're content with receiving the same amount for the rest of your life, for example, you would typically get a larger initial check than if you opted for inflation protection. Other options that reduce your initial check would be signing up for a guarantee that if you died prematurely, your payments would continue for a certain number of years or that money would be refunded to your heirs.

Here's how it might play out. Jose is a healthy seventy-year-old single Californian. He's considering purchasing a $100,000 fixed immediate annuity from Vanguard that promises him payments for life. His monthly check would be $763.

But Jose lived through the inflation of the late 1970s and early 1980s and remembers how hard it was for seniors on fixed incomes to cope with ever-rising prices. He looks into getting the inflation-protection option. That would reduce his initial monthly check to $596. He could also lock in his payments for ten years, even if he died before then. That shrinks the check a bit, to $546.

Now let's say Jose isn't single at all, but married to the sprightly Josephina, who's sixty-five years young. They not only want inflation protection, but they want to make sure that if one of them dies, the other continues to get at least two-thirds of the original check amount. Now the initial payment is reduced to $462.

As with most financial decisions, deciding on an annuity is a balancing act that requires juggling competing options. You'd be smart to consult a fee-only financial planner for help.

WHAT TO DO AS RETIREMENT APPROACHES

Speaking of financial planners, even the most die-hard do-it-yourselfer needs to find and consult a good one in the years leading up to retirement. "Winging it" might have worked okay during most of your working life, but ignorance or mistakes in retirement can cost you dearly. Retiring too soon, choosing the wrong investments, withdrawing too much money, tapping accounts in the wrong order or failing to plan appropriately for health care costs can all turn your golden years to brass. You have far too many decisions to make, and the penalty for mistakes is far too great, to go it alone.

Here's my timeline of what you need to do when.

Twenty Years from Retirement

Find your planner. This is a great time to have an initial sit-down with a fee-only financial planner. (You can get referrals from www .garrettplanningnetwork.com, www.napfa.org and www.aicpa.org; search there for Find a CPA/PFS, for a CPA who is also a financial planner.) The planner can review your overall plan to make sure you're on track for retirement and give you suggestions about your investment portfolio.

Adjust your investment mix. This is particularly true if you've been using target-date maturity funds and other "no-brainer" options. These are fine for people just starting out who are nervous about investing, but as you close in on retirement you'll want to make sure that the investments you own are truly a good match for your plans. If that target-date maturity fund gets too conservative too fast, for example, you might be giving up needed growth. If it stays aggressive too long, on the other hand, you could be looking at a big dip in your portfolio value right when you want to retire. A planner can help you fine-tune your mix using the investment options available to you.

Ten Years Out

Think about where you'll live. Demographic surveys show most retirees "age in place," meaning they continue to live in the same house, or at least the same community, in which they retired. But downsizing or moving to a cheaper community, as you know, can help your retirement assets last longer. Since where you live has a strong impact on your expenses, you'll want to consider your options carefully.

Imagine what you'll do. Some people don't think about how they'll spend their time in retirement until they wake up jobless. That's a bad idea psychologically as well as financially. Retirees who fare best are generally the ones who have absorbing interests to pursue, says Ralph Warner, author of *Get a Life*. Those who wait until retirement often find themselves casting about for something to do, and many discover that the hobby or pastime they thought they would love isn't quite so engaging when they can indulge in it full-time. As Warner says, "There's only so much golf you can play."

Speaking of golf, your activities in retirement also influence how much money you'll need. If you want to play the finest courses or travel the world, you'll need to save more than if you like to play canasta and visit relatives.

Review your retirement contributions. This is your last decade to take full advantage of workplace and individual retirement plans. Loading up now could help you pull the plug a bit earlier or live more comfortably.

Consider paying down your mortgage. If you still have some cash left over after paying off your other debt and maximizing your retirement contributions, think about getting that mortgage retired before you do. Having the house paid off helps many retirees sleep better at night. Not having a mortgage also means you may have to draw less from your retirement accounts, allowing them to grow, tax deferred, longer and reducing your overall tax bill.

Cut your risk. You'll still need to have your portfolio tilted toward stocks, but you may want to ratchet back your exposure. Now is also the time, if you haven't done so already, to lighten up on company stocks and stock options. Consult with a CPA or other tax pro before you sell so you understand the tax implications.

Five years out

Find out what income you can expect. Retirement experts often refer to the "three-legged stool" of postwork income, which is typically made up of Social Security payments, pensions from employers and your own savings:

- Review your annual Social Security benefit statement or contact Social Security at 800-772-1213 for an estimate of your monthly check.
- Contact current and former employers to see if you have any pensions accrued and, if so, how much you can expect to receive.
- Calculate your income from investments.

The latter can be a bit tricky. The longer your expected retirement, the lower your initial withdrawal rate should be. You might not be able to tap more than 3 to 4 percent of your investments in your first year without dramatically increasing the risk you'll run out of money. You can use T. Rowe Price's retirement income calculator (www.trowe price.com/ric) to see what withdrawal rates are likely to be sustainable.

Think about health care and long-term care expenses. Medical costs are spiraling, and you may not have enough coverage:

- Medicare, the government program that covers most health care costs for seniors, doesn't kick in until age sixty-five. (Even then, some significant expenses aren't covered, so you'll want to investigate private Medigap polices; you'll find more information from AARP.)
- The number of employers who extend health care coverage to their retirees is rapidly diminishing, and many of those that do are increasing their former workers' premiums or co-pays. If your employer offers the coverage now, it may not in the future or it may cost more, so have a plan B.
- Medicare doesn't cover most nursing home expenses, which means you may want to consider buying long-term care insurance.

Create a tentative budget. Now that you have an idea of your expected lifestyle and income, you can start to put together a budget that reflects those elements. You may well discover you'll need to work longer than you expected, or you could get some happy news and decide you want to accelerate your retirement plans. Before you do either, though:

Run your plans by your planner. Should you apply for Social Security benefits early or opt for bigger payments later? Will you take a lump-sum pension or monthly checks? Will you need to tap your retirement funds when you quit work, and what's the best way to do so? You can, and should, educate yourself about these topics. (Books like Twila Slesnick and John Tuttle's *IRAs, 401(k)s and Other Retirement Plans* can help.) But once again: planning for retirement is so complex, and the consequences of making a mistake so potentially severe, that it's worth hiring a pro to review your plan.

Two years out

Refine your plan. You're close enough now that you can refine your budget, tweak your asset allocation and get a clearer idea of how much income you can expect. If your plan no longer works, consider other options: working longer, moving somewhere cheaper, living on less.

Review your Social Security statements. Your Social Security check is based on your thirty-five highest-earning years, so you'll want to make sure your wages over the years have been reported properly. You'll want to repeat this review next year.

Take a vacation at your retirement destination. When people are contemplating moving after retirement, the standard advice is to take a few extended visits to the proposed destination in different seasons. The idea is to find out if you still like the place once you're more familiar with it. You might take the same advice even if you don't plan to move. You may find your town has more to offer workers and families than seniors with time on their hands.

One year out

Put the finishing touches on your plan. Figure out what you're going to do with your 401(k) and other retirement accounts—leave them where they are? Roll them over into an individual retirement account? Update your budget and review your asset allocation. Consult again with your planner to make sure you're on track.

Three months out

Notify your employer. Most companies appreciate having more than two weeks' notice when a worker retires, and there may be pension-related paperwork that takes time to process.

Make arrangements for your rollover. Transferring money from a workplace retirement plan to an individual retirement account can take weeks, and sometimes months. If you'll be tapping that money soon, you'll want to put the process in motion.

If you're moving, start getting the house ready. If you've lived in your house awhile, you'll probably have some work to do before you can put it on the market. Pack up the clutter, perform any necessary repairs and consider cost-effective fixes to get the best price.

There are two other deadlines you need to know about that may or may not coincide with your retirement:

The Social Security deadline. Apply for Social Security three months before you want your first check. You won't be eligible until age sixty-two at the earliest, so if you're retiring before then, make sure to note this important date on your calendar. You can apply for retirement benefits online or by calling the administration's toll-free number.

The Medicare deadline. Sign up for Medicare three months before your sixty-fifth birthday. If you're already receiving Social Security checks, your enrollment should be automatic. Otherwise, you should enroll online or by phone with the Social Security Administration.

ACTION STEPS

The road to retirement can be long and rocky, but the following steps will help you get there:

- Calculate how much you need to save for retirement using the tools and calculators mentioned in this chapter.
- Start where you can, even if the amount you're contributing is small.
- Contribute to any available workplace retirement plans, such as 401(k)s and 403(b)s. Chip in at least enough to get the full company match.
- Contribute to a Roth IRA if you're eligible.
- If you're self-employed or have a side business, use a SEP to boost your retirement savings. If you're earning a lot, talk to your tax pro about other options, such as a solo 401(k), profit-sharing plan or defined benefit plan.
- Leave your retirement money alone. Don't raid it to pay bills or debts and don't cash out your accounts when you leave a job—roll it into your next employer's plan or an IRA.
- Consider buying an immediate annuity in retirement with a portion of your savings to give yourself a pensionlike stream of guaranteed income.
- Hire a fee-only financial planner to review your retirement plan and your portfolio. Do this well before you plan to retire.

Get a College Education
You Can Afford

THE OLD-SCHOOL RULES:
Not everybody needs a college degree to get ahead. There are plenty
of good-paying, secure jobs for people with high school diplomas.

THE BUBBLE ECONOMY RULES:
Get the best education you can, regardless of the cost.
Student lenders will give you as much money as you need.

THE NEW RULES:
You need at least a two-year degree to get ahead,
but limit how much you borrow for any education.

During the depths of the Great Recession, I got several interview requests from reporters who wanted to know: is a college education still worthwhile?

Unemployment rates had spiked to levels not seen since the early 1980s. Once-lucrative white-collar jobs were being lost or outsourced overseas. The recruiters who used to flood college campuses had disappeared, and recent graduates returned home to Mom and Dad rather than striking out on their own because they couldn't find work. The journalists covering these trends were feeling the pinch firsthand, as the recession accelerated the contraction of their industry.

But the idea that a college education isn't a good investment is pretty absurd. By every important financial measure, college graduates are vastly better off than people who only have a high school diploma. Their weekly earnings are 64 percent higher, according to the

Bureau of Labor Statistics, and their lifetime earning potential averages over $2 million—nearly twice that of people who didn't get an education past high school. They are far less likely to live in poverty: only 1.4 percent of college graduates lived below the poverty line in 2006, compared to 6.3 percent of high school graduates and 13.8 percent of those who never finished high school. College graduates also have longer life expectancies and enjoy better health overall than those without degrees.

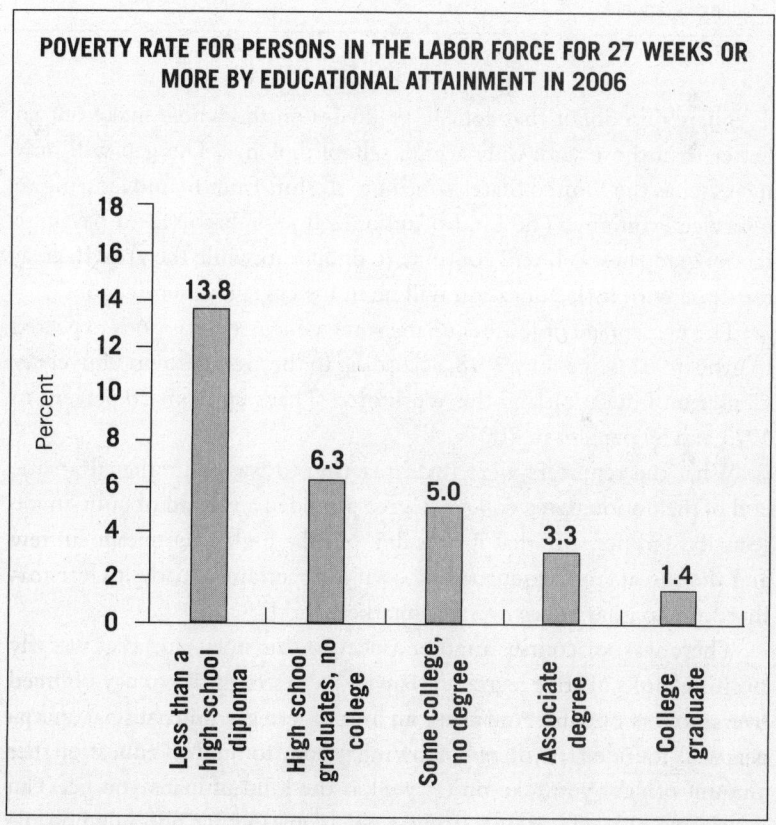

POVERTY RATE FOR PERSONS IN THE LABOR FORCE FOR 27 WEEKS OR MORE BY EDUCATIONAL ATTAINMENT IN 2006

Source: Bureau of Labor Statistics.

And they fared far better during the recession. The unemployment rate for college graduates peaked at about 5 percent. The rate for those with just a high school diploma was twice as high.

SEASONALLY ADJUSTED UNEMPLOYMENT RATE	
	February 2010
Less than high school diploma	15.6%
High school graduate	10.5%
Associate's degree or some college	8.0%
College graduate	5.0%

Source: Bureau of Labor Statistics.

There's no doubt that college graduates on the whole make out far better than those with only a high school diploma. The gap will only increase, as the United States continues to shift from manufacturing to a service economy. The kind of unionized jobs that used to pay high school graduates well will continue to disappear, while the growth areas for those with little education will be in lower-paying service jobs.

The percentage of jobs requiring some college education is expected to grow to 62 percent by 2018, according to the Georgetown University Center on Education and the Workforce. That's up from 28 percent in 1973 and 59 percent in 2007.

What the reporters were (over)reacting to was the rather dramatic end of the notion that a college degree provided any kind of built-in job security. I'm not sure that it ever did, but the high unemployment rate and the threats to the journalists' own jobs certainly made it clear that there are no guarantees in a free-market world.

There was, of course, another aspect to this story, and that was the swelling ranks of college graduates who were struggling to pay off massive amounts of debt. And that's an area where the journalists' concern was well-founded. If you're borrowing money to fund an education, the amount of debt you take on (as well as the kind of loans you get) can skew the whole education-as-investment equation. It's not only possible to buy an education that won't pay off, it's becoming far more common, thanks to largely hidden changes in the world of student loans.

If you're not a recent graduate, the parent of a recent graduate or someone who pays really close attention, you may not be aware of how much the student loan game has changed. You may know that college costs continue to rise and loans have pretty much replaced grants in financial aid packages. But you may not realize how aggressively these loans are peddled to teenage and young adult borrowers; how tough it is to get rid of this debt once it's accrued; and how very, very profitable the whole game has become for many private companies.

So profitable, in fact, that:

- Federal and state regulators investigated allegations of kickbacks and conflicts of interest in college financial aid offices after several schools admitted that lenders showered their financial aid officials with gifts, consulting fees and stock options in return for being added to the colleges' all-important "preferred lender" lists, which determine where most students get their loans.

- Consumer advocates complain that some lenders mislead students into opting for more-expensive private loans when the borrowers are eligible for much-lower-rate federal loans. One study by the U.S. Public Interest Research Group found half of private-loan borrowers failed to exhaust federal loan sources before turning to private borrowers, and 24 percent received no federal loans at all.

- As the amount of student loan debt soars, borrowers are learning to their chagrin that lenders have blocked off the exits. There is no statute of limitations on student loan debt, so collectors can pursue you indefinitely for unpaid loans. Furthermore, in 1998, Congress made federal student loans all but impossible to discharge in bankruptcy. In 2005, lenders persuaded lawmakers to make private student loans just as difficult to shake—even though there are no government guarantees or taxpayer subsidies involved and the lenders' rates are based on the risk involved in making the loans.

For many years, there were three basic types of loan programs for undergraduate students: direct loans made by the federal government; federal loans made through private lenders but subsidized and guaranteed by the federal government through the Federal Family Education Loan (FFEL) Program; and private loans made by private lenders, with no federal guarantees or taxpayer subsidies.

The FFEL program was eliminated in 2010. Now all federal student loans are made directly by the government, a change that's expected to save $68 billion over ten years, since the feds will no longer pay subsidies to banks for handling the loans.

Federal student loans are a classic example of "good" debt. The interest rates are low and fixed, you can get a tax break on the interest and the payoff is (usually) higher lifetime earnings. (Federal student loans come in two flavors—subsidized, where the government pays the interest while you're in school and your interest rate is lower once you're out, and unsubsidized, where you pay all the interest, but you can defer payments until graduation.)

But the total amount undergraduates could borrow was frozen at 1992 levels for fifteen years. Even today, the federal limits for most undergraduate borrowers max out at $23,000 for subsidized loans, and $31,000 for all federal loans—which wouldn't pay for a year at many private schools. Meanwhile, average college costs have more than doubled. So students increasingly have turned to private lenders to pay their bills.

And by increasingly, I mean shockingly so: amounts borrowed from private lenders soared 1,846 percent between the 1995–96 academic year and 2007–08, according to the College Board, from $1.3 billion to $24 billion.

Unlike federal loans, private student loans have variable rates. In 2010, the typical private student loan rate was close to 12 percent, while unsubsidized federal loans carried a 6.8 percent fixed rate. Furthermore, the rates and terms of these private loans often aren't disclosed before a student submits an application, says Mark Kantrowitz of FinAid.org, making it tough for borrowers to comparison shop.

Funding an education with private student loans is a lot like paying for it with credit cards—except credit card debt can be erased in bankruptcy, whereas private student loans are yours for life.

When it comes time to pay off the loans, the differences between federal and private loans are equally stark. Federal loans have far more payment options. You can opt for graduated payments that start small and rise over time, extended payments if you need more time to pay back your loans or plans that base your payments on your income. You can get deferrals or forbearance if you get laid off or suffer other economic setbacks. Private student loan repayment plans are much less flexible, which is why graduates who have trouble paying their student loan bills often wind up with debt that swells over time to 150 percent or more of what they originally borrowed.

Federal student loans now also offer more forgiveness options. If you work in a public service job and make payments for ten years, the remainder of your federal student loan debts can be forgiven. Even if you're not in public service, there's a limit to your financial servitude: any remaining balance is forgiven after twenty-five years of payments. These options are in addition to older forgiveness programs that erased or reduced debt for teachers in inner cities, Peace Corps volunteers and others who served the public good.

Private loans can be a worthwhile investment when they help students pay for an education that will enhance their lifetime earning potential. But because there are few limits to what students can borrow—if they have a creditworthy cosigner, students can borrow the full cost of any education they choose—such loans also can be used by naïve students to pile up mounds of debt for careers that won't pay off. I've heard from more than a few recent graduates with six-figure debts who received liberal arts degrees that qualified them for jobs that earn less than $50,000 a year. Many newly minted graduates find their loan payments are so big that they can't save for other goals, such as a house or retirement.

Fortunately, there are still plenty of ways to ease the burden and to get an affordable college education, if you know how. If you're already burdened with student loan debt, I'll provide some options and strategies later in the chapter.

WHAT IF YOU AREN'T COLLEGE MATERIAL?

College teaches critical thinking, an important skill in a world where workers need to adapt to a constantly changing environment. But you don't always have to have a bachelor's degree or better to survive and thrive in this economy, as long as you're smart about the field you choose and the training you get.

Consider an associate's degree. These two-year degrees typically pay off quickly in higher earnings. They're offered by community colleges, which are far less expensive than four-year schools and usually offer flexible schedules, geared to working students. If you're motivated, you can go to night school and get an associate's degree while working a full-time job.

Focus on high-touch careers. Any job that can be automated or outsourced overseas probably will be, whether the position is high paid or low. A job is at risk of automating if there is little skill involved and contact with customers isn't necessary (one example: parking lot attendants, who are being replaced by automated attendant systems). Jobs may be outsourced, even if considerable skill is involved, if the work is technical with objective standards that make success or failure easy to assess. For example, many people long considered tax preparation to be a "high-touch" job—one that requires human-to-human contact—but turns out, it isn't. Accountants in India now prepare U.S. tax returns for corporations and individuals. Jobs that don't require a four-year degree and that are unlikely to be outsourced include those in health care that require patient contact; auto, motorcycle and small-engine repair; construction and home repair (including plumbers and electricians); personal services such as pet grooming, dog obedience training and fitness training.

Get some skills. If a job requires only a short period of training, chances are good there will be a lot of competition for those positions—which will keep the pay low. Home health aides, who care for the elderly or disabled in their homes, are a classic example. There's a growing demand for these positions as the population ages, and the work certainly can't be outsourced overseas or automated (at least not yet). But there are plenty of people willing and able to perform this relatively low-skill job, so the wages aren't great—the median full-time pay in 2009 was just $21,440. By contrast, a position as a dental assistant—which often requires a one- or two-year certificate program or extensive on-the-job training—paid a median $33,170. And physical therapist assistants, who in many states are required to have an associate's degree in addition to on-the-job training, made a median $46,300.

The Bureau of Labor Statistics lists the fields and jobs where they expect the most growth on its Web site, www.bls.gov. Search on "employment projections" to get the latest data.

THE BEST WAYS TO SAVE FOR COLLEGE

Many parents worry that if they save for their kids' college educations, they'll be "punished" with reduced financial aid packages. What actually happens if you *don't* save is that your kids may get punished with burdensome debt.

KEEP IN MIND:

- **Income is a huge factor in financial aid formulas.** The formulas assume that the higher your income, the more opportunities you will have had to save money. The fact that you could have saved, but didn't, doesn't change what you're expected to contribute.

- **How you save matters.** Don't save in your child's name if you want to maximize your financial aid package.

Now that you know you should save, you should figure out how much. The answer: probably a lot.

If you want to pay 100 percent of the cost for a private school education that currently costs $40,000 a year, you'd need to put aside $947 a month starting when your child is a year old, according to Savingfor college.com's calculator. The longer you delay, the bigger the monthly savings required to meet your goal. Even saving for a public education that currently costs $20,000 a year will be expensive: $498 a month if you start at age one, $776 if you wait until your child is ten.

MONTHLY SAVINGS REQUIRED BY AGE			
Child's age	Private college	Public college	50% of public college
1	$947	$498	$249
5	$1,167	$584	$292
10	$1,552	$776	$388

Source: Savingforcollege.com's college cost calculator.

If you can't swing that much, consider setting your sights a little lower. Saving enough to pay one-third to one-half of a public college education is an attainable goal for many parents, and you can use loans to fill in any gaps not covered by other financial aid. What if you can't even manage that? Rest assured, anything you can put aside will help reduce the debt you and your child may need to take on later. If you can only put aside $25, start there, and build as you can.

INSIDER TERMS

529 college savings plans: Tax-advantaged programs, run by the states, that allow parents and others to invest money for college educations. Investment gains are tax deferred and withdrawals are tax free when used for qualified education expenses. Contributors can choose from a variety of investment options, and prepaid tuition plans—where contributors pay for education in advance—are available in some states.

MAKE COLLEGE SAVINGS A FAMILY AFFAIR

IF YOU THINK YOUR RELATIVES might be receptive to the idea, consider asking for contributions to a college savings account in lieu of gifts for showers, birthdays, holidays or other events. If your parents are well off, contributing to their grandchildren's educations can have tax benefits as well.

If grandparents pay tuition and other education bills directly, they don't have to worry about filing gift tax returns that are otherwise required when they give more than a certain amount (in 2010, it was $13,000 per recipient per giver, so your parents could give $26,000 to your child without having to file a gift tax return). If they're amenable to contributing to a 529 college savings plan, they can contribute five years' worth of gift tax exemption amounts at once (or $65,000 in 2010). Your folks should talk to their tax pro for details.

Next, you must decide *where* to save: 529 college savings plans? Coverdells? Taxable accounts? Custodial accounts?

INSIDER TERMS

Coverdell Education Savings Accounts: Formerly known as Education IRAs, the Coverdell allows contributors to put aside money for education expenses in a tax-advantaged account. Some important Coverdell benefits are set to expire in 2010 if Congress doesn't act, such as the ability to use the money for elementary and secondary school expenses in addition to college. The amount that can be contributed would also drop from $2,000 a year to $500 after 2010.

The reality is that no single college savings method works well for every family. The best way to figure out how to save for college is to use your income, and your tax rate, as a guide. Before we get into a bracket-by-bracket rundown, though, there are a few caveats you should understand:

Caveat #1: The following breakdowns assume that your child is relatively young. If you've got five years or fewer until your first tuition bill comes due, you may want to skip the tax-deferred options. That's because you don't have enough time to earn much in the way of investment returns, so tax breaks on earnings are of little benefit. Saving in taxable accounts will give you more freedom, because you won't have to deal with the restrictions that come with tax-deferred accounts.

Caveat #2: Loans make up more than half of financial aid packages. So even if your savings reduce your ability to get financial aid for your child later, don't sweat it too much; you're simply sparing him or her future debt.

Caveat #3: These strategies assume the tax laws will remain pretty much the same until your kids are grown. That's a pretty big if. Should Congress make major changes, you'll need to revisit your strategies.

The Lowest Brackets

This category includes folks in the 10 percent and 15 percent brackets, which in 2009 are those with taxable incomes up to:

- $33,950 for single filers
- $45,500 for heads of household
- $67,900 for those who are married filing jointly

If you're in the lowest brackets, you don't benefit all that much from tax-deferred accounts because you don't pay very much income tax to start with. You also probably won't be able to save the huge amounts that might make tax deferral a better deal.

But you do have the best shot at getting significant financial aid. So your guiding principle should be to save in ways that don't mess with your child's ability to earn scholarships and grants later.

Here are some dos and don'ts for your tax bracket:

Keep your savings in your own name. Parental assets weigh less heavily in financial aid calculations. Plus, you have the flexibility to use the money any way you want.

Consider beefing up your home equity or retirement savings. Most colleges don't count these assets at all. If your child makes it into an elite private school that does, you'll still be expected to spend only a small portion of these savings on his education.

Think carefully about Coverdells or 529 plans. These plans allow you to set aside money that can grow tax deferred and that's entirely tax free if used for qualified education expenses. The tax benefits for both make them a pretty great deal for higher-income parents, but they have some potential drawbacks:

- You can't claim two valuable tax credits, called American Opportunity and Lifetime Learning, for school expenses you pay with Coverdell or 529 plan funds. (These credits aren't available to singles and heads of household with an adjusted gross income of more than $80,000 or to marrieds with a combined AGI over $160,000.)
- If you don't end up spending the money on qualified college expenses, you'll face taxes and penalties. Coverdells must be spent by the time the beneficiary reaches age thirty, or the tax consequences kick in. There's more flexibility in state-run 529 plans, where funds can be shifted to another child's account or even used by the account owner for qualified education expenses. Still, if you don't use the money for school or need to withdraw it for other expenses, you'll face income taxes and 10 percent federal penalties.
- Your ability to change your 529 investment mix is limited. Typically you can change your allocation just once a year in the state-run plans.

The good news is that Coverdells and 529s don't have a big impact on your ability to get financial aid. The money typically is treated as the parents' asset, and distributions aren't counted as either the student's or the parents' income as long as the cash is used for qualified education expenses.

Don't invest in custodial accounts. Custodial accounts include UTMAs (Uniform Transfers to Minors Act) or UGMAs (Uniform Gifts to Minors Act). Colleges consider these accounts to be the students' assets, which will count heavily against them when financial aid packages are calculated.

What if you already started saving in custodials? All is not lost. If you spend down your custodial account money before your child is a junior in high school, the money won't count against him or her. (Custodial account money can be spent on anything that benefits your child, from camp to a computer to a car; just don't use it on stuff you're required as a parent to supply anyway, like food, clothes or shelter.)

Spend down the account, though, only if you would have incurred these expenses anyway and can put an amount equal to what you've spent into savings in your own name. You don't want to throw away a dollar in savings just because you might lose thirty-five cents in future financial aid.

Massed in the Middle

Folks in the 25 percent bracket include those with taxable incomes below:

- $82,250 for single filers
- $117,450 for heads of household
- $137,050 for marrieds filing jointly

You've still got a shot at financial aid, but your higher income means you'll be expected to chip in more of your own money. You also get more benefit from tax-deferred accounts than lower earners do. That means tax-advantaged options may make sense for you, despite their restrictions on how and when you can spend the money.

Here are some strategies for your bracket:

Avoid custodial accounts such as UTMAs and UGMAs, which count heavily against your child in financial aid calculations.

Weigh the risks of Coverdells and 529 plans. As noted, Coverdells and 529s can limit your ability to take valuable education credits and may be a factor in slightly reducing financial aid awards. On the other hand, the tax breaks will outweigh the risks for many people in your bracket, particularly if you expect your income to grow.

If you opt for a 529, closely monitor your risk. The most popular investment options in 529s are the age-weighted plans, which start out heavily invested in stocks and are supposed to become more conservative as your child approaches college age. Unfortunately, some plans before the 2008 crash kept a high exposure to stocks to goose their returns even when beneficiaries were close to or already in college. Many have since backed off on their stock exposure, but you'll want to step up your surveillance of your 529 plan as your child gets older. Once he is thirteen or fourteen, the money you'll need for his freshman year of college should be mostly in cash. The next year, the money for the sophomore year should be moved to cash, and so forth. If your age-weighted plan isn't getting conservative fast enough, you can transfer assets from the age-weighted plan to the cash-equivalent plan to make sure the money is there when you need it.

Beef up savings in your own name as well as your home equity and retirement accounts, for the reasons noted previously.

INSIDER TERMS

Savings bonds: Low-risk, government-backed bonds that can be purchased with as little as $25 at local banks or directly from the U.S. Treasury at www .treasurydirect.gov. Interest on savings bonds can be tax free if used for qualified education expenses.

Consider savings bonds. If you don't like risk, U.S. savings bonds offer a safe (if low-return) way to save, plus a potential tax break: the interest on savings bonds is tax free under certain circumstances (the owner of the bond can't be the child, for example, and the money must be used for tuition or fees). The ability to take advantage of this break disappears as income rises; the benefit is phased out completely when a single filer's income exceeds $84,950 and married incomes exceed $134,900.

Movin' on Up

You're in the 28 percent bracket when your taxable income is up to:

- $171,550 for single filers
- $190,200 for heads of household
- $208,850 for marrieds filing jointly

It's not impossible for you to get financial aid. After all, anyone can get loans, and your child may score some merit (rather than need-based) scholarships. If you've got more than one child at pricey schools, you also could get some help. Just don't count on getting much.

Good strategies for you include the following:

Consider Coverdells, particularly if you'll have private school expenses before college. Coverdell money can be used for elementary, middle or high school education expenses or tutoring. The ability to contribute ends for singles with an AGI over $110,000 and marrieds with a combined AGI over $220,000.

Definitely check out 529s. There are no income limitations to contribute, and you'll reap significant tax advantages. You also can customize your investments as never before. Several states give contributors a wide variety of funds and investment options from which to choose.

Choose tax-wise strategies if you save in your own name. After 2010, the top long-term capital gains rate is scheduled to rise from 15 percent to 20 percent, but that will still be lower than the tax rates that will apply to short-term capital gains and dividends. Limiting your trading and investing to low-turnover mutual funds can help cut your tax bill, while tax-free municipal bonds might be an appropriate choice for the fixed-income portion of your savings.

Keep saving for your own retirement, and build up home equity.

Top of the Heap

You're in the 33 percent bracket if your AGI, married, single or otherwise, is up to $372,950. Above that, you're in the 35 percent camp.

These are good strategies for people in your stratosphere:

Invest in 529s. Unlike Coverdells, 529s have no income limits for contributors. Besides the tax breaks, these college savings plans offer a big estate-planning advantage. Money contributed to a 529 plan is considered a completed gift, which means you don't have to worry about paying estate taxes on your account should you die. But you retain control over who gets the money and can change beneficiaries any time you want. In addition, you can make a one-time contribution of up to $65,000 and not have to worry about gift taxes (as long as you make no other gifts to that beneficiary for five years). There are no income restrictions for contributors, and many plans allow you to contribute a total of over $300,000. But read the precautions I listed earlier about monitoring and adjusting your investment mix as your child approaches college.

Consider UTMAs and UGMAs if 529s don't do it for you. If you want even more choice over your investments, old-fashioned custodial accounts give you more control. You can invest in individual stocks and bonds, making all the buy-and-sell decisions yourself. Gains are taxed at your child's presumably lower rate. The big disadvantage: you lose control over the money when your child reaches a certain age, typically eighteen or twenty-one, depending on the state. If you want to fund a Coverdell, you can get around the income limitation by putting the money into a UTMA or UGMA and having the child fund the Coverdell.

WHICH 529 PLAN SHOULD I USE?

STATE-RUN 529 COLLEGE SAVINGS PLANS are a good option for many families, but choosing a plan can be tough. You're not limited to your own state's plans—most plans allow out-of-state contributors—and the money can be used at colleges and universities in every state.

Morningstar.com publishes an annual list of the best and worst plans, and Savingforcollege.com offers in-depth analyses of every state's plans. In general, you're often best off using your own state's plan if you get a state income tax deduction on your contributions. If you don't get a tax break, look for well-run plans with low costs. Vanguard, T. Rowe Price, TIAA-CREF and Fidelity run reasonably priced plans with good investment options in many states.

TALK TO YOUR CHILDREN ABOUT WHAT YOU CAN AFFORD

The time to discuss college expenses is not when your child is holding an acceptance letter from her "dream" school—the one that will consign you both to a lifetime of loan payments. It's far better to have these discussions in advance, and to talk about alternatives, than to have your child set her heart on a school, get accepted and then hear, "I'm sorry, we can't afford that." (But saying no, even at the last minute, is certainly preferably to miring yourself and your child in unpayable debt.)

Ideally, you'll start talking about what you can afford to pay for school before she starts her search for schools. By her sophomore year in high school, you should have a fairly good idea of your resources as well as her talents and strengths and can begin looking for the right college match that will give her a good education without sinking you both financially.

You can get some idea of how much you'll be paying for a college education, and how much financial aid you're likely to get, by using FinAid.org's Expected Family Contribution calculator (http://tinyurl.com/4vnl7q). What you're actually offered, however, will depend on the school, its resources and how much the school wants your child.

Many elite schools, for example, have committed to eliminating or limiting loans in student aid packages for low- and middle-income students. Some have eliminated or capped tuition costs as well. So it's entirely possible that a public school education could wind up costing more than what you would pay to have your child attend an elite private school.

The aid your child gets also can depend on what he brings to the table. If he's a talented soccer player and the school needs competitive players, he's likely to get a more attractive package than if the school doesn't have a team at all. Unfortunately, it's tough to know in advance what a school will offer, and that makes managing expectations difficult. But your child needs to understand that while you'll do the best you can, some colleges may be out of reach.

You may want to discuss some alternatives for making college affordable. Such as:

- **Starting with a two-year school.** Many students save money by getting requirements out of the way at an inexpensive junior or community college, than transferring to a four-year school.
- **Helping pay their own way.** Working part-time during the school year and full-time during the summer can allow students to pay some of their own living expenses.
- **Rushing through in three years.** Some schools offer the option of getting a bachelor's degree in three years instead of four. This option typically doesn't save much tuition, since students usually attend summer sessions to pack in the

WHY ARE COLLEGE COSTS SO HIGH?

IN CLASSIC ECONOMIC THEORY, rising prices are at some point supposed to reduce demand. People find alternatives to the product or service or simply go without, which moderates future price increases. That hasn't happened with college education. Costs continue to outpace inflation by several percentage points.

There are several contributing factors to college inflation, of course, but a big reason prices keep going up is that families continue to be willing to pay whatever it costs. And they've been able to do so thanks in large part to student loans.

needed credits, but it does save on living costs. It could be a good choice for a motivated student, particularly one who wants to go on to graduate school.

HOW TO BORROW THE SMART WAY

Even if you save diligently, you might not accumulate enough.

College costs may rise even faster than expected, or you may not get the return you anticipate on your investments. By the time your child is in high school, though, you can get a pretty good idea of (a) how much you'll have and (b) how much you'll need.

If you haven't saved enough to cover the whole bill—and most parents haven't—then loans are likely in your future, but the less borrowing you have to do, the better.

SOME GUIDELINES:

- If you're a student, your payments shouldn't exceed 10 percent of your expected monthly gross income once you graduate.
- If you're a parent, all your debts—including mortgage payments, credit cards, car loans and education loans—shouldn't eat up more than 35 percent of your gross pay.
- Once you start borrowing, keep track of your debt. It's easy to get confused about how much you owe, particularly if you borrow from a number of different lenders.

Figuring the future cost of loans is pretty simple if you've got federal loans. Interest rates on subsidized federal Stafford loans are 4.5 percent for the 2010 to 2011 school year, 3.4 percent for 2011 to 2012, and scheduled to return to 6.8 percent for 2012 to 2013 unless Congress acts. The unsubsidized rate is 6.8 percent, and PLUS loans for parents and graduate students are 7.9 percent. Predicting interest rates on private student loans is tougher, since the rates can vary considerably over the loans' typical twenty- or twenty-five-year terms.

In general, though, *a student shouldn't borrow more for school, in total, than he or she expects to earn the first year out of school.* This isn't an iron-clad rule. You may be training for a profession where you'll be making relatively little the first few years but your income will spike afterward. A good example: lawyers who spend a few years in the district attorney's office before going into private practice. But focusing on that first-year salary will help most students from overdosing on student loan debt.

Not sure what pay to expect? The National Association of Colleges and Employers conducts an annual survey for many fields. So does the Bureau of Labor Statistics. You also can ask guidance counselors or simply use an Internet search engine. If you want to be an educator, for example, type "starting salaries for teachers" into a search engine and explore the results.

Yes, your salary should go up over time, which should in theory make your payments more manageable. But your financial obligations also will multiply. Chances are you'll be buying a home someday, hooking up with that special someone, perhaps having kids. You'll need cars, furniture, retirement savings, college savings for your own offspring.

Parents, too, need to put limits on their borrowing. Too much debt can keep them from adequately funding their other goals, such as saving for retirement. If you've already got a mortgage, car loans and significant credit card debt, you may already be over the recommended 35-percent-of-pay debt limit. Someone making $60,000 a year with a $1,250 mortgage, $400 auto payment and $200 minimum payments on credit cards wouldn't have any room left under this guideline to borrow for college. If helping to pay for Junior's education is important to you and you understand the risks you're taking, you could push the debt limit to 40 percent or a bit higher—but again, don't go overboard.

Once you've decided the maximum you can afford to borrow over four years, don't take out more than 15 to 20 percent of that amount for the first year. College costs tend to rise over the typical student's undergraduate career, and lenders estimate you'll need as much as two-thirds of the money to pay for the last two years.

OTHER GUIDELINES:

- **Don't borrow unless you're sure you'll stay the course.** A degree won't pay off if you never actually get it. If you don't have a clear sense of what you want to do, consider a few semesters at a community college to winnow your choices while keeping costs down.
- **Exhaust federal student loans first.** You won't find more flexible debt than federal loans. You also should submit a Free Application for Federal Student Aid (FAFSA) each

year to see if you qualify for any grants, scholarships or other help.

- **Consider federal PLUS loans.** These loans allow parents and graduates to borrow the entire cost of an education, less any financial aid the student receives. A basic credit check is involved, and applicants can get turned down if they have recent delinquencies or a bankruptcy within the past five years. However, if a parent fails to get approved for a PLUS loan because of bad credit, the student is allowed to borrow more under the federal student loan program.
- **Apply for private loans with caution.** You'll get the best rates if you or a cosigner has good credit scores. Pay attention to any fees, since they can significantly increase the cost of a loan. Check out the information and rate chart at FinAid.org for details on popular loan programs.

What if you find you can't prudently borrow the amount you need for school? Then you should consider some alternatives, if you haven't already:

- **If you're the student, look for a college that wants you.** Your financial aid package will be much more attractive at a school that's trying to recruit you than at one where you're fighting to get in.
- **Consider lower-cost alternatives.** Attending a two-year school and then transferring to a four-year institution is often a good way to cap costs. So is opting for a top-rated public university rather than a mediocre private one.
- **Get a job.** Most students can help contribute at least some of their college costs. A part-time job during the school year, a full-time job in the summer or alternating a semester of work with a semester of study will all help defray education expenses.

HOW TO MANAGE YOUR STUDENT DEBT

You could be reading all these words of wisdom far too late. You may be sitting on a pile of student loan debt, and wondering if you'll ever be rid of it.

If you're just out of school, you're in luck. There will never be a better time for you to make a real dent in your debt. Here's why:

- If you're just out of college, you're used to living on the cheap. If you can refrain from upgrading your lifestyle, even for a few years, you can make a big dent in your debt and put your finances well ahead of those of your peers.
- You're flexible. You're probably willing to do stuff, like have a roommate or take the bus, that would make you crazy when you're older.
- You'll get used to living within your means. Sound boring? It's the key to a successful financial life, but many people never learn it. They live paycheck to paycheck their entire lives and never get ahead.

If you're not fresh out of college, you may have less wiggle room. You may have committed to expenses, like a mortgage, that limit how much you can devote to paying off your loans.

The earlier chapter on paying off debt has information you'll want to review about how to prioritize your debts and find ways to trim your budget so you can throw more money at your bills. But the basic approach to blitzing your student loan debt is the same, regardless of where you stand:

Start by consolidating your federal student loans. Choose the longest repayment term you can. The more money you owe, the longer that term can be. If you owe $20,000 or more you can consolidate to a twenty-year loan. If you owe $60,000 or more, for example, you can consolidate to a thirty-year loan.

Yes, stretching out the loan term can keep you in debt longer and increase the total cost of your loans. But the rates on these loans are relatively low, and the interest is often tax deductible. If you have other, more expensive debt, you would be smart to pay the minimum possible on your federal student loans and use the freed-up money to tackle your more troublesome debt. Once that's done, you can always make extra payments on your federal student loans to pay them off more quickly. Even if all you have is federal student loan debt, you probably have better things to do with your money than rushing to pay it off.

Make sure you're saving something for retirement. "What? Save for retirement with all this debt hanging over my head?" Absolutely. It's hard to make up for lost time when it comes to retirement savings, so you're better off contributing as much as you can as early as possible, and not halting or delaying your retirement savings for any reason. This is particularly important if you have a workplace retirement plan with an employer match—you don't want to pass up free money.

Tackle your toxic debt. Pay off your credit card debt, payday loans, bounce fees and other high-rate debt. Once your toxic debt is gone, charge only what you can pay off each month.

Build your emergency fund. You don't need to stack up a year's worth of expenses in your savings account, but you'd be smart to shoot for an emergency fund equal to one or two months of must-have expenses to start.

Prioritize your private student loans. Once your toxic debt is dispatched and you've got an emergency fund going, you'll probably want to focus on retiring this variable-rate debt, even if your current rates are fairly low. If you have sufficient equity in your home, explore the possibility of using a fixed-rate home equity loan to pay off this debt. I'm generally not in favor of using home equity to pay off federal student loans, since you lose much of the repayment flexibility those loans offer and you put your home at risk. But the interest-rate risk that private student loans pose can be significant, and the only way to fix the rate may be with home equity debt.

If you can't refinance the debt with home equity, you'll simply need to make higher payments to get the loans retired as quickly as possible.

Let's say you have a $20,000 private loan at 12 percent interest. With a twenty-year repayment period, this loan could cost you more than $52,000—and that's if rates don't rise. So you'd be smart to add an extra $100 or so to your required monthly payments of $220. Doing so will shave twelve years off your loan term and save you more than $20,000 in interest. Once your private student loan debt is gone, you can start making extra payments on your federal student loan debt—or target some other, higher-priority debt.

FORGIVENESS OPTIONS

If you have a ton of federal student loan debt and a low income, there's now a light at the end of the tunnel.

Forgiveness programs for federal student loans have been around for a while, but they were typically available only in certain narrow circumstances—if you taught in an inner-city school, for example, or volunteered for the Peace Corps or similar organizations. Today, *anyone* can get forgiveness for federal student loans after making payments for twenty-five years (or twenty years for loans taken out after July 1, 2014). Those who work in public service jobs can get forgiveness after ten years. Public service jobs include:

- Government jobs (except serving as a member of Congress)
- Police and fire
- Public health
- Public education
- Military service
- Social work in a public child or family service agency
- Public services for the elderly or people with disabilities
- Public interest legal services (including prosecutors, public defenders and legal advocates for low-income communities)
- Public librarians
- Employees of tax-exempt 501(c)(3) organizations
- Full-time faculty at tribal colleges and universities
- Faculty teaching in high-need subject areas and shortage areas

Jason is a Marine Corps chaplain, recently returned from a seven-month deployment in Afghanistan, who called into *Marketplace Money*'s "Getting Personal" segment to ask about his debt. Conventional wisdom says he and his wife should be doing something about paying down the nearly $80,000 they owe in student loans. I was delighted to be able to tell him there was a better option. In a few years, he would be eligible to have all his debt forgiven because his is a public service job. Since he loves his job and plans to stick with it, he's far better off paying the absolute minimum on his loans for now and using any extra cash to build up his savings and investments.

FinAid.org has calculators and other resources to help you educate yourself and strategize about the best way to pay off your loans. In general, though, the forgiveness plans are a good deal for those in public service and for those who have a lot of debt and a relatively low income (or a moderate income with a big family to support).

You can maximize your loan forgiveness possibilities by first consolidating your loans into a Direct Consolidation Loan from the government (visit www.loanconsolidation.ed.gov) and then choosing an income-based repayment plan, which caps your monthly payment at 15 percent of your discretionary income. (Discretionary income is the amount by which your adjusted gross income exceeds 150 percent of the poverty line, which will vary by your family size.) For loans made on or after July 1, 2014, the payment will be capped at 10 percent of your discretionary income.

If you qualify for the ten-year public service forgiveness option, the forgiven debt is not taxable, according to the IRS. If you're not in public service, however, any debt forgiven after twenty or twenty-five years will be considered taxable income to you. Either way, forgiveness is a nonevent for your credit scores; your loan accounts will be closed and reported as if you'd paid them all the way down.

WHAT TO DO WHEN YOU CAN'T PAY

FinAid.org has an excellent page, "Trouble repaying debt" (www .finaid.org/loans/troublerepayingdebt.phtml), that details your options when you're having trouble paying your student loans. This summary is meant to be a primer, but I'd encourage you to visit FinAid.org to learn more details.

If you're facing economic hardship, both federal and private student loans offer options to suspend your payments temporarily. Federal student loans offer both forbearance and deferment. You have to reapply each year, but you can get up to three years' of payment suspension under each option (for a total of six years). You could get another six years after consolidating the loans. Private student loans usually offer just forbearance, with a one-year limit that you must reapply for after every three to six months, and private lenders may charge a per-loan fee for the forbearance. (Forbearance and deferments won't hurt your credit scores, by the way, as long as you start repaying your loans when they end.)

Forbearance and deferment should really be reserved only for dealing with short-term economic setbacks, however, since they swell the cost of your loan as the unmade payments are tacked onto your balance. FinAid.org's Mark Kantrowitz has determined that a three-year deferment would nearly double the total cost of the typical ten-year Stafford loan. A six-year deferment would almost triple it.

If you don't pay on time after your forbearance or deferment, your troubles are just beginning. Student loan collectors have "very strong powers" to go after their money, Kantrowitz writes, including wage garnishments, seizure of tax refunds and the ability to block the renewal of professional licenses. Furthermore, your failure to pay triggers collection charges and fees that just grow your debt.

"When you hear about a $10,000 loan exploding into a $40,000 loan, it's usually because of an extended period of nonpayment followed by default (with 25 percent collection charges) and then by a slower than normal repayment trajectory," Kantrowitz writes.

HERE'S WHAT YOU NEED TO DO:

- **Don't hide.** Ignoring your debt and defaulting will just reduce your options and increase your costs. Contact your lenders as soon as you realize you're going to have trouble paying. If you don't know which lenders hold your debt, use FinAid.org's lost-lender finder at www.finaid.org/loans/lostlender.phtml.
- **Consider alternatives.** Graduated payments, extended repayment plans and income-based or income-contingent plans may be what you need to lower your federal student loan payments enough to stay current on your debt. Under the income-based plans, your required payment may be zero if your adjusted gross income doesn't exceed 150 percent of the poverty line. Private student loans have far fewer options for alternative repayment, but you can ask your lender about options and consider choosing a longer loan term (thirty years instead of twenty, for example) to lower your payments.
- **If your situation is extreme, talk to a bankruptcy attorney.** You have to prove undue hardship, which has turned out to be a very difficult standard to meet. If you're living at the poverty line and have no realistic hope of an improvement in your circumstances, however, you may get some relief. Even if your balances aren't wiped out, fees or interest could be reduced.
- **Settlement may be a possibility.** Because student loan debt is so hard to wipe out, and because there's no statute of limitations on this debt—collectors can chase you until you're dead—student lenders don't have a lot of incentive to settle your debt for less than what you owe. But they do have some incentive to favor cash in hand—in the form of a lump sum settlement—over chasing you for years.

You or your attorney can try negotiating with private lenders. If your loan is in the hands of the Department of Education, you need to find out how much the Direct Loan Program paid for your loan, Kantrowitz says, since the government will never accept less than what it cost to acquire a loan.

You can use the National Student Loan Data System (you'll find a link at www.finaid.org/loans/lostlender.phtml) or your own records to determine what your balance was when you consolidated your loans into the Direct Loan Program. That is the amount the department paid to acquire the loans from your original lender.

Kantrowitz recommends offering to split the difference between that figure and your current balance. Whatever the department counteroffers, accept it.

"That's a reasonable approach that is fair to both the borrower and the taxpayers," Kantrowitz says, "providing the taxpayers with some compensation for the cost of the funds over the years."

Don't spend the rest of your windfall, however. If the government does forgive a portion of the debt, the amount forgiven is considered taxable income to you.

Also, your chances of success depend in large part on your circumstances. If your income is low and unlikely to improve, but you have the cash on hand to make a settlement offer, lenders may be more likely to negotiate with you than if your income is high and you've simply lived beyond your means.

ACTION STEPS

To avoid drowning yourself in education-related debt, do the following:

- Calculate how much college is likely to cost and set your college savings goals. The calculator at Savingforcollege. com can help.
- Start saving for your child's education as soon as you can, even if it's only $25 a month. Anything you save will reduce your child's future debt.
- Choose the right savings vehicle(s). State-run 529 college savings plans are a good fit for many, but not all, families.
- Make sure the money you'll need for your child's freshman year in college is in cash investments by the time she's a freshman in high school.

- When college is a few years off, use the Expected Family Contribution calculator at FinAid.org to see how much financial aid you're likely to get. Start talking to your child about what you'll be able to afford to pay.
- Set reasonable limits on your borrowing. Students typically shouldn't borrow more than they expect to make in their first year out of school.
- Exhaust federal student loans before seeking private education loans.
- Explore repayment and forgiveness options if you have low income and high student loan debt.

Reserve Insurance for the Big Losses

THE OLD-SCHOOL RULES:

Buy plenty of insurance. You never know what will happen.

THE BUBBLE ECONOMY RULES:

Buy insurance so you don't have to pay out of pocket. Make claims whenever you can—why have insurance if you never use it?

THE NEW RULES:

Reserve your insurance for catastrophic expenses.
Make a claim only as a last resort.

Your grandparents may have viewed insurance as a thick, comfortable blanket that covered them thoroughly and helped them sleep at night.

Over the years, though, holes have developed in that blanket. Insurance companies have sliced away great swaths of the protections people used to count on, and you may not discover how skimpy your coverage really is until it's too late.

At the same time, many people have lost the understanding of what insurance is actually supposed to do for them and for their finances. They choose low deductibles, make claims at every opportunity—and then watch in irritation as their premiums rise year after year. They denounce insurance as a racket. Some decide to buy as little as possible or, in the ultimate self-defeating move, go without.

But you shouldn't feel cheated if you never get to "use" your insurance—in other words, if you pay premiums for years and never make a claim. Instead, you should feel delighted. That's what you want to happen with most types of insurance.

Insurance should be thought of as your protection against true financial catastrophe, not as a buffer against the normal ups and downs of daily living. So ideally you would get a payoff from your insurance only if your house burns down, or you get sued after a terrible car wreck, or you die. Those aren't exactly outcomes you should be rooting for.

Once you understand the nature of insurance, you'll know why it's important to

- keep your deductibles high,
- max out your liability protection,
- drop unnecessary coverage and
- avoid making claims whenever possible.

You may think the insurance company is "winning," but you'll be richer in the long run.

You also need to understand how insurance has evolved over the years so you make the right decisions about your coverage.

WHY YOUR HOME IS PROBABLY UNDERINSURED

After each natural disaster, too many people discover an awful truth: they don't have enough insurance to rebuild their homes. Nationwide, 68 percent of homeowners are underinsured, according to a survey by insurance services firm MSB, by an average of 18 percent. That means someone whose house cost $200,000 to replace would find herself short by $36,000.

Where homes and rebuilding costs are higher, the problem can be even more acute. A survey by United Policyholders, a consumer advocacy group, said 75 percent of California homeowners affected by the 2007 wildfires in San Bernardino and Riverside counties were underinsured by an average of *$240,000*.

Trying to figure out the right amount of insurance coverage, however, is a tricky, frustrating process. Your insurance company or agent may be surprisingly little help and may even steer you wrong:

- Many victims of Hurricane Katrina said their agents had told them they didn't need flood insurance when, clearly, they did. Damage from rising water, levee breaches and storm surges isn't covered by homeowners insurance; only those who bought special policies through the National Flood Insurance Program were paid for flood-related claims.

- Likewise, many homeowners who lost property in the 2003 San Diego County wildfires complained that their agents had used a computer survey that vastly underestimated the cost of rebuilding their homes. The survey, called Quick Quote, was part of a larger software package sold to insurers to estimate replacement costs and was later removed from the software.

Homeowners often compound the problem by failing to report renovations to their insurers or by simply assuming their coverage is keeping up with inflation and replacement costs, which probably isn't true.

You might think insurers would err the other way, pushing folks to overinsure their homes. But that's generally not the case. Insurance analyst Brian Sullivan says the annual premiums paid on most policies are too small for insurers to spend much time doing a detailed assessment of customers' needs.

"If you ask most insurance companies what they're insuring—how many hardwood floors, how many fireplaces—they have no idea," says Sullivan, editor and founder of Risk Information, which publishes insurance industry newsletters. "It's only companies like Chubb that have [policies with] premiums in the thousands of dollars that will come out and appraise your home and everything in it."

Homeowners are often lulled into complacency because they have "guaranteed-replacement" or "extended-replacement" policies, which sound like they'll cover the rebuilding of a home regardless of the cost, according to attorney Amy Bach of United Policyholders, the consumer advocacy group.

Many years ago, replacement-cost policies actually did just that. If you covered your home for $100,000 but it cost $200,000 to rebuild, you'd get the $200,000. Some customers and their agents learned to game the system by deliberately underinsuring their homes. Why pay higher premiums, after all, when the insurance company would pay out the higher amount anyway?

Insurers finally got wise, and these days true guaranteed-replacement policies are almost extinct. Virtually all insurers cap their payouts at 100 percent to 150 percent of the amount for which the home is insured. Bach recommends consumers buy the highest cap they can afford and take the following steps:

Use Web tools to estimate replacement costs. Bach recommends AccuCoverage, an MSB site that charges $7.95 and walks you through a questionnaire that usually takes twenty to thirty minutes to complete. Another site, Home Smart Reports, charges $6.95 and takes less time but offers less detail, Bach says. Home Smart Reports gives a low and high estimate of what it would cost to replace your home, plus a standard cost of construction in your area, but it doesn't account for custom features.

Compare the estimate with your policy limits. You'll find them on the declarations page of your policy. If your insurer can't explain discrepancies to your satisfaction, start shopping for another insurer.

Don't be cheap. Make it clear to your insurer or agent that you want the best coverage for your money, not the lowest possible premiums.

Decide on disaster coverage. Floods and earthquakes aren't covered by your homeowners insurance. If you're in an area considered at high risk for hurricanes, you may have to buy insurance from a special windstorm-coverage pool. Unless you're prepared to walk away from your home after a disaster, you need to consider such coverage. (I'll discuss this more in a minute.)

Check your "loss of use." Homeowner policies typically provide money to pay your rent and related living expenses while your home is being rebuilt. Again, you should find this coverage on the declarations page. If the amount offered wouldn't cover you for two full years, Bach recommends asking for a higher limit or finding another insurer. If you can't find one or you like other aspects of your coverage, I'd recommend boosting your emergency fund so you can cover living costs for longer, if necessary.

Get "replacement cost," not "actual cash value." It's not just rebuilding coverage that falls short. Many policies severely restrict how much money you'd get to replace your stuff and limit or even exclude some common household items from your policy. If you have a policy that pays out actual cash value on your home's contents, for example, you'd get a check for what your possessions were worth when they were destroyed, not what they would cost to replace.

It's much better to spring for replacement cost on your contents.

You'd typically still get an initial check for the depreciated value of your items, but after you replaced them (and provided receipts to your insurer), you'd get another check to make you whole. The cost of this coverage is typically about 10 to 20 percent more than actual-cash-value coverage.

However, you still could be vulnerable. Some policies provide replacement-cost coverage for most items but make exceptions for others. Your policy might give you a check to buy a new couch, for example, but decide to depreciate your carpet and give you only a fraction of the replacement cost.

The only way to know how you're protected is to read your policy, front to back. Many policies peg your contents coverage to a percentage of your overall policy limit. If your home is insured for $200,000, for example, your contents coverage might be $80,000 or $100,000 or $150,000, depending on the insurer's policies. Obviously, there's a lot of variation, and these limits don't reflect whether your furniture consists of Chippendale or chipped-and-dented. The only way to be sure you're adequately covered is to do a detailed household inventory, writing down all of your possessions and what they would cost to replace. A drag? Of course. But it's time you'll be glad you invested if you're ever faced with making a claim.

Make sure the good stuff has its own insurance. If you own something truly valuable, chances are good that your policy restricts how big a check you'd get. Most policies put payout limits of $1,000 to $2,500 on such items as jewelry, firearms, artwork, furs and silver flatware. If you want full coverage, you need to purchase a "floater," or "rider," on the items at added cost.

Consider your individual needs. Your policy likely has some other gaping holes. Homeowners insurance typically won't replace equipment you use for a home-based business. Property belonging to a tenant is usually excluded. In these cases, you can get supplemental coverage—and you probably should.

Protect yourself from lawsuits. That's the role of liability coverage. Chances are pretty good that you don't have enough protection, which means you could be in danger of losing everything you own to someone who decided to sue you. But choosing how much liability to buy is tough. You can't predict who is going to sue you or for how much. Although most insurance experts advise buying liability coverage equal to one or two times your net worth, a jury could come back with a whopping award that bears no relationship to what you own or could earn in a lifetime.

Still, trial attorneys tend to go for the easy money and often settle for the amount of your policy—unless you're vastly underinsured. Then they're likely to go to the time and trouble of identifying, and going after, all of your available assets. That's why Steve Vidmar, an insurance defense attorney in New Mexico, recommends that most homeowners have at least $1 million in coverage. He recommends even more coverage for parents with teenage drivers, since they're far more likely to get in accidents. To get enough coverage, you would need to increase the policy limits on your homeowners and auto insurance to the maximum allowed—typically $250,000 to $500,000—and then buy an "umbrella," or personal liability, policy that provides coverage to $1 million and up.

Fortunately, boosting your liability coverage is still relatively cheap. According to the Insurance Information Institute, a $1 million umbrella policy typically costs between $150 to $300 a year. You can buy $2 million of coverage for about $75 more, with each additional million costing about $50 extra.

WHAT YOU NEED TO KNOW ABOUT CONDO AND CO-OP COVERAGE

Condo and co-op associations typically carry master policies that cover the building exteriors, hallways and common areas along with liability coverage for claims affecting the association. Individual owners are responsible for insuring the interiors of their units and making sure they have enough liability coverage for claims made against them as individuals.

The type and amount of coverage you need depends in large part on what the master policy says. Some master policies cover the building all the way to the interior fixtures, installations and additions of individual units, while others exclude everything from the interior walls in. Knowing what's already covered will help you determine how much additional coverage you need. You'll also want to know the master policy's deductible, since you may have to chip in to cover that. (You should have been given a copy of the master policy when you purchased your unit; if not, your association should be able to give you a copy.)

The process of determining what coverage to buy is pretty much the reverse of how you buy homeowners policies. With homeowners coverage, you first determine how much it would cost to rebuild the structure. The amount you would get for your possessions is typically a percentage of the coverage on the structure. Condo and co-op coverage, by contrast, is usually built starting with your possessions (anything that would fall out if you could tip the unit over and shake it). Then you figure out how much coverage you need for the structural items that are your responsibility.

As with homeowners insurance, you don't want to skimp on liability or settle for "actual-cost" coverage of your valuables. Go for replacement cost instead. You'll also want riders for items that might not be adequately covered, such as furs, firearms, jewelry and silverware.

The fact that you share common walls and areas with others can have some interesting repercussions, since problems caused by one neighbor can easily affect others. Let's say your upstairs neighbor is still living in the 1970s and can't part with his water bed. The ancient aquatic playground finally springs a leak, flooding his apartment and damaging yours. In many cases, his policy would cover the damage to his unit and your insurer would be on the hook to pay for your repairs. In some cases, the master policy may pick up some of the bill. If the master insurer or your insurer got huffy, though, it could argue that Disco Stan was negligent and insist that his insurer pay all the costs. These kinds of battles aren't uncommon and can leave policyholders in limbo for months.

NOT A HOMEOWNER? YOU STILL NEED COVERAGE.

IF YOUR APARTMENT OR RENTAL HOUSE BURNS DOWN, your landlord probably has coverage to rebuild. That coverage will not, however, pay to replace your stuff. Many renters are surprised to discover that their possessions aren't covered on their landlord's policy. Unfortunately, too many discover this fact after it's too late.

The good news: renters insurance is relatively cheap. For $150 to $300 a year, you can protect about $35,000 worth of possessions. Your policy will include coverage you should have, such as liability protection against lawsuits and "loss of use," which would pay the cost of staying in a hotel while you look for a new place to live.

DO YOU NEED DISASTER INSURANCE?

I mentioned earlier that another big change in insurance over the years has been the elimination of disaster coverage. Insurers decided that some events were simply too catastrophic to cover.

In your grandparents' day, the big risk that wasn't covered was flooding. Private insurers had long since decided that floods were too expensive and that they couldn't charge a premium high enough to make coverage marketable. As a result, the National Flood Insurance Program was created in 1968 to cover communities and properties at high risk of floods. A few years later, buying flood insurance was made mandatory in certain areas. (Today, if you want to get a mortgage and you live in a floodplain, you pretty much have to buy coverage.)

Eventually, insurers backed away from earthquakes and hurricanes, as well. While a few private insurers offer add-on coverage, people are often forced to buy policies from state-run pools.

Or they go without coverage. Of course, the decision not to buy insurance for earthquakes, floods, hurricanes and other natural disasters isn't always conscious. Some homeowners don't realize they're not covered. But many others, faced with high premiums and policies with limited coverage, gamble that they won't need insurance help to rebuild after a disaster.

So is going bare a smart choice or a dangerous one?

I wish I could offer a concrete answer. In this case, the cost-benefit analysis is trickier than usual. Sometimes the price of catastrophic insurance is chokingly high while the risk remains remote. My husband and I, living in Southern California, have struggled mightily with this issue ourselves.

The answer for us, and for anyone, depends on three factors: your location, your financial situation and your comfort with risk. The key is to make an informed choice.

THE MOST COMMON REASONS PEOPLE OPT OUT OF DISASTER COVERAGE:

- **"It's too expensive."** Disaster coverage can indeed be pricey. The average premium is about $500 a year for flood insurance, although policies start around $120. A windstorm policy might cost hundreds of dollars a year for $100,000 of coverage, or many times that for coastal hom-

eowners. Earthquake insurance can range from a couple of hundred dollars to several thousand dollars a year.

- **"The deductibles are too high."** This is particularly the case for earthquake insurance, which typically has a 10 to 15 percent deductible. That means you have to pay the first $20,000 to $30,000 of damage on a home insured for $200,000 before your coverage would kick in. Deductibles are usually 2 percent for windstorm coverage (or $4,000 on a $200,000 home), although they range from 1 to 15 percent of the insured value of the house. Federal flood insurance comes with a much lower deductible, $500 to $1,000.

- **"The coverage is too limited."** Bare-bones California Earthquake Authority policies, for example, cover only $5,000 in damage for all the contents of your home and don't cover swimming pools, landscaping or outbuildings. Additional coverage can be purchased for a higher premium.

- **"It's not mandatory."** As noted, if you live in a high-risk area for flooding, your mortgage lender will insist you buy flood insurance. (Ask to see the latest floodplain maps, though.) Otherwise, catastrophic coverage typically isn't a requirement for getting a home loan.

- **"The government will help us out."** After a major disaster, the Federal Emergency Management Agency (FEMA) provides small grants for emergency repairs and temporary housing, and the Small Business Administration (SBA) offers low-interest loans for rebuilding. In fact, if you have insurance, your ability to get government help may be limited. Grants are usually reserved for those who are uninsured, and loans are restricted to amounts that your insurance doesn't cover.

SO WHY WOULD ANYONE PAY FOR COVERAGE? SEVERAL REASONS, INCLUDING:

- **The government might not step in.** The president has to declare a major disaster before FEMA and the SBA can step in to help. If the damage is limited, that might not happen, even if you personally suffer a catastrophic loss. The vast majority of floods, for example, are not declared major disasters.

- **The help might not be enough.** FEMA grants may be limited, and SBA loans for home repairs top out at $200,000. (You can expect repair costs to soar after a disaster, by the way, because every available contractor will be working overtime.) You have to have "acceptable" credit to get an SBA loan.

- **You may be adding considerably to your debt burden.** SBA loans are just that—loans. You're required to pay the money back. So, between your mortgage and your SBA loan, you could end up owing a lot more on your property than it's worth.

Now that you've considered some pros and some cons, ask yourself the following questions:

1. *Do I live in a high-risk area?* Most homeowners tend to downplay the risks they face, even if they're living directly above an earthquake fault or on the beach on the eastern seaboard. Coastal states from Texas to Maine are most at risk for hurricanes, as is Hawaii. People who live west or just east of the Rockies are at earthquake risk, as are those in Alaska, New England and near the New Madrid fault area along the Mississippi River. Floods can happen just about anywhere.

2. *Have I really weighed the potential costs?* It takes only one natural disaster to ruin your whole day, and your financial life. Insurance is designed to protect you against financial setbacks you couldn't easily recover from on your own. Clearly, most people couldn't pay for a new house out of pocket.

3. *Have I set up an emergency fund?* If you can get your hands quickly on a lot of cash, you may decide to forgo insurance. Getting a home equity line of credit is one option, if you have plenty of equity and can coax a gun-shy bank into extending you the credit. The time to get such a loan is obviously before disaster strikes. The appraisal might not go so well after your house is flattened.

If you opt for this route, you'll want the line of credit to be big enough to rebuild your house.

4. *Have I invested in mitigation?* Homes both new and old can be fortified substantially with some special construction measures. And truth be told, this is what some earthquake experts do, rather than pay expensive premiums for earthquake insurance.

The type of home you have affects your risk. One-story homes that are "tied together," with the roof bolted to the walls and the walls to the foundation, tend to survive earthquakes and windstorms better than multistory homes that aren't. Likewise, houses with big openings, such as plate-glass windows or large garage doors, fare worse than ones without those features.

At DisasterSafety.org, a site of the Institute for Business and Home Safety, you can learn about building techniques that can help homes better withstand disaster. The institute estimates these safer building methods add about 10 percent to the construction cost of a new house. But the higher price may purchase much less damage if disaster strikes.

5. *Am I prepared to walk away?* If you don't have much equity in your home, and you have no ethical qualms about reneging on your mortgage, you could simply plan to hand your house keys back to your lender if a natural disaster leaves your home a pile of rubble. That's the option many homeowners took in hard-hit Northridge, California. As is typical after a disaster, foreclosures spiked in the area after the 1994 quake damaged thousands of homes (and, ultimately, many credit reports as well).

The incentive for many to buy disaster insurance disappeared along with their equity. By 2010, one in four homeowners with a mortgage was underwater, owing more on their loan than the property was worth. If you still have plenty of equity, though, and your home represents a big chunk of your net worth, the scales start tilting heavily toward the need to pay up for extra insurance coverage.

That's what my husband and I ultimately decided to do. Living in California, we've seen firsthand what an earthquake can do to a home. We don't enjoy paying that hefty premium for earthquake insurance every year, but it does buy us something of substantial value: peace of mind.

WHY YOU NEED TO LIMIT YOUR CLAIMS

You probably know that it's not a good idea to make too many claims on your homeowners insurance policy because your insurer could drop you.

What you might not know is that a claim could make selling your home more difficult down the road. Insurers might balk at covering your house, making it harder for your buyer to get a loan.

Even letting your insurance company know about certain damage can cause problems. Jan and Kevin told their insurer about some minor water damage that happened during a storm, although they hadn't made up their mind whether they planned to file a claim. Not only did their insurer drop them, but it alerted other insurers to the water damage, and the couple had trouble finding an insurer willing to cover them.

Insurers use a huge industry database, called the Comprehensive Loss Underwriting Exchange (CLUE), to drop or deny coverage based on a home's history of claims or damage reports. In previous years, insurers used the CLUE database in large part to watch for fraud and for consumers who had a history of filing numerous claims. Following some bad years when they lost billions on homeowners insurance, however, insurance companies have become more aggressive about screening for other risks—including damaged homes that could spawn future claims.

While you can't do much about insurers' overreactions, you can do plenty to protect yourself in this particularly difficult time. Among them:

Keep your home in good repair. A solid, watertight roof, good plumbing and a decent paint job can protect your home from various water disasters, which tend to be what trigger blacklisting. It's a good idea to regularly check the hoses on your washing machine and dishwasher, because cracked or burst hoses often lead to serious water damage.

Think twice about water-related claims. This is especially true if you plan to sell within a few years. You could be better off paying to repair the problem yourself rather than having your home branded as a high risk.

Don't tell your insurer about problems unless you're sure you'll file a claim. This last piece of advice is unfortunate, because insurers and insurance agents can be a decent source of counsel on whether it's worth filing a claim. Because any damage you report could be passed on to the CLUE database, however, it's smart now to err on the side of caution.

Consider getting a copy of your CLUE report. You're entitled to a free copy of your home's CLUE report every year or if you've been denied insurance. (Visit https://personalreports.lexisnexis.com to order it.) You have the right under federal law to dispute any erroneous information on the report.

WHAT A CAR WRECK COULD COST YOU

When it comes to insurance, the Internet offers a wealth of great information, educational resources and the occasional piece of really bad advice.

I came across the latter recently on a Web site devoted to helping people shop for insurance. The site suggested people save a bundle by buying only the minimum liability coverage required by their state.

Yikes.

Liability covers the damage you do to other people and their property. State-required minimums are pretty low, often $25,000 for bodily injury per person, $50,000 coverage per accident and $10,000 in property damage. If you total someone's car, you'll probably exceed the property damage limit. If the accident really hurts someone, your coverage will quickly be exhausted and you're likely to get sued. Paralyze or kill someone, and you could lose everything you have plus a chunk of every paycheck you ever make in the future.

That's an enormous risk to take for a relatively small amount of savings. Keep in mind that liability coverage costs aren't linear—you don't pay ten times more to have ten times the coverage.

And being a good driver isn't enough to protect yourself from disaster. Most people overestimate their driving skills, and all it takes is a momentary lapse to cause a catastrophe. Clearly, you should drive well and defensively, but that's not protection enough.

I'd say the minimum liability coverage drivers should carry is 100/300/50, or $100,000 in bodily injury coverage per person, $300,000 in bodily injury coverage per accident and $50,000 in property damage coverage per accident. If you're a homeowner or have other assets to protect, such as a business, you'll probably want to max out your liability coverage. If you can't buy enough liability coverage to at least equal your net worth—many auto policies max out at $500,000 of coverage—consider adding an umbrella policy, as recommended in the homeowners insurance section.

(If you're injured by another driver, that driver's insurance should pay the bill—unless, of course, he or she is uninsured or underinsured. Most states don't require you to buy insurance for such drivers, but it's usually a prudent add-on to your policy.)

In addition to liability coverage, the typical auto policy also provides collision and comprehensive coverage. Collision coverage pays for the damage to your car in an accident (although if the accident was another driver's fault, your company might try to get the other insurance company to pay). Comprehensive covers the other bad things that can happen to your car, such as theft or fire.

With comprehensive and collision coverage, it's as easy to have too much coverage as too little. You may not need collision and comprehensive insurance at all, for example, if your car is several years old. That's because even if your car were stolen or totaled, the insurance company likely would give you so little money that it's not worth the premiums you pay for the coverage.

To see what your car might be worth to your insurer, visit a car comparison site such as Edmunds.com or Kelley Blue Book (www.kbb .com). What you'd get from your insurer is probably somewhere between the trade-in value and the dealer retail price for your car. If the amount is just a few thousand bucks, it might be worth dropping the coverage and starting to save for your next car.

One rule of thumb: if the total cost of comprehensive and collision coverage is more than 10 percent of the value of the car, think about dropping it.

Important note: Normally, your auto policy covers you when you rent a car. However, if you drop comp and collision on your own car, your insurer won't provide that coverage on any rental vehicles. If you drop those coverages, be sure to sign up for the rental car company's optional coverage.

Because of the way cars depreciate—and because of the way some people buy cars—many people don't have enough coverage but don't realize it. Chances are good this includes you if:

- You purchased a new car and didn't have a substantial down payment—at least 20 percent and perhaps as much as 50 percent
- You're leasing a car
- You recently financed your car for more than four years
- You rolled debt from your last car into your current auto loan

In any of these cases, the payout from your insurance company if your car is stolen or totaled is likely to be less than you owe your lender.

Here's an example. You buy a car for around $25,000. Several months down the road, it's totaled, but your insurance check covers only the car's current value, which is about $20,000. Not only do you have to find new wheels, but you're on the hook to the finance company for a gap of about $5,000.

If you rolled debt from your old loan into your new one, the amount you owe could be even larger. One out of five vehicles financed typically includes debt rolled over from a previous vehicle, according to vehicle research site Edmunds.com, and the average amount of this "negative equity" is well over $4,000.

Few people would want to have to buy a replacement car while facing thousands of dollars in expensive leftover debt. And if your finances are already shaky, the gap between what you owe and what you're paid might be enough to push you over the edge.

"It could be the difference between staying afloat and having to declare bankruptcy," says Phil Reed, consumer advice editor for Edmunds.com and coauthor of the book *Strategies for Smart Car Buyers*.

In the future, I'd advise avoiding car-buying practices that leave you exposed like this. Buying cars with cash or a large down payment and a short loan will save you money in the long run.

But for now, you can cover your exposed assets with extra coverage known as GAP insurance, short for Guaranteed Auto Protection. These policies bridge the gap between what your insurer will pay and what you owe the lender.

It's possible you may already have this coverage and not know it. Most lease agreements include it. (In some states, including New York, leases by law must include GAP coverage.) Also, your auto policy may be written to cover the gap. This isn't the norm, but some auto policies promise to pay off a loan regardless of the car's worth. You can try reading your policy to see if you're covered for any gaps or simply call your insurer and ask.

If you don't already have it, you typically can buy the coverage:

From the dealership or auto finance company. This is probably the most expensive choice, especially if you roll the cost into your monthly note. You typically pay a one-time premium of $300 to $500 or more, plus interest if it's added to your loan or lease. Another disadvantage: you'll continue paying that interest as long as you pay on the car, even after you're no longer upside down on your loan.

From your current auto insurer. It's usually the best choice if your insurer offers the coverage. You can drop it once you're sure you're in the black.

From another insurance carrier. If your auto insurer doesn't offer GAP insurance, you can look for GAP insurance providers. Make sure they have top marks from one of the rating services such as A.M. Best, Standard & Poor's or TheStreet.com Ratings.

The best time to shop for coverage is before you set foot on the dealer's lot, Reed says. He advises calling your insurer to get a quote for coverage as soon as you decide what car you're going to buy. But all isn't lost if you fail to plan that far ahead.

"It'll be cheaper through your agent than through a dealership," Reed says, "but you can always buy it [at the dealership] and cancel it later," once you've got coverage with your insurer.

THE RIGHT WAYS TO SAVE ON INSURANCE

You know now that skimping on liability coverage isn't the way to go. But there are other ways to save a bundle on most insurance policies. Those include:

Choose higher deductibles. Raising your deductible from $500 to $1,000 can shave 20 percent off your premiums—and will encourage you not to make claims for small expenses, which can cause your premiums to jump. Just make sure you keep enough money in savings to cover any damages below the deductible amount.

Shop around. Insurers aren't all the same, and some charge thousands of dollars more than some of their competitors for the same coverage. (Yes, thousands. Not all insurers view risk the same way, and some are really trying to discourage certain business—like, say, teen drivers.) Shopping is a big old pain, but you can start by seeing if your state offers a premium comparison survey, which can give you insight into which companies are trying to win your business.

But don't choose by price alone. Some companies keep their prices low by being stingy when it's time to pay claims. Before you sign on with an insurer, check its complaint record. Many state insurance departments rank insurers by the complaints they generate—avoid those that consistently anger their customers.

Ask for discounts. You probably know that good drivers and good students typically get breaks. You may know you can save money by buying your auto and homeowners policy from the same place. But some insurers also offer discounts to teachers, engineers or scientists. Certain types of safety features on your car can save you money, too. Review the available discounts listed on your insurer's Web site or ask your agent.

Buy boring cars. As Edmunds.com puts it, the more expensive and high performance the car, the more expensive it will be to insure. You may even pay more for some seemingly run-of-the-mill cars, because they're more likely to be stolen than their competitors and chopped up for parts. Before you buy, check what the vehicle costs to insure. You can talk to your agent or use Edmunds.com's True Cost to Own feature to get a general idea. (Boring colors won't, however, get you a cheaper rate. Although urban legend says red cars get ticketed more often, there's no evidence to support that. There's also no evidence that any car color is "safer" than any other. After reviewing available studies, the AAA Foundation for Traffic Safety concluded that "the relationship between car color and safety is not at all clear . . . the bottom line is that there is presently no scientific evidence supporting the selection of one particular vehicle color as the unambiguous best choice for safety.")

Drop unnecessary coverage. What's necessary will vary by your situation. If you can pay for a rental car for a week out of pocket, for example, rental car coverage is probably unnecessary.

Drive defensively. I've known law enforcement officers who prefer not to use the word "accident," since it implies a crash couldn't have been avoided. In most cases, someone's at fault, and in many cases it's both drivers. One may have been driving too aggressively, for example, but the other may not have been paying close enough attention. Don't use your cell phone while driving, minimize other distractions and expect every other driver on the road to act like a complete idiot, and you may keep your driving record clean enough to qualify for the best rates.

Keep your credit scores in good shape. Fair or not, most auto and homeowners insurers factor your credit record into the premiums you pay. Their experience is that people with poor credit are more likely to file claims and to cost them more than people with good credit.

WHAT YOU NEED TO KNOW ABOUT LIFE INSURANCE

Life insurance can be mind-bendingly complicated. So it may help you to know that there's one guideline that's more important than anything else. And that is:

If you need life insurance, make sure you buy enough of it.

That one guideline short-circuits the whole discussion about which is better: term insurance (which provides only death benefits and is meant to cover a certain period of time) or cash-value insurance (which provides an investment feature and is meant to cover you for a lifetime).

That's because cash-value life insurance is a lot more expensive than term insurance. Cash-value coverage can cost ten times as much as the same amount of term insurance. Most families who need life insurance can't afford to buy an adequate amount of cash-value coverage, so term insurance is the only answer.

If you're the exception—you're swimming in cash, you've fully funded your retirement accounts and you're intrigued by the investment policies of a cash-value policy—then you can well afford to purchase a few hours of consulting time with a fee-only financial planner, who can review the policy you're thinking of buying and offer some objective advice.

Assuming that's not your situation, let's move on.

We should make sure, of course, that you even need to be reading this section. Life insurance is designed to replace your income and/or help your family afford to hire people to replace the services you provide to your family. You probably don't need life insurance if no one depends on your income or the services you provide, or if you have plenty of savings and other assets that your loved ones could tap.

If you're retired and your spouse could live comfortably for the rest of his life on what you've saved, life insurance probably isn't necessary. If you're still working, though, your spouse may need your income to help pay the mortgage, buy groceries and save for your children's education. If you're a stay-at-home parent, your spouse most likely would need to hire someone to provide child care if your children are young.

Once you've established that you need coverage, you have to determine how much.

A family with young children may need insurance equal to ten times their income, or even more. A family with older kids, fully funded college accounts and guaranteed retirement pensions likely would need much less. MSN has a life insurance needs estimator at http://tinyurl. com/ccdmb that can help you run the numbers for your own situation.

Your next step is to determine how long you want the coverage to last—typically term insurance is purchased in ten-year, twenty-year or thirty-year increments. You'll want a guaranteed level term for the duration, which basically means your premiums won't change while you have the coverage. The longer the term, the higher the premiums, but as is usually the case with insurance, the costs don't grow in proportion to the coverage. It typically doesn't cost 50 percent more to get a 50 percent longer term, for example, so stretching a little to get a longer policy often makes sense.

If your primary purpose is to help a partner pay off the mortgage and you've got twenty years left on the loan, then a twenty-year level-term policy may be appropriate. If you have young kids, the thirty-year term may be better. Many insurance experts recommend you time the coverage so that it lasts until your youngest is in her midtwenties, since it can take kids that long to get out of college and get started on their adult lives.

After that—assuming you're healthy—it's just a matter of shopping around. Term life insurance is considered a bit of a commodity, meaning the basic product doesn't vary that much between companies, so they compete primarily on price and reputation (you'll want a company with solid financial ratings). There are several Web sites, including AccuQuote, InsWeb and Insure.com, that can help you compare quotes.

To get the best rates, you'll need to be in pretty good shape—not overweight, not a smoker, with cholesterol and blood pressure readings inside healthy ranges. Life insurance gets a little trickier if you're not in the best of health or if your application contains other factors that tend to spook insurers: you smoke, ride motorcycles, or have parents who died before age sixty of cancer or heart disease, for example.

(You might be tempted to get a better rate by lying, but resist the urge. If the insurer finds out, your coverage will be discontinued—and you may have a tough time getting a replacement. If the deception is discovered after you die, your family won't get the insurance proceeds. The best they'd get is the return of the premiums you paid.)

Because insurer policies differ so much, it can be hard for an individual to know in advance whether her medication-controlled high blood pressure will cost her more with a certain company (as is often the case) or be a nonissue (as is sometimes the case).

A good independent insurance agent would know various insurer policies and keep track of how they change over time. If you have complicating factors, it may be worth seeking out such an agent to help you shop. Just know that they get paid a lot more to sell you cash-value policies than term policies, so make it clear you're not shopping for "permanent" coverage.

How to find a good agent? Ask around. Your friends and family may have recommendations, or you can check with CPAs, financial planners and attorneys you know. Independent agents work with a variety of different companies (unlike captive agents, which work for one) and your best bet is to find someone who has been in business in your community for ten years or more.

DISABILITY AND LONG-TERM CARE INSURANCE

If you're still working, your earning power is your greatest asset, and the one you should worry most about losing. Insurance experts will tell you that you're far more likely to be disabled during your working years than you are to die. The American Council of Life Insurers says one-third of all Americans between the ages of thirty-five and sixty-five will become disabled for more than ninety days, and one in seven workers will be disabled for more than five years.

Government programs provide some disability coverage, but they're pretty restrictive. Workers' compensation funds, for example, will pay you only if you're injured on the job. Get hurt at home or suffer a disabling illness, and you're out of luck.

Social Security disability payments are even harder to get. The system covers only total and long-term disability, not partial disability or short-term problems. You have to prove that you're so disabled you can't do any job—even flipping burgers or telemarketing—to get benefits.

So if your employer offers disability coverage, sign up for both short-term and long-term coverage. If you're given the option, buy enough coverage to replace at least 60 percent of your income.

If your employer doesn't offer group coverage, or doesn't provide enough, you can contact one of the major disability insurers, such as Unum, Hartford or MetLife, to get quotes. Getting an individual policy is tougher, and often more expensive, than buying a group policy. To make it affordable, you may have to settle for a longer waiting period or limit your coverage (to three or five years instead of until age sixty-five, the usual standard).

Another coverage you should at least consider is long-term care insurance, which covers the kind of custodial care you'd receive outside a hospital, such as in a nursing home, at an assisted living facility or from a home health aide.

Medicare, the government health program for people sixty-five and over, doesn't cover these costs after the first one hundred days, and Medicaid, the government health program for the poor, covers these expenses only for the indigent.

And the costs can be steep. A semi-private nursing home room averaged $72,270 a year in 2009, while home health care services averaged $21 an hour. Round-the-clock care at home could set you back $183,960 a year. Long-term care insurance could help you pay those costs, preserving your assets for your spouse or your heirs.

The big problem with long-term care insurance is that it hasn't been around that long, and insurers haven't done that great a job at predicting costs. That means several have jacked up premiums dramatically, sometimes making it hard for people to continue coverage even when they've been paying on a policy for years. Some insurers have coped with higher costs by denying claims, while others have gone out of business.

The health care reform law that passed in 2010 created an alternative—a voluntary, government-run program called Community Living Assistance Services and Supports (CLASS). Starting in 2013, people who make voluntary payroll deductions can, after a five-year vesting period, receive at least $50 a day to offset the costs of home care, adult day care or residential care.

Whether the program is a good option for you, or even if it remains viable—by law, it has to pay for itself—will depend on the cost of premiums. It's certainly worth considering, though.

If you want more coverage or don't want to gamble on the government program sticking around, you should investigate long-term policies by the time you're in your early fifties. AARP has an excellent primer at www.aarp.org/health/longtermcare.

WHY HEALTH CARE INSURANCE IS DIFFERENT

You need health care insurance for the same reason you need liability coverage: to avoid bankrupting yourself. It doesn't matter how healthy you are now: one accident or illness can wipe you out. (Medical bills are a factor in two-thirds of all U.S. bankruptcies.)

Health insurance doesn't just reduce the chances you'll go broke. It reduces the chances you'll die.

THE KAISER COMMISSION ON MEDICAID AND THE UNINSURED HAS FOUND:

- People without health insurance receive less preventive care and are less likely to have major diseases detected early.
- The uninsured are more likely to die prematurely than the insured, with various studies putting the mortality rate for the uninsured somewhere between 1.2 times to 1.6 times the rate for the insured.
- Uninsured infants have relative odds of dying that are 1.5 times higher than infants with private insurance.
- The poorer health associated with being uninsured depresses workers' average lifetime earnings significantly. The commission has estimated that better health would boost earnings by 10 to 30 percent.

Of all the complaints voiced about the health care reform law, to me the least compelling were the ones protesting mandatory coverage. Everyone *needs* health care insurance. Period. End of story.

The question remains whether you can get it—and if you can, if it's affordable. The health care system has long been troubled, both by skyrocketing costs and by insurance practices that made it tough for many people to get adequate coverage.

Employer-provided policies typically offer the best deal, since most companies subsidize a majority of the costs and everyone gets covered, regardless of their health status. But companies have been pushing more of the costs onto their employees and some plans have gaping holes, such as high deductibles or co-pays that could leave a sick worker with crippling debt.

The individual insurance market—coverage for people who don't have policies through an employer—is also problematic. Insurers really pick and choose when it comes to issuing policies to individuals. People who lose or leave their jobs quickly find that coverage is tough to get—taken even a single prescription drug can make you tough if not impossible to insure. People could pay premiums for years and then lose their coverage as soon as they get sick. Costs are often staggering, so many people resort to high deductibles just to have any coverage.

The health care reform bill that passed in 2010 has already made some changes. Insurers can no longer drop people who become sick, a practice known as rescission. Insurance policies no longer have lifetime limits on their coverage; in the past, limits of $1 million to $2 million were common, and some really awful policies had limits as low as $10,000. Also, children up to age twenty-six can remain on their parents' policies.

But it remains unclear whether the reforms will do anything to curb the wildly surging costs of health care in the United States. In just ten years, the cost for family coverage through employers rose 131 percent, with workers bearing most of that cost. In 2009, it cost an average $1,098 a month, or $13,176 a year, to insure a family. Individual policies have seen even steeper increases.

As I mentioned in the first chapter, you can offset some of the costs by using tax-advantaged savings accounts: flexible spending accounts (FSAs), if your employer provides them, or health savings accounts (HSAs), which are tied to high-deductible policies. You also can lower the cost of coverage by opting to pay more of the bills yourself. Choosing higher co-pays and higher deductibles often makes your monthly premiums more affordable. With so-called catastrophic policies, you pay most costs out of pocket until you reach a relatively high deductible—$1,000, $3,000, $5,000 or even more.

I've long been a fan of buying health care policies that way, but lately have realized that they really aren't for everyone. In fact, the tighter money is, the more you may want to reconsider a catastrophic policy. With other types of insurance, a high deductible can make you more careful. Knowing you'll pay for dings out of pocket might make you park your car farther away from others, for example. With health insurance, however, there's a built-in incentive to delay or avoid preventative care and screenings that could save your life.

My friend Anne has a policy with a $5,000-per-person deductible. She's never come close to meeting the deductible, but that didn't matter: she felt covered in case of catastrophe. The problem came the day her doctor told her it was time to get a colonoscopy. The test wasn't one of the limited number of screenings her policy covered. She'd have to pay for the whole thing out of pocket.

So she put off the test. *Even though her mother had died of colon cancer.*

She's a smart, educated woman who made a potentially life-threatening choice, because of the cost. If you could see yourself making the same mistake, opt for more coverage, or at least make sure you have a savings account specifically set aside to cover your deductible.

Also, be wary of any policy that doesn't cap the amount you pay out of pocket. Some policies, for example, have a 30 percent co-pay, with no limit. One high-risk birth or car accident could put you on the hook for a six-figure bill.

In a few years, getting adequate coverage should get easier. The biggest changes are scheduled for 2014. Starting that year:

- Insurers will no longer be able to deny coverage based on preexisting conditions or charge people more based on their sex or health status.
- State-run exchanges will be created to allow businesses and certain individuals—the self-employed, the unemployed and those whose companies don't provide insurance, among others—to shop for coverage from private insurers. The exchanges won't be allowed to set premiums but will select the insurers that are allowed to participate.
- Policies available on these exchanges will be required to cover a variety of services, including preventative care and screenings; doctor visits and hospital and emergency room care; rehabilitation; maternity and newborn care; and mental health and substance abuse treatment. (Employer-provided plans won't have to meet those same standards, however.)
- Four levels of coverage will be offered on the exchange policies: platinum plans that cover 90 percent of costs, gold plans that cover 80 percent, silver plans that cover 70 percent and bronze plans that cover 60 percent, with steeper premiums for more coverage. Out-of-pocket costs for all the plans will be capped at $5,950 for individuals and $11,900 for families.
- If employer plans cover less than 60 percent of costs, or an individual would pay more than 8 percent of his or her income to purchase the employer coverage, he or she would be eligible to buy insurance on the exchanges.
- Sliding-scale subsidies will be available to help families with incomes up to four times the poverty level ($88,200 for a family of four, in 2009). The subsidies will ensure the families pay no more than 2 to 9.5 percent of their incomes, with the government paying the rest.

- Eligibility for Medicaid, the health care program for the indigent, will be expanded to include anyone with income 133 percent or less of the poverty level (in 2009, that was $29,327 for a family of four). Medicaid payments to health care providers will be increased to the levels used by Medicare, which should increase the number of providers willing to accept Medicaid.

ACTION STEPS

We've covered a lot of ground in this chapter, but these are the most important things to remember about insurance:

- Opt for higher deductibles and keep cash equal to your deductibles in a dedicated savings account.
- Get enough liability protection. Liability coverage on your home and auto should at least equal your net worth. Buy an umbrella policy if necessary.
- Make sure your home is adequately covered. Talk to your agent and double-check your coverage amounts using AccuCoverage.
- If you have considerable equity in your home, opt for disaster coverage.
- Maintain your home and don't procrastinate on repairs, lest they turn into a larger problem.
- Get GAP coverage if you owe more on your car than it's worth.
- Shop around. Compare premiums for home and auto insurance every few years to make sure you're still getting the best deal.
- If you need life insurance, make sure you buy enough. You may need coverage equal to five to ten times your salary if you have young children.
- Investigate disability and long-term care insurance. If these are offered by your employer, strongly consider buying them.
- Get adequate health insurance. If you're in good health, a high-deductible policy may be an appropriate way to keep costs down, but don't skimp on preventative screenings.

Treat Your Marriage
Like a Business

THE OLD-SCHOOL RULES:
The husband should be in charge of the money.
The wife should live within the budget he sets.

THE BUBBLE ECONOMY RULES:
Talking about money isn't worth the fight.
As long as it keeps coming in, it'll work out somehow.

THE NEW RULES:
One spouse should be in charge of day-to-day money management,
but both need to agree on goals and keep to the budget.

Marriage makes people richer.

Not all marriages, of course, and "richer" is relative. But overall, people who get married and stay married build significantly more wealth than those who are single.

- The median net worth of married-couple households in a Census Bureau wealth study was $101,975. For single men, median wealth was $23,700. For single women, $20,217.
- A fifteen-year study of nine thousand people found that during that time, people who married and stayed married built up nearly twice the net worth of people who stayed single. The study, by Ohio State University's Center for Human Resource Research, found that even when all other factors are held constant—variables such as income and education—

just the fact that they were married contributed to a 4 percent annual rise in these couples' wealth.

- Divorce destroys wealth. Declines in people's net worth typically started four years before a divorce was final, the Ohio survey found, and the breakup dramatically reduces the typical person's wealth, compared to that of a single person the same age.

Of course, most people don't marry for money, and we have some nasty names ("gold digger," "black widow," "gigolo") for people who do. But marriage is far more than a romantic arrangement; it has legal and financial ramifications as well. Those who ignore the business aspects of marriage do so at their own peril, as that divorce statistic shows.

Probably fewer marriages would end if people in the beginning would think more objectively about finances and how they were going to handle them. Love really does not conquer all, as any long-term married person will tell you. When times are good, you might be able to ignore your differences. In bad times, though, you really want to be working together as a team.

That means treating your marriage more like a business. You don't have to excise the romance, but you should take advantage of the systems businesses have in place to assure progress and reduce conflict. Such as:

A plan. Successful businesses tend to have business plans that include their goals for the coming years and how they propose to achieve those goals. Married partners need to agree on goals as well and craft a plan together to attain them.

A chief financial officer (CFO). Smart business owners learn to delegate and specialize, which usually means having a CFO. Having one person in charge of the day-to-day financial details, such as paying bills and monitoring accounts, also can help your marital finances stay on track.

Regular reports to stakeholders. Publicly traded businesses are required by law to reveal the details of their financial situation every three months, along with a comprehensive annual report. It's also important for married couples to regularly review their finances together. Ethical businesses don't try to fudge or hide unpleasant details in the fine print; honesty about financial matters is crucial in marriage, too.

I speak not just as someone who has covered issues surrounding couples and money. I speak also as someone who's been happily married for more than a dozen years. I've learned that you don't have to have the exact same approach to money to succeed (I'm a saver; my husband's more of a spender), but you do have to be willing to listen to each other, compromise and put a plan into action.

My husband delights in telling people, including complete strangers, about his "pittance." That's his word for the cash that is automatically whisked from our joint account into his separate checking account every week. I withdraw a similar sum for myself, and we use these weekly allowances as no-questions-asked spending money.

We had a few false starts—and some tense moments—before we hit on this system. But when it comes to merging money when you're married, many financial planners will tell you that trial and error is often the best approach. "There are no rules," says Delia Fernandez, a financial planner in Los Alamitos, California, who advises many couples about their money. "That's the wonderful thing about marriage—you get to make it up as you go along."

The challenges of marriage and money are complex because of the interaction of love, emotion and practical realities. How we were raised, our temperaments and personalities and our life experiences with money all inform how we think about and deal with money. Our differences about money are usually profound enough that we shouldn't assume money matters will simply fall into place without effort. Successfully merging your finances in marriage requires honesty, communication, flexibility and trust.

If you can't agree or aren't clear about the right path, take your time. Couples in general should consider merging their finances slowly, says Washington, D.C., psychotherapist Olivia Mellan, as they get to know each other and build trust. This is particularly important if your money styles are different, which is often the case.

Here are the issues you should talk about, whether you are just contemplating marriage, already starry-eyed honeymooners or struggling to mesh your money styles after years of conflict.

Basic banking and bill paying. When it comes to handling money and bills, couples' styles are as different as their relationships. They range from the roommate approach, with each spouse maintaining separate accounts and dividing up bills, to a mix of joint and separate accounts, to the two-shall-be-as-one style where every checkbook, credit card and brokerage statement in the house is in both names. Once again, there's no right answer. But couples need to figure out what works for them by asking these questions:

Should we have a joint account? Most couples have at least some joint accounts, and about half have *only* joint accounts. Separate accounts can give each partner a sense of freedom and autonomy, but some people feel these private accounts can undermine the sense of all-for-one unity they were hoping for in marriage.

HOW WE HANDLE BANK ACCOUNTS	
All bank accounts are combined	50%
All bank accounts are separate	18%
Some accounts are separate	29%
No bank accounts	3%

Source: Harris Interactive.

Where will our paychecks be deposited? Some couples who have both joint and separate accounts have their checks deposited in the joint account to cover the bills, and they transfer spending money to separate accounts. Some do just the opposite, depositing their checks in their own accounts, then moving enough money to cover bills into the joint account.

How will we make spending decisions? Most couples don't want to debate every $5 purchase. On the other hand, you probably wouldn't want to see a new car in the driveway when you hadn't been consulted. (This, by the way, actually happened to a friend of ours. And it was a Jaguar, no less. They're no longer married.)

Many people starting out set a limit of how much they can spend without consulting the other: $50, $100, $500, depending on how tight their finances are. Working out a budget of how much is to be spent on groceries, clothes, household items and other sundries each month can also help avoid fights.

Allowances, of course, are yet another option. It was fountain pens, of all things, that led to our decision to try allowances. My artist husband fell in love with one expensive pen after another. Since I couldn't tell a $175 Namiki Falcon from a Bic, the amounts that kept popping up on our charge card were driving me nuts.

At the same time, my husband was feeling a distinct lack of privacy. With a joint account and joint credit cards, he couldn't buy me a present without my knowing exactly where he bought it and how much it cost—sometimes within a few hours, since our personal finance software is so efficient at tracking transactions.

So now we have the pittance system—and a lot more money harmony. I get surprised with lovely gifts, and he gets to have his lovely pens, with no carping from the Wife.

How will we pay the bills? If you have separate accounts and are dividing up the bills, you need to decide whether you'll contribute equally toward your expenses or proportionately to your incomes. Again: there's no one right way, as long as you both feel comfortable with your approach. If your main household accounts are joint, you'll probably want to make one person responsible for most money matters. This is usually the most efficient approach, but the partner who's not handling day-to-day bills shouldn't be left in the dark. Regular business meetings, where finances are discussed, are essential, planners say. "You should know what's going on," Fernandez says. "If something happens [to the CFO], you're going to need to step in and take over."

WHY YOU NEED A FAMILY CFO

The TV show *Mad Men* gives today's viewers a fascinating glimpse of life in the early 1960s among a certain slice of upper-income New Yorkers—and how drastically different women, children, minorities and money were treated back then. When it came to finances, married men typically called the shots, often without even consulting their wives. In one telling scene, a character brightly informs his wife that he's enlisted in the military to become an army surgeon—a decision that promises to uproot and dramatically alter her life. She is one of the smartest and most capable characters on the show—if she were born thirty years later, she might be on her way to being a CEO—but she swallows her objections and smiles, ever the supportive wife.

Now, some relationships back then were more partnerships than command-and-control arrangements—my parents had one such marriage, where decisions were worked out together. And some marriages today follow the "Father knows best" model. But more often today marriages are collaborative and require both partners to be involved in the finances.

Still, it's usually more practical to have a single person in charge of the everyday practicalities of paying bills and monitoring the budget. Chances are one of you is more comfortable with these duties than the other, and having a chief financial officer reduces the chances that bills or other important details will slip through the cracks because you each thought the other was handling it.

That doesn't mean the other partner is left out of the loop. It's important for married couples to review their finances together at least every few months (every few weeks may be better if you're digging out of debt or money is tight), with an overall financial review each year. Even if the non-CFO has absolutely no interest in financial matters, he or she at least needs to know where to find the important information, including account IDs and passwords, if something should happen to the chief financial officer.

Another area to review is your credit and debt situations.

There's no such thing as a "joint" credit report—everybody has his or her own reports at the three major credit bureaus—but your credit is still likely to get intertwined after marriage. Technically, you could try to keep things separate. But if you apply for a mortgage together, add each other to your credit cards or even buy stuff that benefits you both, your partner's credit past can affect your future. If one or both of you has bad credit, improving it should be a priority.

HOW YOUR PARTNER'S CREDIT AFFECTS YOU

IF YOU APPLY FOR A MORTGAGE or other major loan together, your lender will typically pull credit scores for both of you—and use the lower score to determine your rates and terms.

If you're jointly responsible for a debt and your partner misses any payments, those "lates" will trash your credit scores as well as your partner's.

On the other hand, if your credit scores are good and you want to improve a partner's credit, you can add him or her as an authorized user to one of your credit cards. Your positive history with the card often will be imported into his credit files.

WHAT DO OUR CREDIT HISTORIES LOOK LIKE, AND HOW CAN WE MAKE THEM BETTER?

Here's a profoundly unromantic idea for a date: sit together at a computer and pull your credit reports from AnnualCreditReport.com. You can also get your reports and your FICO credit scores by visiting My FICO.com. Talk about what you see on the reports, make plans to correct any errors and read the information at MyFICO about ways to improve your creditworthiness. Paying bills on time, reducing debt and applying for credit sparingly are all ways to improve your ability to get credit when you need it.

I know a lot of people who wish they had taken this step earlier in their marriage, or even before their marriage, instead of getting blindsided too late by their partner's debts. Even if you aren't technically responsible for the debt, it will affect your life together and how much money you have for other things, so you need to know about it and discuss how to tackle it if you want your financial partnership to be as strong as it can be.

WHAT DO WE OWN, AND WHAT DO WE OWE?

Creating a net worth statement is the first step in financial planning. You start by listing all your assets and their current value. Assets include bank accounts, investment accounts, retirement funds, real estate, the cash value of any life insurance and any other property of value. Then list your liabilities—everything you owe (you'll find a list of possible debts in the third chapter). Your credit reports may remind you of any debts you may have forgotten. Subtracting those liabilities from your assets will give you a snapshot of where you are now and can help point you where you need to go.

NET WORTH BY AGE			
Age	Median	Top 25%	Top 10%
20 to 29	$6,400	$35,000	$132,000
30 to 39	$51,200	$184,000	$436,000
40 to 49	$133,100	$371,000	$840,000

Age	Median	Top 25%	Top 10%
50 to 59	$229,300	$605,000	$1,350,000
60 to 69	$256,300	$710,400	$2,030,000

Source: Federal Reserve's Survey of Consumer Finances, 2007.

Use this balance sheet as a starting point for discussions about your goals. Do you want to retire early? Have kids? Buy a home? Travel the world? Figure out together what's important to you, and prioritize your goals. Then you can use personal finance software like Quicken to start planning for those goals, or you can consult a financial adviser.

WHAT'S OUR PLAN FOR PAYING OFF OUR DEBT?

Not many people come to marriage without some financial baggage, often in the form of credit card debt, car payments and student loans. Each dollar you spend on interest, though, is a dollar you don't have for your other goals. And as you know, debt is often a signal that you're living beyond your means, which could mean never achieving your dreams.

Creating a debt repayment plan will require that you first find out how much you spend and then determine a realistic budget for future spending. This is a joint effort, not something either one of you can do alone.

Some couples decide that payments for premarriage debts be made from separate accounts, rather than the joint account. Others take a more all-for-one approach, reasoning that they're a team now and that whatever benefits the team financially is the right thing to do. Discuss which way you want to handle it.

Debts incurred during marriage, of course, are a whole different matter. You're often on the hook for a spouse's spending, whether you knew about it or not. That's why financial planners say honesty and continued communication are so important.

What if you just can't seem to agree?

Jennifer tried to work things out with her spouse, a compulsive spender. They experimented with joint accounts, separate accounts and an allowance system in which each got a weekly infusion of "no-questions-asked" spending money. But Jennifer's husband kept overspending, and he sulked when she reminded him that they were trying to save for a house. One of the last straws: he decided he "needed" a new

$40,000 car, and he stopped speaking to her when she pointed out that the vehicle cost twice his annual income. After four years, Jennifer gave up and filed for divorce.

"I should not have let it go as long as I did," says Jennifer, a financial professional in her midthirties. "I should not have let myself be emotionally bullied."

Others hang in there longer, sometimes to their regret. One poster on the Your Money message board, who has been married twenty-nine years, recounted how she refinanced a mortgage to pay off $45,000 in credit card debt her husband secretly had incurred.

"I just found out that 4 years later, he has run up his credit cards again to $36,000 and can't help me pay taxes or any emergency expenses that come along. I am sooooo mad, frustrated, and resentful of him I can hardly stand it," poster "purse" wrote. "We are at retirement age and he doesn't have ANY money saved. . . . The sad thing is I never saw anything new to indicate he was spending. He was supposed to cut up his credit cards after the refinance. . . . I just feel so betrayed."

Another couple I know kept their accounts separate from day one because of her extensive credit card bills and student loans. When her husband asked about the debt, the wife always assured him she was taking care of it. Then the collection calls started, and he discovered she had instead maxed out all of her credit cards and had turned to payday loans to try to pay her bills. He was furious at the deception and couldn't believe she would hide the magnitude of the problem from him. But she was angry, too, claiming his holier-than-thou attitude about debt prevented her from talking to him honestly about what was going on.

Few couples are on exactly the same page when it comes to money, but some partners are so far over the edge that their destructive habits can sabotage the family finances. How can you tell whether your partner just needs a little persuading or is a total financial basket case? You're facing an uphill battle if:

There's an underlying addiction. If your partner has problems with alcohol, drugs or gambling, he or she literally can't think straight. Financial progress takes a backseat to feeding the addiction. Recovery is always possible, of course, but you'd be smart to get counseling (even if your partner won't go) and attend a support group such as Al-Anon, Nar-Anon or Gam-Anon. (Our message board poster wrote that her husband had a longtime drinking problem, and no interest in pursuing treatment; last we heard, she was pursuing a divorce.)

There's a mental disorder. Overspending can be a symptom of a number of mental problems, including depression, bipolar disorder and attention-deficit/hyperactivity disorder (ADHD). Adults with these conditions may not be able to resist impulse spending or to tend to the details of their finances, leading to big debts, late fees and other fallout. Again, progress is possible, but the underlying disorder must first be properly diagnosed and treated. (After a huge fight about their finances, the woman who had taken out payday loans sought help from a counselor, who diagnosed her with ADHD. Treatment and medication helped reduce her symptoms. She decided she couldn't handle credit cards and now uses a debit card linked to a checking account with no overdraft privileges.)

There's no acknowledgment of the problem. This may be the hardest nut to crack. Your partner either doesn't see what you're worried about or blames the problem on you. Counseling and sessions with a financial planner may help, but if your partner takes no responsibility and instead blames others, prospects for improvement may be dim. That was Jennifer's situation with her husband, and she counts herself lucky that the marriage lasted only as long as it did.

Many people try to insulate themselves from an overspending spouse by keeping separate accounts, but there's a big danger in that: you can't see what he or she is up to. Separate accounts can allow profligate partners to run up big secret debts. In any case, simply setting up separate accounts while you're still married may not protect you from your spouse's financial missteps.

In community property states, which include Arizona, California, Idaho, Louisiana, Nevada, New Mexico, Texas, Washington and Wisconsin, debts incurred during marriage are typically considered joint debts. In other states, debts can be considered joint if they were incurred for family necessities, such as food or shelter. Even when a debt is the sole responsibility of one partner, some states allow creditors to go after jointly owned property if the debt is not paid.

You can get an idea of your liability, and what you can do to protect yourself, by talking to an experienced bankruptcy attorney who knows your state's laws. You may be able to legally wall yourself off from your spouse's debts, even in community property states, through a document known as a postnuptial agreement. Or you may decide to divorce rather than incur further liability.

For most couples, though, the picture isn't nearly so bleak. Even those with drastically different money skills and approaches can find a compromise that works. Couples who work out their financial differences usually do so by taking the time to understand each other's point of view and being willing to compromise, financial experts say.

"It comes down to . . . how they deal with conflict," says Sandra Wang, a financial adviser with Morgan Stanley Smith Barney in Palo Alto, California, who is also a licensed marriage therapist and a certified divorce financial analyst. "It takes a lot of work, and a lot of people don't want to do that."

Besides, money can be extremely tough to talk about, says financial planner Tracy B. Stewart of College Station, Texas. Many couples with financial disagreements find they need a third party, such as a counselor or a financial planner, to help them navigate these tricky issues.

"They're better off with a third party, because it's going to be emotionally charged for both of them," says Stewart, a CPA who is also a personal financial specialist and a certified divorce financial analyst. "Money is up there at the top of emotionally charged issues."

Some ways you can get on the same page:

Understand where your partner is coming from. Talk about how your families dealt with money growing up. Share your first memories of having or spending money, discuss each of your parents' attitudes about money and talk about what you wish had been done differently in your family. Chances are you'll gain valuable insights into your partner's current approach to finances (and probably into your own, as well).

Appreciate your partner's strengths. Often spenders are "seize the day" kind of people who are spontaneous and fun, Wang says. They can be an important counterweight to savers, who tend to value the future over the present. My husband's insistence that we live life today, as well as save for the future, has resulted in some terrific vacations—and much nicer furniture than I'd have bought had I been left to my own devices.

Agree on goals. Talk about short-term goals, such as your next vacation, as well as longer-term plans like paying for the kids' college and saving for retirement. People who live for today need to have something to look forward to in the near future; too much delayed gratification makes them grumpy and unwilling to cooperate with the longer-term plans.

Track where the money is going. Stewart asks married clients to bring in at least three months' worth of bank and other account statements so they can see exactly how much income has come in and how much has been paid out. Sometimes this evidence is enough to get an overspending spouse to realize that changes need to be made, particularly if the outgo greatly exceeds the income.

Solicit solutions; don't impose them. If your expenses exceed your income or you're not saving enough for your goals, cuts will have to be made. But the spender should have an active role in deciding exactly where to cut. "The key is for the person we're dealing with to own the reduction in spending," Stewart said.

Attack the problem, not each other. No one is blameless here. "It takes two to tango" and create the dynamic that causes financial problems, Wang notes. Attacks and accusations are counterproductive. Instead, she suggests, focus on working as a team.

Tell the truth—always. Most of us understand that physical infidelity is devastating to a relationship. But many people don't understand that financial infidelity is a big deal, too.

FINANCIAL INFIDELITY—WHY THERE ARE NO "LITTLE WHITE FINANCIAL LIES"

A survey that Lawyers.com and *Redbook* magazine commissioned from Harris Interactive in 2005 tells the tale. Harris interviewed 1,796 adults, ages twenty-five to fifty-five, who were married, engaged or living together. Among the findings:

- Virtually all the people interviewed (96 percent) said it was both partners' responsibility to be completely honest about financial issues.
- Nearly one in four (24 percent) believed so strongly in this principle that they said openness about money is *more* important than being faithful. (As the legal editor for Lawyers.com, Alan Kopit, put it, "They're saying, 'It's one thing to fool around. It's another thing to fool around with my hard-earned cash!'")
- Despite the previous statistics, almost one in three (29 percent) admitted they had lied to their partner about finances, most often about personal spending (21 percent) or spending on the kids (12 percent).
- One in four (25 percent) said a partner had withheld financial information, usually about personal spending (20 percent) and spending on children (11 percent).

When I asked my MSN readers about ways they lied to their partners, I got an earful. Several confessed to hiding purchases or shopping bags or pretending that a recent purchase wasn't recent—the "what, this old thing?" response to a partner's query "Is that new?"

They usually justified their deceptions by saying they wanted to avoid a fight, or even a bout of retaliatory spending, where their partner would go out and buy something to "even the score."

Some took their deceptions further. A few had secret bank accounts. Some deliberately didn't tell their partners about raises or even inheritances, for fear it would ramp up the partner's spending. One woman who was hiding money from her husband insisted she had no qualms about doing so—"it would be gone by now if it were up to him," she said.

Most of us would feel queasy about such a big deception. But financial planner Diane McCurdy thinks *any* marital lie about money is a red flag. "I do not think it is all right to fudge numbers," McCurdy said.

I tend to agree, and here's why:

Lies erode trust, compromise the teller's integrity—and can make the person who's lied to feel really, really bad. A poster on the Your Money message board offered a perspective about what it feels like to be lied to. Shortly after they were married, her husband told her he'd won a new PlayStation in a raffle. She later found a statement from a credit card he'd opened secretly to buy the toy.

"I was crushed for many reasons," she wrote, most importantly because "he thought his PlayStation was more important than our joint goals, ones we'd written together, talked about and set out to accomplish, together."

Lies may signal significant problems in the relationship. In the Harris poll, people who said they were happy in their relationships were far less likely to have lied or been lied to than those who were less happy. Nearly half of those who responded that they were "not satisfied" in their relationships said they had lied or been lied to; only one in five of the "very satisfied" crew reported that they or their partner had been untruthful.

Do the lies cause the unhappiness, or the unhappiness the lies? The poll doesn't say; all that's clear is that lying can be an indicator of trouble. Also, financial infidelity often accompanies sexual infidelity, notes Ruth Houston, author of *Is He Cheating on You?* A cheating spouse often hides spending on a lover and may hide assets in anticipation of divorce.

Lies can prevent couples from getting on the same page. Many times, McCurdy says, couples have settled into potentially destructive black-and-white attitudes about their partners. People who are natural savers can see their freer-spending spouses as childish and irresponsible, while the spender spouse may view the saver as a miser and a killjoy.

In these cases, she says, both spouses need to work hard to understand their partner's perspective and be willing to make compromises. The spender may need to curb the shopping trips, but the saver may have to loosen up the purse strings.

The PlayStation lie, for example, resulted in a long talk that helped the woman realize the couple needed a little more flexibility in its budget. From her husband's perspective, using all their money for joint goals didn't leave room for the fact that they were individuals, with different wants and needs. "To him . . . I wasn't respecting he was still his own person, in addition to being a partner," she wrote. "He didn't excuse away the lying or blame it on anyone, he accepted his deceit," she wrote. "After that we started getting an allowance and have done it ever since!"

People who lie rather than risking a confrontation are missing out on a chance to get closer. Talking about these issues, rather than trying to avoid them with lies, can help a couple work out their differences and create a plan that gives both what they need, McCurdy says. The saver can still be assured that the family is building financial security, while the spender doesn't have to delay all gratification.

"Remember goal setting, the common family goals, can be accomplished together," McCurdy says, "with a little family planning and discussion."

Little lies tend to lead to bigger ones. When deception has snowballed into serious debt, professional help might be needed, Kopit says. A financial planner and a couples therapist may need to be called in to help straighten out both the money mess and the behavior that led to it.

If you think you can fix the problem before your significant other finds out, you're probably wrong. The money problems that caused the debt are likely to persist as long as you're hiding the problem. Typically, the bills will grow until you can no longer keep up. "The judgment day will arrive," Kopit warns. "It's going to happen."

The first step, he says, is to "fess up" to the problem. Then work jointly to fix it. The confession probably will be painful, as will the spending changes needed to pay off the debt. But concealing problems, financial or otherwise, is no way to solve them.

"Your mother and dad told you to tell the truth," Kopit says, "and that was good advice."

The one exception: if you fear your partner will physically harm you. If that's the case, you need to talk to a counselor or call the nearest women's shelter for help (men can call these shelters, too, if they are victims or potential victims of spousal abuse).

FINANCES FOR BLENDED FAMILIES

Working out money issues is tough enough for most couples. Add in financial entanglements from previous relationships, and a real quagmire can result.

The first step: disclosure. It's essential to talk to your current partner about all your financial obligations to your ex, including the amount and term of any spousal support and child support, plus any promises that have been made about helping children with college costs. You can't plan together as a couple unless everything is on the table.

Work the budget around the realities. I hear from too many people who resent the amount their spouses are required to pay to care for their children from previous relationships. Those amounts are usually set in accordance with state laws that are trying to prevent children's standard of living from plummeting when their parents divorce. Yes, those payments cut into the money you'd like to spend on other things, but your partner has a responsibility to support a child he or she has created. If the child support payments are too high given your partner's current income, they can be adjusted by a court. Otherwise, you have to work your budget around them.

Try to sever credit relationships. Ideally, joint accounts would be closed and any joint loans refinanced into the responsible person's name before the divorce is final. If that hasn't been done, try to do so now, although getting a mortgage refinanced may be difficult if the responsible party doesn't have the income, equity or credit scores to get the deal done.

Understand the financial aid implications. Your child's financial aid package for college will depend on the income and assets of her custodial family. If your ex's new spouse makes a lot of money but is unwilling to contribute, and that's the house where she spends the most time, your child could find herself with no financial aid and no way to pay the bills, other than borrowing. Conversely, a low household income could result in more aid, even if you have ample funds set aside for her. Consider using the Expected Family Contribution calculator at FinAid.org to see how much financial aid your child is likely to get, and try to coordinate savings strategies with your ex.

Fair doesn't necessarily mean equal. Favoring one child or set of children over another can cause lifelong resentments and even permanent rifts in families. A parent who pays child support reluctantly, and late, while lavishing toys and vacations on the children of the current marriage has a name: jerk. But that doesn't mean you have to spend exactly the same dollar amount on each child. Consider that children from an intact family may pursue different interests and go to colleges with dramatically different costs. Shoot for an equitable division of spending that acknowledges the differences among children as well as your desire to treat them fairly.

THE MYTH OF THE MARRIAGE PENALTY

If you believe the myth about the marriage penalty—the one that says you pay more taxes when you're married than if you'd stayed single— you might be baffled by the whole gay marriage thing. Why are gays and lesbians trying so hard to get married, you might ask, if marriage is so hard on the wallet?

The reality is that marriage has plenty of legal and financial benefits, including tax breaks. Even before Congress changed tax rules in 2001 to deal with the so-called marriage penalty, more married couples got a tax bonus from being married than paid a tax penalty:

- Fifty-one percent of married couples paid less tax jointly than if they had not been married, according to a 1996 Congressional Budget Office analysis. The average amount these couples saved: $1,300.
- Forty-two percent of married taxpayers paid more by filing jointly than they would have if they'd remained single, the office said. The average penalty: $1,380.

If one spouse made more than the other, they were likely to get a tax break. The wider the gap between the paychecks of the husband and wife, the bigger the bonus. If the spouses made similar incomes, though, they often paid a penalty. Typically, the more they made, the bigger the penalty they paid.

But the couples who faced the worst penalties as a portion of their income were the working poor, according to tax expert Edward Mc-Caffery, a law professor at the University of Southern California and the author of *Taxing Women*. A husband and wife who each earned $10,000 could end up with a marriage penalty of more than $4,000.

Those low-income couples still face the potential for a tax penalty, says Mark Luscombe, a principal analyst for tax research firm CCH. That's because the earned income credit, a tax break designed to keep the working poor out of poverty, can be less for a two-earner household than for singles.

But Congress effectively eliminated the penalty for the majority of couples with its 2001 legislation, which has since been extended (but not made permanent; more on that in a minute). The standard deduction for married couples is now twice that for singles, and, for the 2010 tax year, the 15 percent income tax bracket has been widened for marrieds to $68,000, twice the limit for singles. There's still a potential for a marriage penalty once joint incomes reach the 25 percent bracket, but the widening of the 15 percent tax bracket means that even those who pay a penalty will pay a less significant one than in the past.

The legislation eliminating the penalty for most couples is set to expire in 2010. Congress will be under plenty of pressure to make the change permanent, but that doesn't mean it will happen. Even without income tax breaks, though, there are plenty of financial benefits to marriage, regardless of the couple's income tax situation. Among them:

Workplace health and pension benefits coverage. Some companies offer health coverage to domestic partners, but this benefit is typically taxable as income. When spouses are covered, the benefit is tax free.

Social Security retirement and survivor benefits. A husband or wife is entitled to one-half of the spouse's Social Security benefits and to additional benefits in the event of death.

Lower insurance rates. Married people usually get a discount on auto insurance and may pay less for other types of insurance.

Automatic inheritance rights. Die without a will, and your spouse gets your stuff. In many states, the surviving spouse has a legal right to at least one-third to one-half of your estate.

Preferential estate tax treatment. The richer you are, the better a deal this is. Essentially, estates worth more than a certain amount—it was $3.5 million in 2009—are subject to estate taxes. But this exemption amount doesn't apply to married people: you can leave an unlimited amount to a spouse without generating a penny of estate tax. In certain states, this benefit is multiplied by special capital gains tax treatment for homes and other assets held by married couples as community property.

One marriage penalty that remains has to do with Social Security taxes and working spouses, particularly women. The Social Security Administration says 62 percent of the women over age sixty-two who receive benefits do so based on their husband's work records, rather than their own. A little more than half of these women didn't earn enough to qualify for payments based on their own work records. The rest opted to take half of their husbands' benefits because they were larger than the checks they could qualify for based on their own earnings.

Now, in one very real sense, these women are better off married because they benefit from their husbands' larger Social Security checks. In another sense, they're severely penalized because all the Social Security taxes they contributed over the years essentially yielded no additional benefit. They'd get the same payments if they'd never worked and never paid into Social Security.

This is no small potatoes. Social Security taxes now eat up 6.2 percent of every worker's paycheck, up to an annual maximum of $6,622 on earnings of $106,800 in 2010, while employers contribute an equal amount. As more women work and earn better salaries, the proportion claiming benefits based on a spouse's record may decline somewhat. But because men still earn more on average than women, this phenomenon certainly won't disappear. Given the precarious state of Social Security and political realities, this is one marriage penalty that's likely to persist.

FINAL THOUGHTS ON MARRIAGE

Your financial obligations to your spouse don't end at death. And should you die prematurely, you could be leaving behind a real mess.

If both of your incomes are needed to pay the mortgage, for example, you both should have life insurance. Otherwise, your mate could end up homeless. You should also check—and usually change—the beneficiaries of any existing life insurance policies as well as beneficiaries for all your bank, brokerage and retirement accounts. Marty Kuritz, creator of the estate-organizing workbook *The Beneficiary Book*, tells of a man who failed to change his beneficiary when he remarried; when he died unexpectedly, his life insurance and retirement accounts went to his ex-wife.

It doesn't take a second marriage to foul things up. I once got a letter from a young widow with three children who tried, unsuccessfully, to get her mother-in-law to give up the proceeds of a life insurance policy the mother received because her son forgot to change the beneficiary on his life insurance policy when he got married. In most cases where this happens, the parents want to give the money to the surviving spouse. But this often creates gift tax problems for the parents. This is not the legacy you want to leave behind.

Here's the checklist of what to talk about:

Do we need a will? Typically, the answer is yes. Otherwise, your state will distribute your assets, and its plan might not jibe with your wishes. Wills become particularly important if you have minor children and you both die together. If you haven't named a guardian, you could be setting up a devastating court battle over custody, or your children could wind up in foster care.

Do we need life insurance? If your spouse depends on your income, or vice versa, the answer is yes. See the previous chapter for more.

Are all our beneficiary designations current? Call your brokerage, your bank and your life insurance agent, if you have one, to update their files. Your human resources department at work can help you check and update the beneficiary for any company-provided life insurance or retirement accounts.

As you can see, a lot of work lies ahead. But calm discussion and a workable plan can help head off lots of money conflicts later. The time you spend taking care of these issues is an important investment in your marriage.

ACTION STEPS

To build your marital finances, you should do the following:

- Work out a budget together. Both of you need to agree on goals and how to get there, including any spending cuts.
- Set a "talk to me" limit for purchases above a certain amount.
- Designate a family CFO to handle bill paying and other day-to-day financial chores.
- Have regular meetings—at least once a month, but more

often if necessary—to review your progress toward your goals and make any necessary tweaks in your spending.

- Be honest. Don't hide purchases or lie about your spending. Consider allotting "no-questions-asked" money to each partner to minimize fights over small items.
- Draft a will, name a guardian for any minor children and update the beneficiaries on your retirement plans and life insurance benefits.
- When conflict arises, remember to attack the problem, not each other.
- Get professional help if you can't resolve your conflicts on your own.

Defend Yourself in the War on Consumers

THE OLD-SCHOOL RULES:
Follow the rules and you'll get a square deal.

THE BUBBLE ECONOMY RULES:
It's buyer beware, baby. If you get ripped off, it's your own fault.

THE NEW RULES:
Be a careful consumer, but support laws and regulations
that insist corporations play fair.

Ernestine the Telephone Operator was a comedy icon for a generation of viewers who watched the TV show *Laugh-In*. Created by comedienne Lily Tomlin, Ernestine embodied the indifference that AT&T, which at the time had a monopoly on telephone service, held toward its customers. "We're the telephone company," Ernestine would snort. "We don't care. We don't have to."

AT&T's monopoly didn't last, but its business model survives. Throughout the United States, businesses are irritating, ignoring and angering their customers—if not for fun, certainly for profit. What was once enough of an anomaly to be parodied is now standard operating procedure.

Who hasn't waited hours for the cable guy, or signed up for cell service that was vastly more expensive than the advertised price? Who hasn't snapped up a bargain airline seat or a good rental car rate, only to get pummeled by extra charges? Who hasn't tried to get help from a customer service line only to be put on hold, cut off, transferred to the wrong department or sent off to a call center in the nether reaches of the world, only to get a phone rep who seems as baffled by your problem as you are (but is unwilling to admit it)?

It wasn't supposed to be this way. The Internet was supposed to help us become better consumers, allowing us to search for the best deals, research the companies involved and make informed decisions.

Instead of competing transparently on price and service, though, too many companies advertise one price and then slam you with hidden fees and costs once you're a customer. Phone and pay television providers tack on "taxes" and "services charges" that aren't either, but instead are pure profit. Airlines, hotels and car rental companies lard their contracts and services with fees and other gotchas. Hidden expenses at investment companies and 401(k) providers siphon off your returns at such an egregious rate that you could end up working years longer than necessary.

There are laws against deceptive and misleading business practices, but for years they have been barely enforced. Twenty years ago, the Federal Trade Commission (FTC) had two thousand full-time employees to help with its mission of protecting consumers, according to MSNBC columnist Bob Sullivan, author of *Stop Getting Ripped Off*. Today, despite a vast expansion of its duties, including policing the Internet and fighting identity theft, the FTC has about one thousand full-time workers, says Sullivan.

Other agencies with consumer protection roles—including the Federal Communications Commission, which polices the airwaves; the Consumer Product Safety Commission; and the Securities and Exchange Commission, which protects investors—have been similarly gutted. Getting assigned to consumer protection duties in some agencies came to be considered a career cul-de-sac, since so little attention was paid to this area.

Is it any surprise, then, that financial companies in particular have made ripping off consumers a virtual art form?

Take the credit card industry. Like schoolyard bullies, they initially focused on beating up their weakest customers—those with poor credit and little sophistication. When regulators failed to step in, card issuers began seeking out more profits—and victims. They introduced ever more egregious ways to gouge their customers, from double-cycle billing (a method of charging interest even when you don't carry a balance) to universal default (a clause that allowed them to raise your rate if you fell behind with any of your other creditors).

INSIDER TERMS

Credit card issuers: Banks and other lenders that provide credit cards to customers. Credit cards that bear the Visa or MasterCard logo are issued by banks, and the leading issuers include Bank of America, JPMorgan Chase, Citigroup, Capital One, and HSBC Bank. Credit cards with the Discover logo are issued by Discover, while those labeled American Express are issued either by Amex or by a bank, depending on the card.

For most of the decade, lawmakers and regulators responded with a collective shrug. If you were dumb enough to rack up credit card debt, the feeling seemed to be, you got what you deserved. Then the credit card companies started beating up on their best customers—those with good credit scores—who suddenly saw their lines of credit cut or their rates doubled for any or no reason. Finally, the political environment changed and the tolerance for financial institution misdeeds wore thin.

In the interim between the passage of credit card reform and its implementation, the credit card companies went all out. Instead of cleaning up their act, issuers innovated brand-new ways to jerk around their customers. They imposed new fees, implemented more rate hikes, chopped credit lines and abruptly closed accounts for their best, most creditworthy customers. Their behavior in those months became a vivid illustration of how lenders had abandoned ethics, fairness and even common sense.

And it wasn't just on the credit side of their operations that financial institutions targeted the little guy. When banks saw how much money payday lenders were making—offering loans as short as two weeks for triple-digit interest rates—they tried to get in on the action. Some partnered directly with payday outfits (which now have more outlets than McDonald's, Burger King and Wendy's combined). Others began offering "payday advances" for slightly lower but still egregious fees.

But most financial institutions simply and quietly altered their overdraft policies, without notifying their customers or offering them a chance to opt out. Instead of denying overdraft transactions, banks approved, even encouraged, purchases over a depositor's limit. Some banks added hundreds of phantom dollars to the balance customers saw when they checked in at the ATM—dollars that equaled the amount of their "bounce protection"—to increase the odds people would overdraw their accounts.

Even without such tricks, keeping track of a bank balance became more challenging. Instead of writing checks for cash and spending that, or withdrawing money at an ATM, more people—encouraged by the banks—started using their debit cards for most of their purchases, vastly increasing the number of transactions whirling through their accounts.

Banks also sped up how quickly they processed checks, reducing the "float" time—between when you wrote a check and when they deducted the money—to a matter of hours, instead of days. At the same time, banks continued to put long "holds" on certain deposits, meaning that although they may deduct a check you wrote from your account the same day, when it came to a check written *to* you, they might not credit that toward your balance for as long as two weeks.

Thanks to banks' new overdraft programs, customers who misjudged their balance a single time often got slapped with hundreds of dollars in bounce fees. Instead of true overdraft protection, which taps a savings account or line of credit to cover over-limit transactions, these programs lent money directly to the customer for a fee of $35 or more per transaction, plus interest on any unpaid balances. Banks reaped a windfall of billions of dollars, mostly on the backs of the young, those with a low income and the elderly on fixed incomes.

Banks insisted consumers liked the new program because it prevented people from being "embarrassed" in the checkout line when their over-limit transactions were denied. Polls of consumers, however, repeatedly showed that the majority wanted to have the option of shutting off this feature—an option many banks refused to offer.

Again, the regulatory and legislative response for years was a collective shrug. Too few people understood how dramatically bank policies had changed or how much the most vulnerable consumers were paying for those changes.

In 2010, regulators finally pulled on the reins, requiring banks to make bounce protection an "opt-in" feature. Faced with having to sell these programs on their merits, some banks realized they couldn't put lipstick on this particular pig and abandoned the programs altogether.

While it's true that regulators and lawmakers are finally waking up after years of benign neglect, that doesn't mean open season on consumers has ended. If you don't want to continue being a victim, you need to arm yourself with the facts, an eye for fine print and a willingness to stand up for your rights. I'll start with tips for dealing with particularly "gotcha"-prone services and contracts, then follow up with advice about how to complain and win every time.

HOW TO PUSH BACK, AND WIN, AGAINST YOUR CREDIT CARD COMPANIES

The credit crunch that started in late 2007, and the recession that quickly followed, transformed the credit card industry.

Unable to tap investment markets and reeling from higher defaults, credit card issuers shut down lines of credit and jacked up rates. Customers who carried balances—once the darlings of the industry for all the interest they paid—were suddenly viewed with suspicion by some issuers. Many people saw their rates spiral, which was a disaster for their pocketbooks, and their limits cut, which was a potential disaster for their credit scores.

But all credit card issuers are not alike, and they proved that during the recession. Some trimmed credit lines prudently and protected their lowest-risk customers, while others slashed credit lines across the board, regardless of their customers' credit scores or history. Having all your credit cards with a single issuer has always made you vulnerable to that lender's whims, but the recession showed how such loyalty could be devastating to your credit if all your accounts were reduced or frozen at once.

It became abundantly clear that we need to diversify our credit accounts just as much as our investments. I'd recommend having cards from at least two different issuers, and there's nothing wrong with having more—the typical American adult has four to five major credit cards, and you can have many, many more without hurting your credit scores, as long as you don't run up big balances on those accounts.

The people who rode out the credit crunch the best were those with good credit scores and cards from several different issuers. If they didn't like how they were treated by one company, they could easily switch their business to another. And far from hurting their credit, having several major credit card accounts helped their scores.

While good credit scores didn't protect some customers from their card issuers during the recession, a sterling credit rating still is your best leverage when you're fighting back against a rate increase, a new fee or any other action you don't like. Anyone with scores of 700 or above on the 300 to 850 FICO scale is generally considered to have good credit;

scores of 750 or above mean you have excellent credit and can easily move your business elsewhere. Point that out to the card issuer that's trying to lower your limits. If the issuer won't budge, follow through on your threat.

By the way, if you have good credit, you shouldn't be paranoid about closing accounts. I'm hearing from too many people who are afraid to tell their credit card companies to take a hike after being slapped with rate increases or annual fees. There are a lot of e-mails like this one, from Betty:

"If I'm notified that an annual fee will be assessed and I cancel the card, doesn't this hurt my credit score? I don't need the card but I am afraid to cancel and ruin my good score."

It's good that Betty knows that closing accounts can hurt her scores, but she's probably more worried than she needs to be. If she has good credit scores and several other open credit card accounts, then closing a single account is unlikely to have a huge impact on her scores.

In other words, people like Betty are the last people who should be worried about telling their card issuers to take a long walk off a short pier. Yet they are. And I wouldn't put it past the credit card companies to exploit those fears. Card issuers know that their most desirable customers, the ones with the great scores, are likely to be concerned about preserving those scores. Card companies are probably banking on those good customers meekly accepting whatever fees, rate increases or other changes issuers want to impose.

There are, of course, times when you really shouldn't close a credit card account if you can possibly avoid it:

You're in the market for a major loan. When you're seeking a big loan such as a mortgage or auto financing, every credit score point may count in helping you get better rates and terms. Hold off on closing accounts until after your loan has closed.

You're trying to resuscitate a battered score. You probably want to avoid shuttering accounts, particularly credit card accounts, until you're well into the 700 range. You particularly want to preserve your oldest and highest-limit accounts when you're in credit improvement mode.

You have only one or two credit cards. Closing an account in this case may dramatically alter your so-called credit utilization ratio, which is the credit you're using compared with your open, available credit limits. Reducing that gap substantially can really hurt your scores. If you feel strongly about wanting to close a card in this situation, consider opening another credit card before you shutter the existing account.

If you aren't in any of these categories, though, you don't have to keep open an account if you don't want to. Saying no sends a powerful message to credit card issuers that there's a limit to what you'll put up with from them. If enough of their good customers walk out the door, the card companies might reconsider some of their most egregious actions.

And put your closure request in writing. Don't trust the phone reps to follow through on your request to close the account or to pass on to the higher-ups your explanation of why you're closing it. Take matters into your own hands by writing a letter to the issuer explaining exactly why you closed the account. Send one copy to the address indicated on the back of your statement and another to the card issuer's chief executive.

The next time you open an account, do a little research into which issuers treat their customers well. Policies vary widely, and some issuers do a better job than others of meeting their customers' needs. In a 2009 survey by J.D. Power, for example, American Express and Discover were the two highest-rated cards for customer satisfaction, while Capital One and HSBC ranked at the bottom.

FOR BETTER BANKING, DITCH YOUR BANK

Many people are perfectly satisfied with their banks. But a lot of you aren't. You're sick of getting socked with fees or tripped by hidden penalties or earning lousy interest rates. You're tired of being treated like a nuisance rather than a customer. And yet you have little hope that the bank down the street is any better.

But who says you have to settle for a bank? Relief could be as close as the nearest credit union. Because so many people are fuzzy about the differences between banks and credit unions, I'll highlight the three most important distinctions:

Credit unions are member owned. If you have an account at a credit union, you're a part owner in the enterprise. That may not entitle you to use the executive washroom—your CU probably doesn't even have an executive washroom—but you're likely to be seen as a person rather than as a "cost center."

Credit unions are not-for-profit. This status helps explain why interest rates tend to be significantly better, and fees fewer and smaller, at credit unions than at banks. Any profits credit unions do make are distributed as dividends to their members. Contrast that with banks, which continually invent new fees and policies to boost profits (and to pay those stunning executive salaries).

Banks really hate credit unions. President Franklin D. Roosevelt signed the Federal Credit Union Act into law in 1934 to "promote thrift and thwart usury," and banks have pretty much been gunning for them ever since. Because of their not-for-profit, cooperative structures, credit unions are exempted from most state and federal taxes. Banks have convinced themselves this is an unfair advantage and have spent a lot of effort, plus a fortune in lobbying fees, trying to legislate credit unions out of existence or at least limit who can join. (I guess they thought the money was better spent there than on, say, improving their interest rates, reducing their fees or slashing their telephone hold times.)

Fortunately for you, banks have failed pretty miserably in their efforts to contain the competition. That's why the Credit Union National Association, the CUs' trade group, can brag that virtually everyone in the United States can belong to a credit union, thanks to where they live, where they work or the associations to which they belong.

The nation's credit unions count ninety million members, and their trade association estimates that members save $8 billion a year thanks to better interest rates and reduced fees. Credit union–issued credit cards, for example, tend not to have annual fees or to charge punitive interest rates for a single late payment. Most credit unions offer free checking accounts, and penalties for overdrawing those accounts tend to be lower: a $20 or $25 fee is typical, compared with up to $39 a pop charged by banks.

Yet many people discover the benefits of credit unions almost by accident, says Pat Keefe, a spokesman for the credit union association. They join because they can get a decent rate on a car loan, say, and only gradually discover that the checking account has far fewer fees, the credit cards offer better interest rates and the mortgages aren't bad, either.

But you don't have to wait until you need a loan. Usually, finding a credit union is as easy as visiting your employer's human resources department. If you don't have an employer or you want more options, you can use the "CU Matchup" tool at Findacreditunion.com.

Based on where we live, where my husband works and our various other affiliations, the matchup tool spit out thirty-one local credit unions that might accept us. Some of them had fairly narrow membership requirements, like America's Christian Credit Union, which requires attendance at certain evangelical churches. Others were pretty darned broad, like Wescom Credit Union, which allows anyone who lives, works, worships or goes to school in Southern California to become a member.

Like bank deposits, money in credit unions is insured. Instead of the Federal Deposit Insurance Corporation, which insures bank deposits, the coverage typically is provided by the National Credit Union Administration, but both agencies are backed by the full faith and credit of the federal government. And you typically aren't restricted to using your own credit union's ATMs. Most CUs either offer fee-free access to a huge network of ATMs or reimburse your fees if you use other institutions' machines.

Are credit unions perfect? Of course not. No institution run by humans and their computers could possibly claim to satisfy everyone all the time. Occasionally I'll hear of a credit union that's instituted some silly fee, and too many opted for the bounce protection I excoriated earlier. But most of the folks I talk to who have abandoned banks for credit unions are thrilled they made the switch. If you're sick of your bank, why don't you follow suit?

HOW TO GET A BETTER DEAL FROM YOUR PHONE PROVIDERS

There's a reason your phone bills make you want to scream. Phone service is a classic example of the "gotcha" contract. You think you're signing up for one price, but when the bill comes it's much higher, larded with overage fees, unexpected charges and services you didn't authorize. Fortunately, you can do something about all this. Here's your game plan:

First, consider your home phone service. Unless reception in your home is poor, you typically can save money by using your cell for your long-distance calls, says Jody Rohlena, editor of *ShopSmart* magazine, a sister publication of *Consumer Reports*.

You might save even more by dropping your landline entirely, but Rohlena worries you may regret that decision if you ever need to call 911. Emergency operators can find landline addresses easily if you can't talk, because those are wired into the system. Not so cell numbers, so you should at least weigh the risk before you terminate your landline service. MSNBC columnist Bob Sullivan uses only a cell and isn't worried about the 911 issue "because I'm young and able. If I were my parents' age, I'd think twice about it."

Some options:

1. An easy solution for people who want the wired-in 911 service is to downgrade their landline to basic phone service with no long-distance privileges, which typically costs about $15 a month, Sullivan says. The phone companies don't advertise basic service, he says, but most offer it.

2. If it's just the convenience of the home handset you'd miss, you can find Bluetooth-enabled cordless phones that allow you to use your cell service with a home handset. The handsets can also help you make calls in any cell "dead zones" of your house.

3. Internet phone service can offer significant savings for those who want or need a landline. MagicJack, which connects your phone to your computer for unlimited calling, costs $40 a year (but the software you download allows magicJack to display ads on your computer). Vonage plugs into your high-speed modem and allows you to use your existing phone system for about $25 a month. To use Skype, you can either use a computer microphone and speakers or purchase a Skype-enabled phone. Unlimited calls to U.S. and Canadian landlines costs $2.95 a month; for $12.95 a month, you can get unlimited calls to landlines in more than forty countries worldwide.

4. Digital phone service, offered by cable companies and other providers over broadband connections, usually includes unlimited local and domestic long-distance calling, as well as features such as call forwarding and caller ID, all for around $40 a month. You typically can register your number with your carrier to get 911 address location service.

But these services have another downside: if the Internet goes out or the power goes off, you have no phone. With old-fashioned landline service, you can plug a nonelectric handset into the wall and still have service.

If you're intrigued by digital phone service, check into whether you can save by bundling it with your high-speed Internet and/or television service, Rohlena recommends.

Reevaluate your cell plan. An informal *Consumer Reports* poll found two-thirds of respondents failed to use all their cell plan minutes each month. So "the A–No. 1 way to save on your cell phone is to get the right plan for your calling pattern," says Elisabeth Leamy, ABC News consumer correspondent and the author of *Save Big*. The variables include:

- How many "anytime" minutes you use
- Whom you call frequently
- How many lines you need
- How much data capacity you need (for e-mail and Web browsing)
- How much texting you do

The problem, Leamy says, is that cell phone companies "offer a zillion different plans that are all just slightly different, making it almost impossible to compare plans at one carrier, not to mention at multiple carriers."

Impossible, that is, unless you have help. *ShopSmart* recommends two Web sites, BillShrink and Validas (www.myvalidas.com), to aid you in figuring out how to save. BillShrink is free but requires you to input some data from your bills. For $5, Validas will download your latest cell phone bill and do a detailed analysis.

Leamy used Validas to find a better phone plan for a Virginia family of nine (two parents and seven kids) as part of a savings makeover series for ABC's *Good Morning America*. The family had so many lines that they qualified for a small business plan and will save nearly $1,300 a year.

When I tested the sites, I was impressed with the results. Validas recommended a plan that saved us $10 a month with our current carrier. BillShrink suggested a variety of options at other carriers that could save us as much as $1,346 annually when our contract is up.

Validas also notes which numbers you call the most. This can help you take maximum advantage of "friends and family" plans that allow you to talk free to five or ten other people. If you use this option, don't include people who have the same carrier you do, Rohlena advises, because those "in-network" calls are free anyway.

Consider prepaid options. Neither BillShrink nor Validas will mention prepaid phones, but they can be a great solution if you're not a big talker, Rohlena says. Anyone who uses fewer than two hundred minutes a month and many people who talk less than three hundred minutes a month should consider prepaid, Sullivan says.

Prepaid service doesn't require a contract and usually costs $30 a month or less, with unlimited talk and text plans topping out at $50 a month. Instead of paying a monthly bill, you can:

- Pay as you go (minutes usually cost 5¢ to 25¢ each, often with a per-day access fee of $1 to $2)
- Buy blocks of minutes
- Buy a monthly plan with a set number of minutes for a fee

Prepaid carriers include MetroPCS, TracFone and Virgin Mobile. The big four carriers, AT&T, Sprint Nextel, T-Mobile and Verizon, also offer prepaid service. Parents often use prepaid services when buying phone service for their kids so they can limit the bill—but more on that in a bit.

Adjust on the fly. Carriers will typically let you switch plans to one that better suits your needs even if the change is only temporary. Going to Canada? Ask if they have a North America plan, Sullivan recommends. For $20 extra, you could avoid hundreds of dollars in roaming fees. Family crisis? You can bump up your plan to one that offers more anytime minutes, then bump it down again once the crisis has passed.

You can even ask for these accommodations after the fact. Many times, carriers are willing to retroactively change your plan. Even if your carrier won't accommodate you that way, it may be willing to knock down the cost of your mistake—requiring you to pay only half the bill for all those extra texts your daughter sent, for example.

Just make sure the carrier doesn't extend your contract in exchange for making these changes, Sullivan warns. Consider asking twice: first when the phone rep you're talking to agrees to the change, and again before you hang up. You might say, "This doesn't extend my contract, right?" and then at the end of the call ask, "When does my current contract expire?" just to make sure.

Scrutinize the add-ons. Don't pay for what you're unlikely to use. Some carriers offer roadside assistance, for example, but you don't need it if you have auto club coverage. You may not even need a national long-distance plan if most of your calls are local, Leamy says. Ditto for international plans if you rarely call out of the country. You can add additional coverage should you need it, but you shouldn't pay monthly for a feature you don't typically use.

Also, cell phone insurance is a waste of money, Leamy declares.

"Most people never use this insurance, and there are lots of exclusions that make it hard to exercise. In most cases you can get a new handset or parts easily and cheaply just by searching Craigslist or eBay."

Deal with kids and phones. Most kids will be agitating for a phone by middle school, if not before. For the youngest kids, limited-access phones like the Firefly allow parents to decide which numbers can be called. Older kids will want more freedom to call and text. (A Nielsen study published in early 2010 found that most mobile users use more texts than calls, and the typical teenager sends 3,146 monthly texts, or ten per waking hour. Kids under twelve sent 1,146 messages per month.) There are two main philosophies:

1. Give them limits. Sullivan is a big believer in limiting the minutes and texts you provide. That means monitoring your kids' cell usage pretty closely to avoid overage charges, if you use a family plan, or opting for prepaid service. Virgin Mobile's Pay As You Go option, for example, allows you to buy two hundred texts for $5 or one thousand texts for $10 when you add them to a prepaid phone plan, which start at $20 for two hundred minutes.

2. Kids will talk. Teenagers will find a way to communicate with each other, which means if they run out of texts they'll spend all their time on the computer instant-messaging each other, Rohlena says. Families may be better off buying large blocks of texts or unlimited texting as part of their service.

Other ways to cut the texting bill:

Turn it off. Your children may report you to Child Protective Services, of course, but it's one way to ensure you don't get slaughtered with texting charges. If you don't have kids and don't use texting, shutting it off will keep you from paying for unwanted incoming texts, Leamy says.

Turn off premium texting. Some texts are way more expensive than others, because they actually sign you up for subscriptions and other services (weather alerts, sports alerts, jokes, coupons, interactive radio) that trigger a fee. The carriers will allow you to turn off premium texting, but the services are imperfect, and some may slip through. So make sure your kids know not to sign up for these services, which are typically initiated through special four-, five- or six-digit numbers called "short codes."

Use your computer. You can send a text via e-mail or instant message to a cell phone and avoid texting charges (although the receiver will still pay). Most instant-messaging services allow you to send a text to a cell simply by entering "1" plus the person's ten-digit number as the contact's username. To send via e-mail, you have to know the recipient's carrier and put his or her number in front of the carrier's suffix. An AT&T user's suffix is txt.att.net, so someone with the 555-123-4567 phone number would have the address 5551234567@txt.att.net. Other carriers' suffixes include:

- T-Mobile: @tmomail.net
- Virgin Mobile: @vmobl.com
- Sprint: @messaging.sprintpcs.com
- Verizon: @vtext.com

Some of the carriers also provide the ability to send a text message via their Web sites, Leamy says. For example, Nextel (now part of Sprint) has long provided this service for others to easily contact their subscribers.

Use an iPhone app. The textPlus app offers free, unlimited texting between iPhone users who have it loaded. The app's creator, GOGII, claims millions of users—"including a huge teen fan base."

Finally, make sure to review your cell service at least once a year to see if you can get a better deal. Plans change frequently, as may your calling patterns. A little vigilance can pay off in a lot of savings.

TRAVEL INDUSTRY GOTCHAS

If you want decent service, plenty of perks and fewer fees, there are two ways to go. One is to qualify for elite traveler status with an airline or hotel chain, which typically involves flying more than twenty-five thousand miles each year and spending dozens of nights on the road. If you travel that much, then concentrating your business with one airline and its partners and one hotel chain is a savvy move.

The other way is to be a smarter traveler, able to see and avoid the gotchas in advance. To be a smarter traveler, here are some to the traps you need to avoid.

Trap #1: Limiting your search

The biggest "gotcha" is paying too much. Unfortunately, there's no single Web site that always has the best deals. To find a good rate, you'll need to scour the Web. You might start with major travel sites like Expedia, Travelocity or Orbitz and then check out the prices at Hotwire and Priceline.com. Or you can go to Kayak, which aggregates results from those sites as well as from travel providers, like JetBlue and Southwest, that don't appear on other travel sites. But you still may want to visit the individual sites of airlines, hotels and rental cars to see if you can find better deals there. If you're signed up for a travel provider's frequent traveler program, you'll get e-mails about special deals; if you're on Twitter and Facebook, you can sign up to get special offers, as well.

With hotels and cars, the earlier you book, the better. Booking weeks in advance allows you to hedge against future price increases, but you're not locked in if rates should drop. (In most cases, there's no penalty for canceling a reservation if you find a cheaper rate later. Some hotels offer somewhat lower rates if you pay in advance and agree to forfeit your payment if you cancel; I avoid those like the plague, since the discount usually isn't enough to compensate for the risk.)

With airlines, when you book matters. Bing Travel (www.bing .com/travel/) offers a "farecast" feature that lets you know if airfares are likely to rise or fall so you'll have a better idea when to book.

Trap #2: Not factoring in fees and taxes

Most of the major travel sites, including Expedia, Travelocity, Orbitz, Kayak and Hotwire, show you total costs that include fees and taxes paid by every traveler so you can make a general comparison. But they won't tip you off to every fee you're likely to face.

Airlines are famously charging for virtually everything that used to be free, from food to checking bags to the privilege of selecting a seat, and their fees differ substantially. Concentrating your travel with one provider will help familiarize you with its fees, but you'll want to do some extra research on a provider's Web site before booking the flight. Airline A might seem to offer the best fare, but once you add in its $25 baggage fee and $50 "seat selection" charge, Airline B, which doesn't charge either, might be the better choice.

Still, trying to make apples-to-apples comparisons is tough when the fees vary so much. Here's just a small sample of the huge variation in bag fees that make comparison shopping tough:

- AirTran charges $15 for the first bag but a whopping $50 for the second and each additional bag.
- Alaska used to charge $15 for the first bag; now it charges $20 plus $20 for the second and third and $50 for each additional bag.
- American charges $25 for the first bag, $35 for the second, $100 each for bags three to five and $200 for each bag beyond that . . . unless you're flying to or from Canada, in which case the first bag is $15 and the second is $25.

Got that? I've covered only three of the twelve major domestic airlines, each of which has different policies on number of bags, how much to charge when bags are over fifty pounds and what exact measures qualify a bag as "oversized" and trigger additional hefty fees.

Hotels have gotten in on the act with "resort fees" (which may pay for a tiny fitness center and a copy of *USA Today* in the morning), Internet access charges, outrageous phone fees and exorbitant parking charges. Again, scour the hotel's Web site for these fees before you book. Don't fire up your laptop or pick up the hotel phone before you determine how much it will cost you. If you get slapped with an unexpected charge, ask that it be removed. Most hotels interested in repeat business will accommodate you (and that's yet another reason to sign up for their frequent traveler plan—to show you plan to return).

Interestingly, it's the expensive hotels that are more likely to ding you with a bunch of add-on charges. Lower-budget hotel chains aimed at business travelers often offer the best overall deals, with reasonable room rates combined with free Internet, free fitness rooms and often free breakfast. Go figure.

Some of the most stunning fees you'll find are in your rental car contract. State and local governments have discovered rental car drivers are the perfect patsies: in many areas, various government-mandated charges make up 20 to 40 percent of the total bill. Even airports that didn't have such fees in the recent past, including Los Angeles International (LAX) and New York's John F. Kennedy, now lard them on. At LAX, for example, car renters pay "airport concession" and "customer facility" fees as well as a "California Tourism Commission assessment."

In other words, tourists to La La Land get to pay the state to lure other tourists to La La Land. Government agencies have been able to add these charges with impunity because they're levied on rental car drivers who don't live or vote in the area—a classic "taxation without representation" situation.

You may be able to reduce the fees by renting away from major airports. You'll still pay taxes and some fees if you rent from a chain's downtown or suburban location rather than its airport site, but the total is likely to be less. You'll have to weigh the cost and hassle of getting to the alternate location against any savings.

You also need to be on the alert for other tack-on fees, including:

Late fees. Most agencies use a twenty-four-hour clock that starts when you pick up the car. If you get the vehicle at noon, you're expected to return it by noon on the final day of your contract. Get stuck in traffic on the way to the airport and you could face a hefty fine. Be late enough, and you'll be charged for an extra day. The best cure? Prevention. Check local traffic conditions and leave plenty of time to get to the airport.

Fuel charges. If you fail to fill your tank before returning, the agency could charge you $5 a gallon or more for the missing fuel. Prepaying for a full tank isn't usually the best alternative, though, since any gas you don't use is essentially a donation to the car rental company's bottom line. Most of the time, you're better off skipping the prepaid options. Instead, look for a convenient gas station as you leave the airport and use it when the time comes to return your car. And *make sure the tank is full when you get the car.* If it's not, insist that the agency rep note the fuel level on your rental contract so that you don't wind up paying for the last driver's gas as well as your own.

Additional or young drivers. Some rental companies allow you to add another driver at no charge; others slap on a fee of $25 or more. Drivers under twenty-five often face a surcharge that can range from $10 to $80. These fees may not be disclosed before you book; you'll need to ask.

One-way charges. If you're not going to drop the car off at the same location where you picked it up, you may pay a lot more—or you may not. The cost depends on a number of factors, including the agency, the cities involved and even the type of car. Don't assume you'll have to pay through the nose; cast a wide net and check out the prices for various types of cars at various agencies before you book.

Mileage fees. You can still find these charges at smaller agencies and specialty rental companies. Typically, you're allowed a set number of miles, with an added fee of 15¢ to 50¢ for every mile you drive over the contract's limit. If you're renting from a small company, inquire about mileage limits and try to stay within them. Or, better yet, opt for an agency that offers unlimited mileage.

Extra cleaning charges. Do something really disgusting in or to your rental, and you may pay dearly for it. Most rental agencies reserve the right to charge you a premium for any deep cleaning that's required before they can rent the vehicle to another customer. So if somebody gets sick in the car, spills something gooey or doesn't quite make it to the potty, you might save some money (and embarrassment) by paying an auto detailer to clean up the mess before you return the car. Even if the mess isn't egregious you should clean it up and discard any garbage before returning the car if you want to keep the agency employees happy. A happy employee may be less likely to turn you in for that scratch or rat you out for a not-quite-full tank.

Various equipment rentals. Navigation systems, ski racks, child car seats and satellite radio can each boost the cost of a rental by several dollars a day. Whether the convenience is worth the cost is an entirely personal matter. You should also know that your request for a certain item doesn't guarantee its availability. If it's really important—like that car seat—consider bringing your own.

Damage that's not your fault. Most major car rental agencies now hold renters responsible for damage caused by "acts of nature," including hailstorms, floods, tornadoes, hurricanes and other disasters. Even if you couldn't have predicted the act or prevented the damage, you're on the hook. Less catastrophic damage can get you in trouble, too. Many rental agencies charge drivers hundreds of dollars for relatively minor dings or scrapes.

If you don't do a careful walk around your vehicle and report existing damage to the company before driving away, you could end up shelling out for damage caused by the last driver. When you return the car, consider taking a few photos or a short clip with your camcorder or video-enabled phone as proof you brought it back in good shape. If it's dark and you're stuck without a flash camera, ask a car rental employee to drive it to a better-lit spot for your inspection.

If you do get saddled with a repair bill, you may have insurance or other coverage that will pay it, but even that is problematic.

Trap #3: Getting lost in the car insurance maze

The usual advice you hear—skip the coverage the rental car company offers you—is way too simplistic. In general, the coverage you've got on your personal vehicle will carry over to a rental, says Loretta Worters of the Insurance Information Institute. Your homeowners or renters policy probably covers your personal property if it's stolen from the car.

But if you've dropped comprehensive and collision coverage on your own car, something many people do to save money on older vehicles, you don't have that coverage for your rental, either. That means you could be held responsible for damage to or the theft of your rental. You might be saved by your credit card if you used a Visa or Diners Club or one of the higher-end MasterCard, Discover or American Express cards that promise to pay for damage to a rental car. Even then, though, there are limits. For example:

- Certain vehicles, including SUVs, luxury cars, pickups and vans, often aren't covered.
- Long-term rentals (over two weeks, for example) may not be covered.
- Losses caused by an unauthorized driver or a driver who violates the rental agreement typically aren't covered.

If you get popped for driving under the influence, for example, or you take the car out of the geographic area designated by the contract, your credit card issuer probably won't pay.

There's no shortcut: you need to review both your auto insurance policy and your credit card's benefit guide. (If you don't have those handy, call the companies and have them send you copies.)

And then there's the whole "loss of use" issue. If you wreck your rental, the company may bill you for the money it supposedly loses while the car is being repaired or replaced, along with "administrative" charges and "diminution of value" fees. You don't want to be on the hook for these charges, which can total hundreds of dollars, so check to see if your insurance or your credit card covers them. Even then, you may still face a tussle, because credit card companies often balk at paying these fees, says Michelle Crouch, who investigated credit card coverage for CreditCards.com.

"The credit card companies say, 'We'll pay it, but we want to see the rental car company's fleet utilization log' to prove there were no cars available to replace the damaged one," Crouch says. "But a lot of times the rental car company won't provide that log because they say it's proprietary."

Judging from her research and response to the column, Crouch says Visa has the best reputation for covering these fees. Discover doesn't cover them at all. With other cards, the bigger the stink the cardholder made, the more likely they were to get some concessions, she says. "Most of the ones who really made a fuss about it ended up at least getting some of the fees waived," Crouch says.

If you don't want the fight, you aren't covered for loss of use or your coverage has other gaps, you should at least consider buying the rental car company's coverage, usually called a "loss damage waiver" or "collision damage waiver." (Don't just buy everything that's offered, though. Coverage for personal effects, illness and extra liability protection often duplicates what you already have.)

Or you could change the card you use. Diners Club offers no-cost primary insurance to all cardholders, meaning that you don't have to use your auto coverage first or even notify your insurer that there's been an incident (which could protect you from a premium increase). You can get the same type of coverage from American Express by enrolling in its Premium Car Rental Protection, which charges a flat $24.95 fee each time you rent a car ($17.95 for Californians).

You also might consider taking the rental car agency's coverage if you've had an at-fault accident recently or a series of other claims against your auto insurance. That way, you won't have to notify your insurer if you have yet another incident. The few bucks you'll pay for the coverage could be dwarfed by higher premiums or the hassle of finding another insurer after yours drops you cold.

HOW TO COMPLAIN AND WIN

No matter how careful a consumer you are, sooner or later you will get stung with a product that doesn't work, a fee you shouldn't have to pay or a policy that simply doesn't make sense.

The good news is that you can complain effectively, and get results. You just have to know how. You must:

Know your rights. Sometimes companies get away with egregious behavior simply because their victims don't know the law. It's illegal, for example, for a company to knowingly report false credit information or for collection agencies to keep calling you after you've told them in writing to stop. Knowing the law, and letting the companies know you know, is sometimes effective in getting bad behavior to stop.

If your complaint involves a contract, warranty or guarantee, read all the fine print that came with it. You don't necessarily have to limit yourself to the remedies prescribed in these documents, but you should at least know what the company promised.

Know what you want. Be clear in your mind and in all your communications with the company about what you want to happen. That way you won't get sidetracked. After all, the customer service rep's job, typically, is not to make you happy. It's to get you off the phone.

If the rep suggests ways to fix your problem at all, it will usually be ways that don't cost her or the company much. When my new laptop's hard drive failed for the second time, Dell wanted to send me yet another replacement part. But I knew from the start of my call that I wasn't getting off the phone until a replacement computer was on its way.

I'm assuming, by the way, that what you want is both reasonable and doable. Your definition of those two terms may vary from the company's, but you can't be ridiculous about it. The dry cleaner that ruined your jacket, for example, should be expected to buy you a new one. You shouldn't expect free dry cleaning for life.

Be concise. Boil your story down to its essential elements; you might even practice first with a friend before you pick up the phone. Nattering on about irrelevant details will just make it easier for the rep to tune out or miss the point. Besides, you're going to have to repeat your story over and over and over to get results. Might as well save yourself some time by editing in advance.

Don't be a jerk. My husband, the most effective complainer I know, puts it this way: You don't have to be nice, necessarily. You do have to be polite. Hubby has used this not-nice-but-polite approach to get us a 50 percent discount on a garage door that was incorrectly installed, a free upgrade on our TiVo service (again, botched installation) and a number of other concessions from companies that initially insisted there was no way to accommodate us.

He isn't sweet, understanding or particularly patient when he deals with people who resist giving him what he wants. But he is unfailingly civil. Rude behavior just gives the rep an opportunity to hang up on you or feel justified in not helping you.

I've found being nice sometimes greases the wheels. Some reps are so used to being berated by customers that they melt pretty quickly when dealing with someone who's pleasant. My favorite ploy is to chat them up, then ask them how they would handle my problem if it were theirs, instead of mine. Many times, they'll respond to this treatment by connecting me with someone who can actually solve my dilemma.

Know that the company's problems are not your problems. Customer service reps love to tell you exactly why the company's procedures don't allow them to do what you need them to do. Guess what: you don't have to care. How the company chooses to conduct its business is not your concern. What is your concern is getting your problem fixed, however the company ultimately decides to do it.

Carve out some time. I'm convinced some companies try to wear you out with excessively long hold times. You can't force them to pick up the phone, but you can fight back by outwaiting them. Get yourself a portable phone or, better yet, a portable with a headset. That way you can do other things to keep your sanity while waiting for the company to see reason.

It took me three hours on a Saturday morning to persuade Dell to see things my way. I survived innumerable transfers, two disconnects and endless stretches on hold largely because I wasn't tethered to a desk the whole time. Thanks to my portable headset, I was able to play with my daughter, sort mail and even do a little light housekeeping while I talked to Sandy, Matt, Phyllis, Jason, Raina and the rest of the Dell crew about how they were going to get me a replacement computer.

Get names and call-back numbers. Sometimes you don't have three hours in a row to spend on the phone. Rather than start over from the beginning each time you dial, make sure you know how to get back in touch with the people who handled your last call. Having a name and number also comes in handy when you get transferred into voice-mail hell or the phone simply goes dead—not that a customer service rep would ever, ever deliberately hang up on you. (*Ahem*, Sandy.)

Take notes. I don't know why, but reps are inordinately impressed when you can tell them exactly when you were told what by whom. These details can also help when you're enlisting others to come to your aid (see the next page).

When in doubt, get it in writing. Consumer advocates usually recommend putting disputes in writing. The reality is that most problems get handled over the phone, and you don't necessarily have to conduct business by snail mail. If the issue involves a lot of money, taxes, legal issues or your credit report, however, put everything in writing and send the letters by certified mail, return receipt requested. Keep a log of all your communications with the company and copies of every relevant piece of paper.

Keep moving up the ladder. You probably know that if you can't get what you want from a phone rep, you should ask to speak to a supervisor. But the folks with the real power may be several rungs up the ladder. If you strike out, try the company's marketing or public relations division. A letter sent to the company's president or CEO can often break through a logjam like nothing else. If a quick Google search doesn't turn up the name and address, check the Web site. Don't fall for the customer service address that's prominently listed; you want the address where the CEO actually does business. If it's a publicly traded company, you'll find that in its SEC filings in the "Investor Relations" tab.

Social media may help you, or it may not. Social media expert Peter Shankman tells of the time he tried to get Delta's attention about a travel problem with repeated tweets to @Delta, only to get a response (and an offer to help) from @SouthwestAir. At least somebody was monitoring Delta-related tweets on Twitter, he says—too bad it wasn't Delta.

If the company is violating the law, you may need to contact the appropriate regulator. You'll need to do some research to find the right office (a Google search such as "Who regulates banks?" can get you started), but you can't necessarily count on results. The Federal Trade Commission, for example, collects complaints about credit bureaus, but typically only acts if it sees a pattern of problems emerging. You may get a better response from your state's attorney general or office of consumer affairs.

The situation may get better for consumers once the Bureau of Consumer Financial Protection, which was created as part of the 2010 financial reform bill, gets up and running. The bureau will take over consumer protection duties from a number of other federal agencies, including the Federal Reserve Board, the Federal Trade Commission and the National Credit Union Administration, and will provide a single toll-free number consumers can call for help.

If you're having a problem with the government itself, the ultimate resource may be your local, state or federal representative. Many lawmakers pride themselves on taking care of their constituents on this grassroots level.

Then there's always the option of alerting the media. If the company's behavior has been particularly terrible or you think you might be part of a trend, you can seek out a sympathetic blogger or try contacting your local newspaper or television station to see if you can interest them in your plight. That's the way one of my former colleagues at the *Los Angeles Times* discovered that a local phone utility was charging many of its customers for broadband service that didn't work. The utility kept insisting that there was no problem, or that customer complaints were "isolated incidents." After the reporter heard from a bunch of victims of these "isolated incidents" and wrote a front-page story about them, the company was forced to stop billing people for something they never got.

If nothing else works, you can always hire a lawyer. It's not the easiest or most cost-effective way to get what you want, but sometimes it pays off. When a company is particularly entrenched in ignoring its consumers, sometimes that law firm letterhead is the only thing that will get their attention. For lawyers versed in consumer issues, visit the National Association of Consumer Attorneys at www.naca.net.

These tips and techniques can help you level the playing field, but you're still David in a valley of corporate Goliaths. There is no substitute for effective regulation and consistent enforcement of laws already on the books that prohibit unfair, deceptive and misleading practices. Those who say regulation isn't necessary simply aren't living in the same world as the rest of us, where the typical family pays nearly $1,000 a year in unnecessary and hidden fees, according to Bob Sullivan's research.

You can support effective consumer protection in several ways:

Stay informed. The Consumerist (http://consumerist.com) offers a wealth of informative and entertaining updates "about dealing with everything from non-existent customer service to onerous cell-phone contracts to ever-shrinking (and ever-more-expensive) grocery products." The Consumerist doesn't accept advertising and is owned by the nonprofit Consumers Union, which publishes *Consumer Reports* magazine. Speaking of which:

Sign up for *Consumer Reports*. The magazine's site, www.consumer reports.org, is another good place to find advice, tips and information about consumer-related legislation and regulation. Much of the content is free, but it's well worth paying the $26 annual subscription for access to detailed reviews and other data.

Voice your opinion. You can find your congressional representative at www.house.gov and your U.S. senators at www.senate.gov. You can weigh in on proposed financial regulations being considered by the Federal Reserve at www.federalreserve.gov/generalinfo/foia/proposed regs.cfm. Find out how to contact state and local lawmakers for the issues that concern you, and speak up.

ACTION STEPS

Here are some ways you can be a savvier consumer:

- Diversify your credit accounts so you have cards from different issuers. Get cards from at least two different lenders.
- Don't be afraid to close an occasional credit account if you have good scores and plenty of other open accounts and you won't be looking for a major loan in the next few months. Shuttering an account is sometimes the best way to get your message across that you don't like how you're being treated.
- If you're not happy with your bank, consider switching to a credit union. Findacreditunion.com can help you locate credit unions you may be able to join.
- Make sure your phone service still fits your needs. Drop unnecessary services and let Validas analyze your cell phone bill for possible savings.
- Search broadly when looking for airfares, hotel rooms and rental cars. Don't forget to factor in add-on fees, which can really increase the cost of travel.
- Check back two weeks before your trip to see if hotel or rental car costs have dropped, and rebook if so.
- Review your auto insurance and credit card coverage before renting a car. In addition to getting a written copy of your benefits, call and ask, "Am I covered for loss of use, administration fees and diminution of value?" Consider signing up for the rental company's loss damage waiver or collision damage waiver if there are holes in your coverage.
- When you need to contact customer service, know your rights, what you want and how to move your complaint up the ladder.
- Be a better consumer by staying informed and urging your lawmakers to support effective regulation.

CONCLUSION

At the beginning of this book I warned you about the "Money Fundamentalists"—those who believe in black-and-white, one-size-fits-all solutions. But the world of personal finance, and the broader world of our economy, is complex and ever changing. What works for one person may not work for another, and the rules that guided one generation may not serve the next.

Money Fundamentalism really falls short when it attributes complicated problems to simple causes. For example, some have tried to lay the blame for the subprime meltdown and subsequent Great Recession entirely on "stupid, greedy homeowners" who took on loans they shouldn't have. But focusing just on individuals ignores Wall Street's role in pushing these loans and then creating dangerous derivatives and other financial instruments that multiplied the impact as defaults climbed. The "stupid, greedy homeowners" explanation also ignores lawmakers who made it easier for "too-big-to-fail" banks to make these big bets, and regulators who failed to spot those risks or protect consumers from unethical, predatory companies.

Similarly, soaring bankruptcy rates have been attributed to profligate, immoral consumers—a worldview that conveniently airbrushes out the irresponsibility of lenders, the stagnation of incomes over the past decade and the burgeoning health insurance crisis that left millions vulnerable to catastrophic medical bills.

We need to take responsibility for our own financial lives. We should live within our means, eliminate toxic debt, protect ourselves with insurance and savings and invest for our futures. The ten commandments of money are all about making the most of what you have and positioning yourself for a prosperous life.

But the Great Recession has vividly demonstrated that personal responsibility alone isn't enough, since what others do can have profound impacts on our lives, our employment prospects and the value of our investments. Your efforts to build prosperity may be undermined by a neighbor who doesn't understand those concepts, a lender who gives that neighbor a too-expensive mortgage, Wall Street speculators that make dangerous bets based on that neighbor's shaky finances and regulators who allow all this to happen.

Personal financial literacy—educating ourselves on the realities of the new world we live in and implementing the financial strategies that will work in it—will allow us to weather the bad times better and maximize our fortunes in the good times. But we'd all be better off if our efforts to be more personally responsible were met with corporations that acted responsibly as well—and regulators who were empowered to strike against those who would mislead and deceive.

RESOURCES

If you want to read more about some of the topics and issues discussed in this book, here's where you can go.

CHAPTER 1

Budgeting: Harvard University bankruptcy expert Elizabeth Warren outlines the 50/30/20 budget in a book she wrote with her daughter, Amelia Warren Tyagi, called *All Your Worth: The Ultimate Lifetime Money Plan* (New York: Free Press, 2005). Their earlier book, *The Two-Income Trap: Why Middle-Class Parents Are Going Broke* (New York: Basic Books, 2003), reviews the macroeconomic trends that have led to increased bankruptcy filings.

If you're self-employed or have a side business, check out *The Money Book for Freelancers, Part-Timers, and the Self-Employed: The Only Personal Finance System for People with Not-So-Regular Jobs* by Joseph D'Agnese and Denise Kiernan (New York: Three Rivers Press, 2010). These two freelancers offer advice honed by trial and error on budgeting methods that work when your income isn't regular.

Saving money: *The Complete Tightwad Gazette: Promoting Thrift as a Viable Alternative Lifestyle* by Amy Dacyczyn (New York: Villard, 1998) remains in print all these years later because it is jam-packed with money-saving advice and tips—some of them pretty far out, but most of them usable by a typical American household.

Worthy successors with great money-saving ideas include:

Debt-Proof Living: The Complete Guide to Living Financially Free by Mary Hunt (n.p.: DPL Press, 2005); *Miserly Moms: Living Well on Less in a Tough Economy* by Jonni McCoy (Bloomington, MN: Bethany House, 2009); *365 Ways to Live Cheap!: Your Everyday Guide to Saving Money* by Trent Hamm (Avon, MA: Adams Media, 2008) of Simple Dollar; and *10,001 Ways to Live Large on a Small Budget* by the writers of Wise Bread (New York: Skyhorse, 2009).

Revising attitudes about money: The bible of the voluntary simplicity movement, and an important read for anyone wanting greater control over finances, is *Your Money or Your Life: 9 Steps to Transforming Your Relationship with Money and Achieving Financial Independence* by Vicki Robin and Joe Dominguez with Monique Tilford (New York: Penguin, 2008).

For more inspirational reading, check out *Get Satisfied: How Twenty People Like You Found the Satisfaction of Enough* edited by Carol Holst (n.p.: Easton Studio Press, 2007).

But you'll also want to check out *The Ultimate Cheapskate's Road Map to True Riches: A Practical (and Fun) Guide to Enjoying Life More by Spending Less* by Jeff Yeager (New York: Broadway, 2007) and his follow-up, *The Cheapskate Next Door: The Surprising Secrets of Americans Living Happily Below Their Means* (New York: Broadway, 2010).

If you're serious about growing your wealth, another classic is *The Millionaire Next Door: The Surprising Secrets of America's Wealthy* by Thomas J. Stanley and William D. Danko (Atlanta: Longstreet Press, 1996). Stanley's follow-up, *Stop Acting Rich . . . and Start Living Like a Real Millionaire* (Hoboken, NJ: John Wiley & Sons, 2009), is another good read.

The financial crisis: Some terrific books are available that explain what happened and why. One of the first to appear was *The Wall Street Journal Guide to the End of Wall Street as We Know It: What You Need to Know About the Greatest Financial Crisis of Our Time—and How to Survive It* by Dave Kansas (New York: Harper, 2009); Kansas is a longtime financial reporter and *Wall Street Journal* veteran. Another early arrival, *Chain of Blame: How Wall Street Caused the Mortgage and Credit Crisis* by Paul Muolo and Mathew Padilla (Hoboken, NJ: John Wiley & Sons, 2010), was recently updated. For a real page-turner, though, you can't beat *The Big Short: Inside the Doomsday Machine* (New York: W. W. Norton, 2010); author Michael Lewis finds fascinating characters to help tell the tale and he manages to explain concepts like credit default swaps and collateralized debt obligations in ways that won't make your head spin.

CHAPTER 2

Credit and credit scoring: Allow me to recommend my first book, *Your Credit Score: Your Money and What's at Stake: How to Improve the 3-Digit Number That Shapes Your Financial Future* (Upper Saddle River, NJ: FT Press, 2009). Currently in its third edition, it's the best-selling book on the topic and explains how credit scores work, why they're important and what to do to improve yours.

Dealing with a financial crisis: If you're in the midst of a financial crisis, read Sally Herigstad's excellent *Help! I Can't Pay My Bills: Surviving a Financial Crisis* (New York: St. Martin's Griffin, 2007), a practical how-to to surviving a fiscal crunch by a CPA who lived through one. And if you're wrestling with creditors and collection agencies, be sure to check out consumer advocate Gerri Detweiler's helpful site, Debt CollectionAnswers.com.

CHAPTER 3

Troubled mortgages: The best book I've read on dealing with unaffordable home loans is attorney Stephen Elias's *The Foreclosure Survival Guide: Keep Your House or Walk Away with Money in Your Pocket* (Berkeley: Nolo, 2010). Elias's experienced, clear-eyed advice can help you determine whether to fight for your house, how to do so and, if foreclosure is inevitable, how to get through the process in the best financial and mental shape possible.

Bankruptcy: Another of Elias's books, cowritten with attorneys Albin Renauer and Robin Leonard, is *How to File for Chapter 7 Bankruptcy* (Berkeley: Nolo, 2009).

CHAPTER 4

Investing: One book, *The Little Book of Common Sense Investing: The Only Way to Guarantee Your Fair Share of Stock Market Returns*, by John Bogle (Hoboken, NJ: John Wiley & Sons, 2007), encapsulates the philosophy behind low-cost index fund investing.

The Great Depression: *Freedom from Fear: The American People in Depression and War, 1929–1945* by David M. Kennedy (New York: Oxford University Press, 1999) is a classic and immensely readable tome about a frightening time in America's history. Another great read about the same time period is *Traitor to His Class: The Privileged Life and Radical Presidency of Franklin Delano Roosevelt* by H. W. Brands (New York: Anchor, 2009). Last but certainly not least, Studs Terkel's *Hard Times: An Oral History of the Great Depression* (New York: New Press, 2000) should be required reading for every American.

Choosing a financial planner: Finding someone you can trust— and who knows what he or she is doing—isn't easy. Arm yourself with money columnist Chuck Jaffe's *Getting Started in Finding a Financial Advisor* (Hoboken, NJ: John Wiley & Sons, 2010).

CHAPTER 5

Buying and selling homes: Ilyce Glink has written a number of books about real estate; her latest is *Buy, Close, Move In!: How to Navigate the New World of Real Estate—Safely and Profitably—and End Up with the Home of Your Dreams* (New York: Harper, 2010). Also check out Elizabeth Razzi's *The Fearless Home Buyer* (2006) and *The Fearless Home Seller* (2007), both subtitled *Razzi's Rules for Staying in Control of the Deal* (New York: Stewart, Tabori & Chang). Once you have a house, get *Home Maintenance for Dummies* by James Carey and Morris Carey (Hoboken, NJ: John Wiley & Sons, 2009).

Rental property: Pick up a copy of *Every Landlord's Legal Guide* by Marcia Stewart, Ralph Warner and Janet Portman (Berkeley: Nolo, 2010). Another helpful guide is *First-Time Landlord: Your Guide to Renting Out a Single-Family Home* by Janet Portman, Marcia Stewart and Michael Molinski (Berkeley: Nolo, 2009).

CHAPTER 6

Long-term care: This is a tricky area and one likely to change dramatically if the federal government's experiment in long-term care insurance takes off. In the meantime, read *Long-Term Care: How to Plan and Pay for It* by Joseph L. Matthews (Berkeley: Nolo, 2008).

Planning for retirement: Lots of good books are out there, but I like *Saving for Retirement (Without Living Like a Pauper or Winning the Lottery)* (Upper Saddle River, NJ: FT Press, 2007) by Gail MarksJarvis, a *Chicago Tribune* money columnist who helps you make sense of it all.

Social Security benefits: You should find everything you need to know about the current system from *Social Security, Medicare and Government Pensions: Get the Most Out of Your Retirement and Medical Benefits* by

Joseph Matthews and Dorothy Matthews Berman (Berkeley: Nolo, 2010).

Living in retirement: Two good books about making the most of your golden years include *The AARP Retirement Survival Guide: How to Make Smart Financial Decisions in Good Times and Bad* by Julie Jason (New York: Sterling, 2009) and *Get a Life: You Don't Need a Million to Retire Well* by Ralph Warner, founder of Nolo (Berkeley: Nolo, 2005).

CHAPTER 7

College planning: *The College Solution: A Guide for Everyone Looking for the Right School at the Right Price* by Lynn O'Shaughnessy (Upper Saddle River, NJ: FT Press, 2008) is the go-to book for parents, while *Debt-Free U: How I Paid for an Outstanding College Education Without Loans, Scholarships, or Mooching Off My Parents* by Zac Bissonnette (New York: Portfolio, 2010) should be required reading for high school students *and* their parents.

CHAPTER 8

Insurance: You wouldn't expect to find a page-turner about this topic, but there is one. It's called *Against the Gods: The Remarkable Story of Risk* by Peter L. Bernstein (New York: John Wiley & Sons, 1998). Less about insurance and more about how our brains trick us into worrying about the wrong things is *Risk: A Practical Guide for Deciding What's Really Safe and What's Really Dangerous in the World Around You* by David Ropeik and George Gray (Boston: Houghton Mifflin, 2002).

Emergency preparedness: If you want a bit more than a FEMA checklist but don't want to wade through a survivalist tract, read *The Complete Idiot's Guide to Disaster Preparedness* by Maurice A. Ramirez and John Hedtke (New York: Alpha, 2009) for a practical, balanced and immensely helpful guide to dealing with emergencies big and small.

CHAPTER 9

Communicating about money: Old but hardly outdated is *Money Harmony: Resolving Money Conflicts in Your Life and Relationships* by Olivia Mellan (New York: Walker, 1995). More recent is Mellan's *Overcoming Overspending: A Winning Plan for Spenders and Their Partners* (n.p.: Money Harmony Books, 2009), which she cowrote with Sherry Christie.

Issues for unmarried couples: Two good books include *Money*

Without Matrimony: The Unmarried Couple's Guide to Financial Security by Sheryl Garrett and Debra A. Neiman (Chicago: Dearborn, 2005) and *Living Together: A Legal Guide for Unmarried Couples* by Ralph Warner, Toni Ihara and Frederick Hertz (Berkeley: Nolo, 2008).

Estate planning: It's hard to beat *Plan Your Estate: Protect Your Loved Ones, Property and Finances* by Denis Clifford (Berkeley: Nolo, 2010), unless you combine that helpful tome with *Get It Together: Organize Your Records So Your Family Won't Have To* by Melanie Cullen with Shae Irving (Berkeley: Nolo, 2008).

CHAPTER 10

Keeping more of your hard-earned money: Two must-reads, both by MSNBC Red Tape columnist Bob Sullivan: *Gotcha Capitalism: How Hidden Fees Rip You Off Every Day—and What You Can Do About It* (New York: Ballantine Books, 2007) and *Stop Getting Ripped Off: Why Consumers Get Screwed, and How You Can Always Get a Fair Deal* (New York: Ballantine Books, 2009). Round out your book list with *Living Rich by Spending Smart: How to Get More of What You Really Want* by Gregory Karp (Upper Saddle River, NJ: FT Press, 2008).

Traveling smart: I read the first edition of *The Penny Pincher's Passport to Luxury Travel: The Art of Cultivating Preferred Customer Status* by Joel L. Widzer (Palo Alto, CA: Travelers' Tales, 2008), and I am so glad I did. If you travel more than a few times a year, you need to know these strategies for scoring the best travel upgrades and freebies.

INDEX